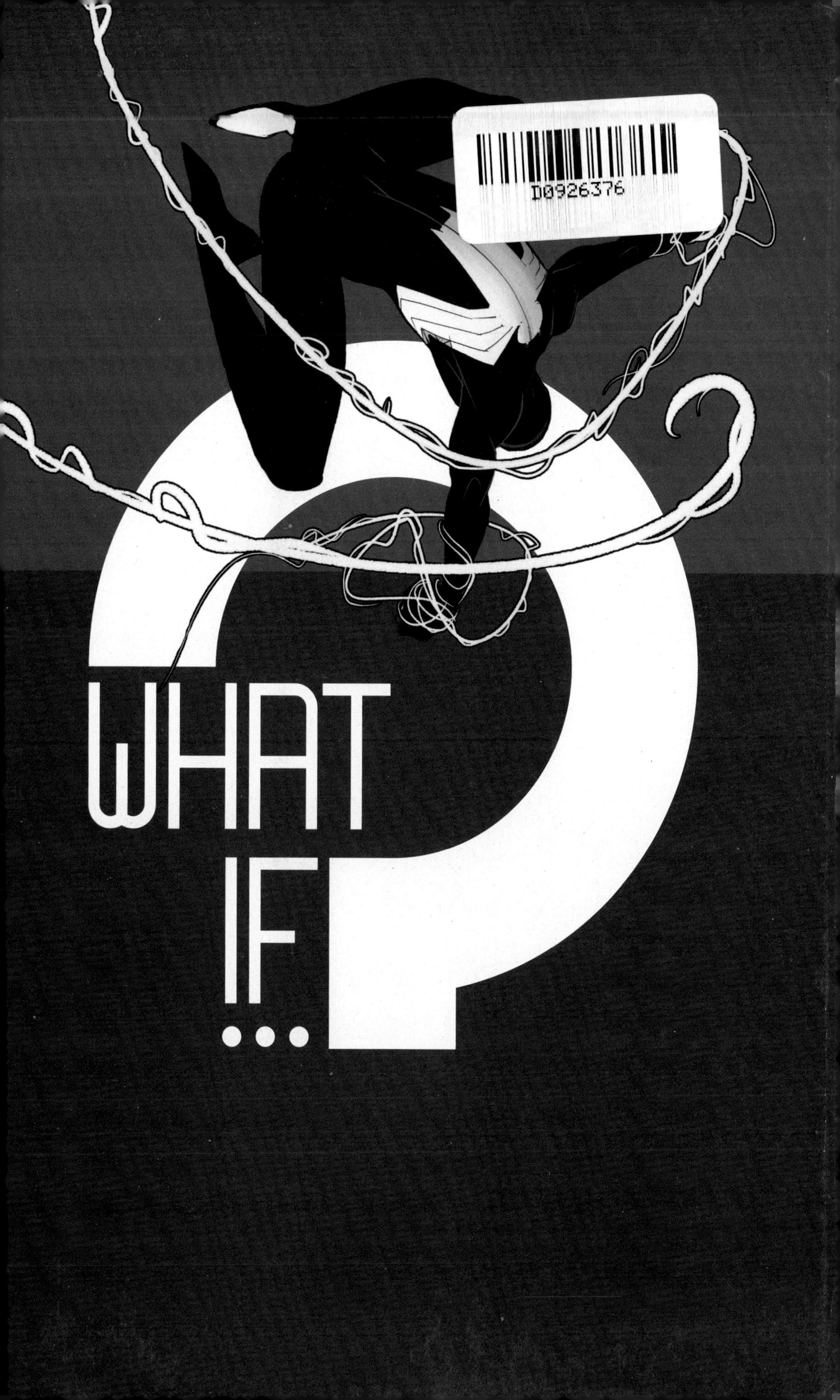
WHAT
IF
...

Some time ago, during an adventure on an alien world, Spider-Man found a new black costume that responded to his every thought. When he eventually learned it was actually a symbiotic life-form and that it was trying to permanently bond with him, Peter got rid of it. The symbiote then found a new host, Eddie Brock, creating a dark, monstrous new foe for Spider-Man: Venom.

But what if Spider-Man had kept the suit...?

[Note: This story takes place around the time of AMAZING SPIDER-MAN #258, available on Marvel Unlimited.]

SPIDER-MAN CREATED BY
STAN LEE & STEVE DITKO

JENNIFER GRÜNWALD COLLECTION EDITOR
DANIEL KIRCHHOFFER ASSISTANT EDITOR
MAIA LOY ASSISTANT MANAGING EDITOR
LISA MONTALBANO ASSISTANT MANAGING EDITOR
JEFF YOUNGQUIST VP PRODUCTION & SPECIAL PROJECTS
JAY BOWEN & CHIP ZDARSKY BOOK DESIGN
DAVID GABRIEL SVP PRINT, SALES & MARKETING
C.B. CEBULSKI EDITOR IN CHIEF

SPIDER-MAN: SPIDER'S SHADOW. Contains material originally published in magazine form as SPIDER-MAN: SPIDER'S SHADOW (2021) #1-5. First printing 2021. ISBN 978-1-302-92091-3. Published by MARVEL WORLDWIDE, INC., a subsidiary of MARVEL ENTERTAINMENT, LLC. OFFICE OF PUBLICATION: 1290 Avenue of the Americas, New York, NY 10104. © 2021 MARVEL No similarity between any of the names, characters, persons, and/or institutions in this magazine with those of any living or dead person or institution is intended, and any such similarity which may exist is purely coincidental. **Printed in Canada.** KEVIN FEIGE, Chief Creative Officer; DAN BUCKLEY, President, Marvel Entertainment; JOE QUESADA, EVP & Creative Director; DAVID BOGART, Associate Publisher & SVP of Talent Affairs; TOM BREVOORT, VP, Executive Editor; NICK LOWE, Executive Editor, VP of Content, Digital Publishing; DAVID GABRIEL, VP of Print & Digital Publishing; JEFF YOUNGQUIST, VP of Production & Special Projects; ALEX MORALES, Director of Publishing Operations; DAN EDINGTON, Managing Editor; RICKEY PURDIN, Director of Talent Relations; JENNIFER GRÜNWALD, Senior Editor, Special Projects; SUSAN CRESPI, Production Manager; STAN LEE, Chairman Emeritus. For information regarding advertising in Marvel Comics or on Marvel.com, please contact Vit DeBellis, Custom Solutions & Integrated Advertising Manager, at vdebellis@marvel.com. For Marvel subscription inquiries, please call 888-511-5480. **Manufactured between 7/30/2021 and 8/31/2021 by SOLISCO PRINTERS, SCOTT, QC, CANADA.**

10 9 8 7 6 5 4 3 2 1

SPIDER-MAN
SPIDER'S SHADOW

CHIP ZDARSKY
WRITER

PASQUAL FERRY
ARTIST

MATT HOLLINGSWORTH
COLOR ARTIST

VC's JOE CARAMAGNA
LETTERER

PHIL NOTO
COVER ARTIST

CHIP ZDARSKY
LOGOS & DESIGN

KAT GREGOROWICZ
ASSISTANT EDITOR

WIL MOSS
EDITOR

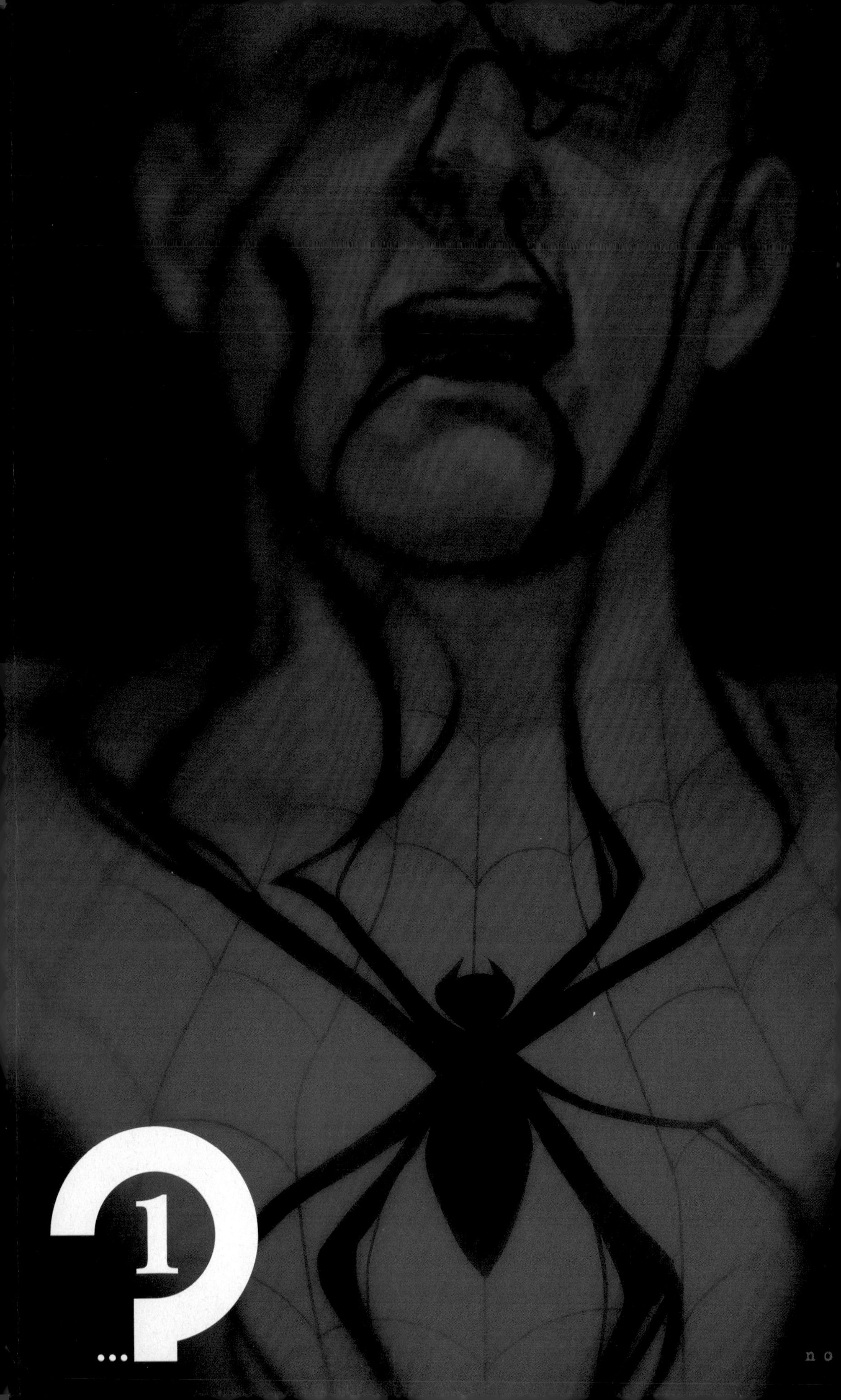

1
...

no

"HURRY,
PETER."

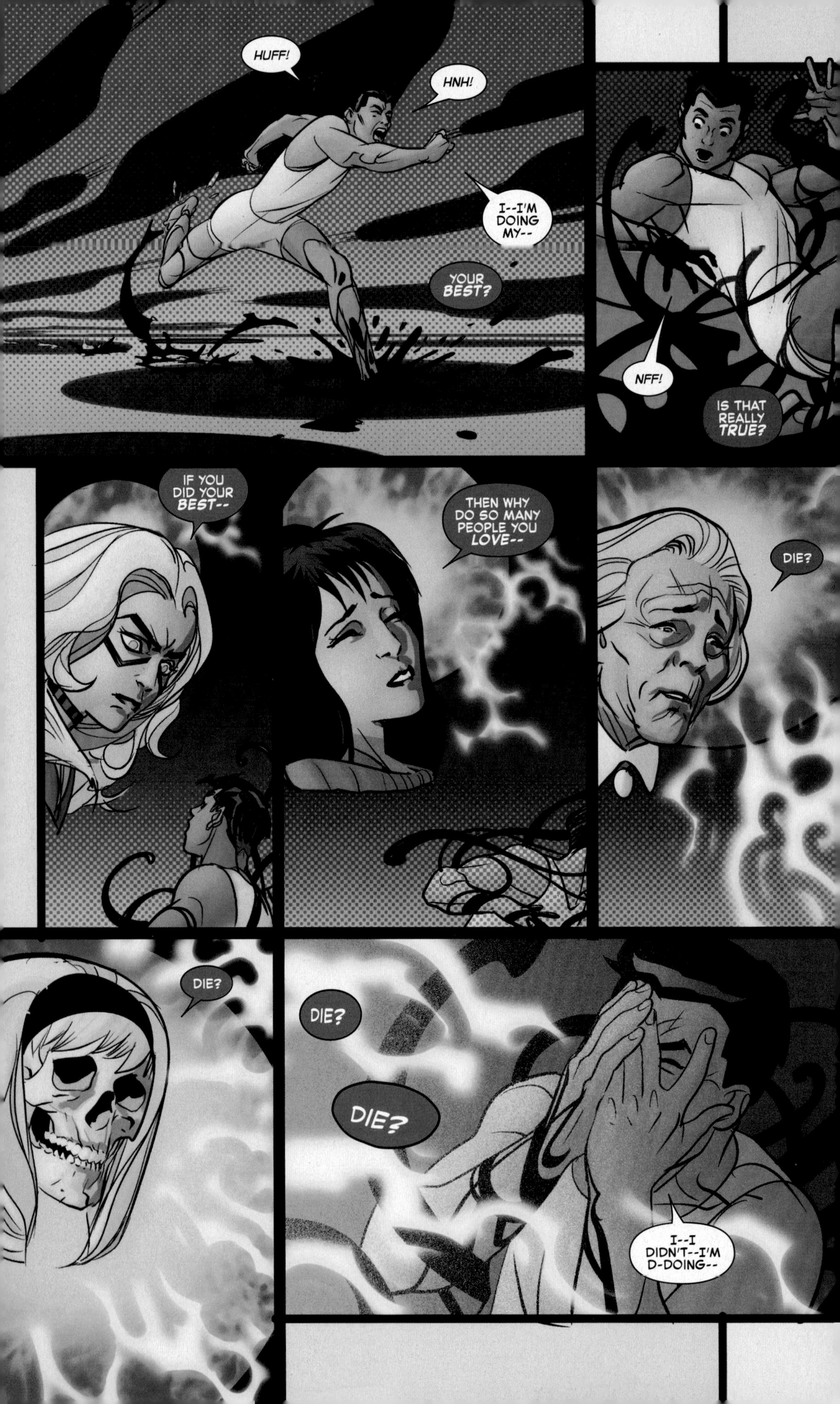
HUFF!
HNH!
I--I'M DOING MY--
YOUR BEST?
NFF!
IS THAT REALLY TRUE?
IF YOU DID YOUR BEST--
THEN WHY DO SO MANY PEOPLE YOU LOVE--
DIE?
DIE?
DIE?
DIE?
I--I DIDN'T--I'M D-DOING--

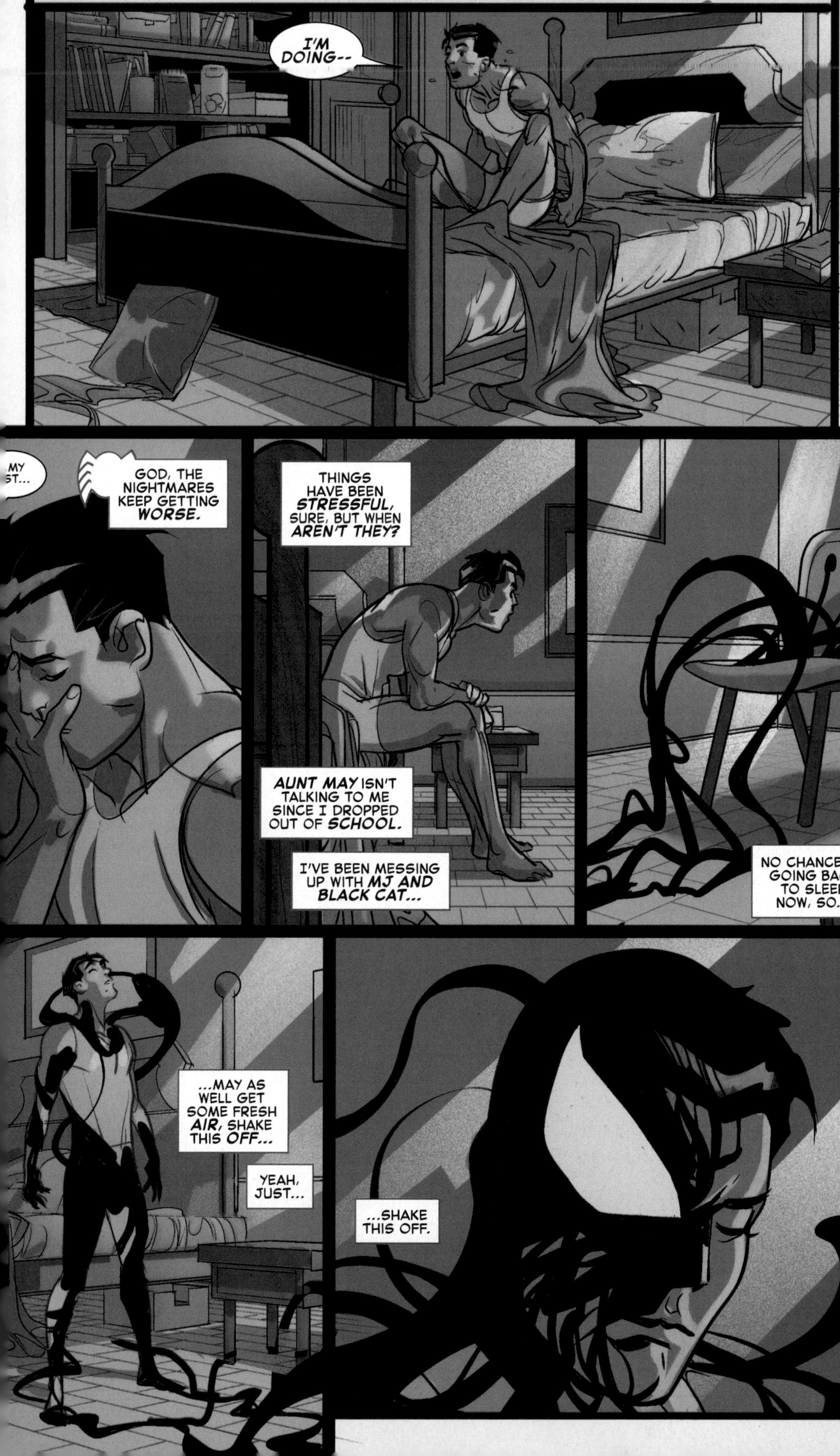
I'M DOING--
GOD, THE NIGHTMARES KEEP GETTING WORSE.
THINGS HAVE BEEN STRESSFUL, SURE, BUT WHEN AREN'T THEY?
AUNT MAY ISN'T TALKING TO ME SINCE I DROPPED OUT OF SCHOOL.
I'VE BEEN MESSING UP WITH MJ AND BLACK CAT...
NO CHANCE OF GOING BACK TO SLEEP NOW, SO...
...MAY AS WELL GET SOME FRESH AIR, SHAKE THIS OFF...
YEAH, JUST...
...SHAKE THIS OFF.

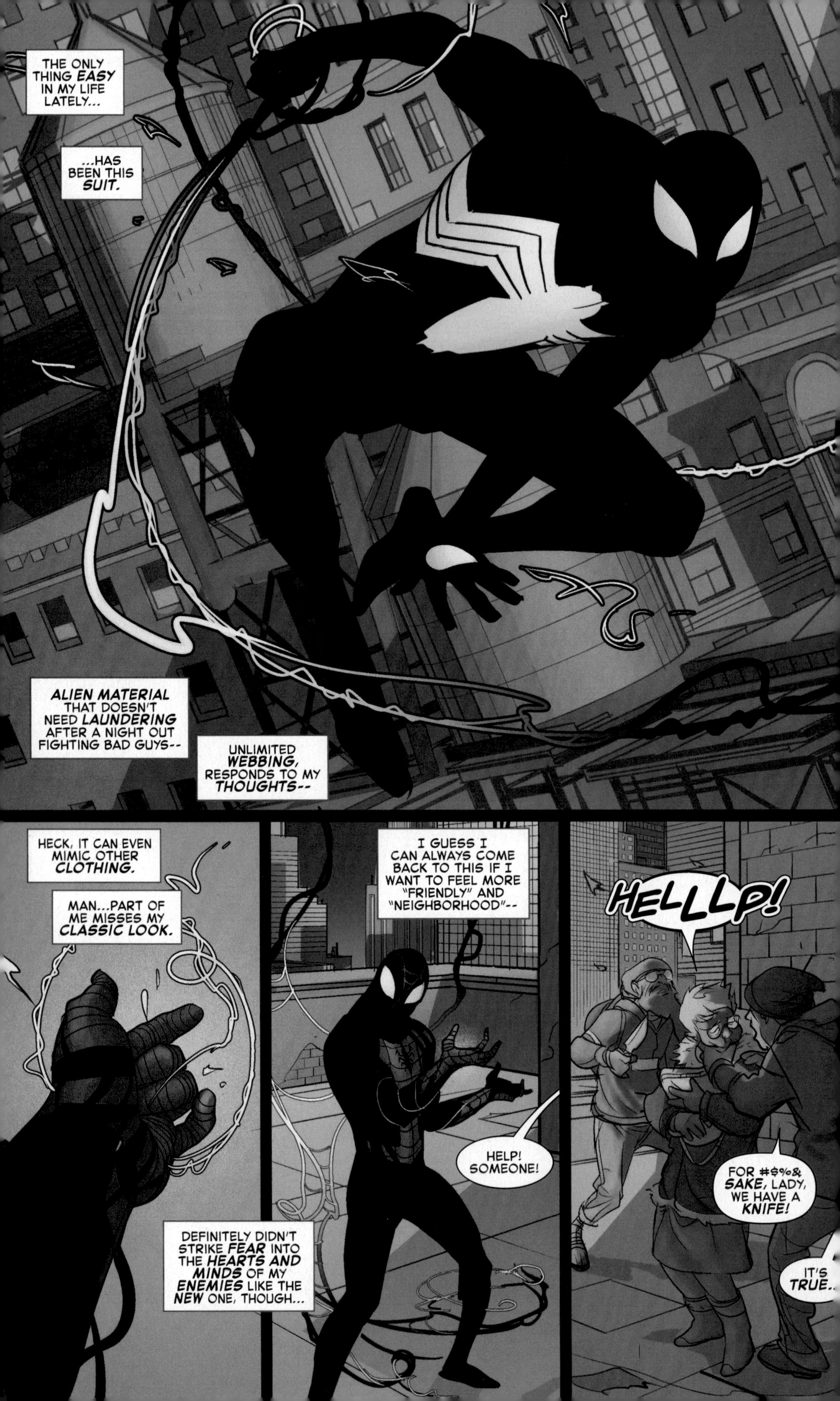
THE ONLY THING EASY IN MY LIFE LATELY...
...HAS BEEN THIS SUIT.
ALIEN MATERIAL THAT DOESN'T NEED LAUNDERING AFTER A NIGHT OUT FIGHTING BAD GUYS--
UNLIMITED WEBBING, RESPONDS TO MY THOUGHTS--
HECK, IT CAN EVEN MIMIC OTHER CLOTHING.
MAN...PART OF ME MISSES MY CLASSIC LOOK.
I GUESS I CAN ALWAYS COME BACK TO THIS IF I WANT TO FEEL MORE "FRIENDLY" AND "NEIGHBORHOOD"--
HELP! SOMEONE!
DEFINITELY DIDN'T STRIKE FEAR INTO THE HEARTS AND MINDS OF MY ENEMIES LIKE THE NEW ONE, THOUGH...
HELLLP!
FOR #$%& SAKE, LADY, WE HAVE A KNIFE!
IT'S TRUE...

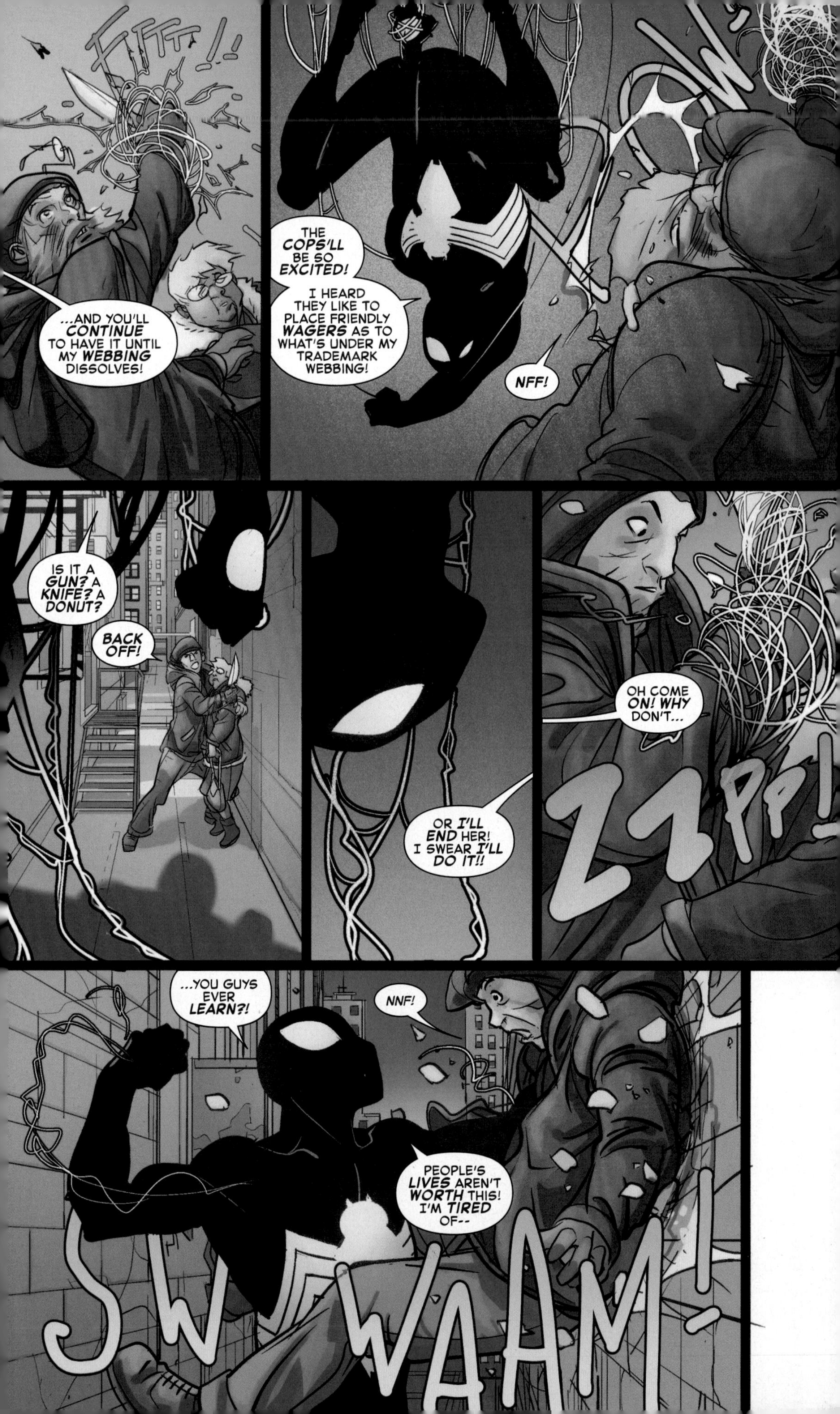
FFFT!!
...AND YOU'LL CONTINUE TO HAVE IT UNTIL MY WEBBING DISSOLVES!
THE COPS'LL BE SO EXCITED!
I HEARD THEY LIKE TO PLACE FRIENDLY WAGERS AS TO WHAT'S UNDER MY TRADEMARK WEBBING!
NFF!
IS IT A GUN? A KNIFE? A DONUT?
BACK OFF!
OR I'LL END HER! I SWEAR I'LL DO IT!!
OH COME ON! WHY DON'T...
ZZPP!
...YOU GUYS EVER LEARN?!
NNF!
PEOPLE'S LIVES AREN'T WORTH THIS! I'M TIRED OF--
SWWAAM!

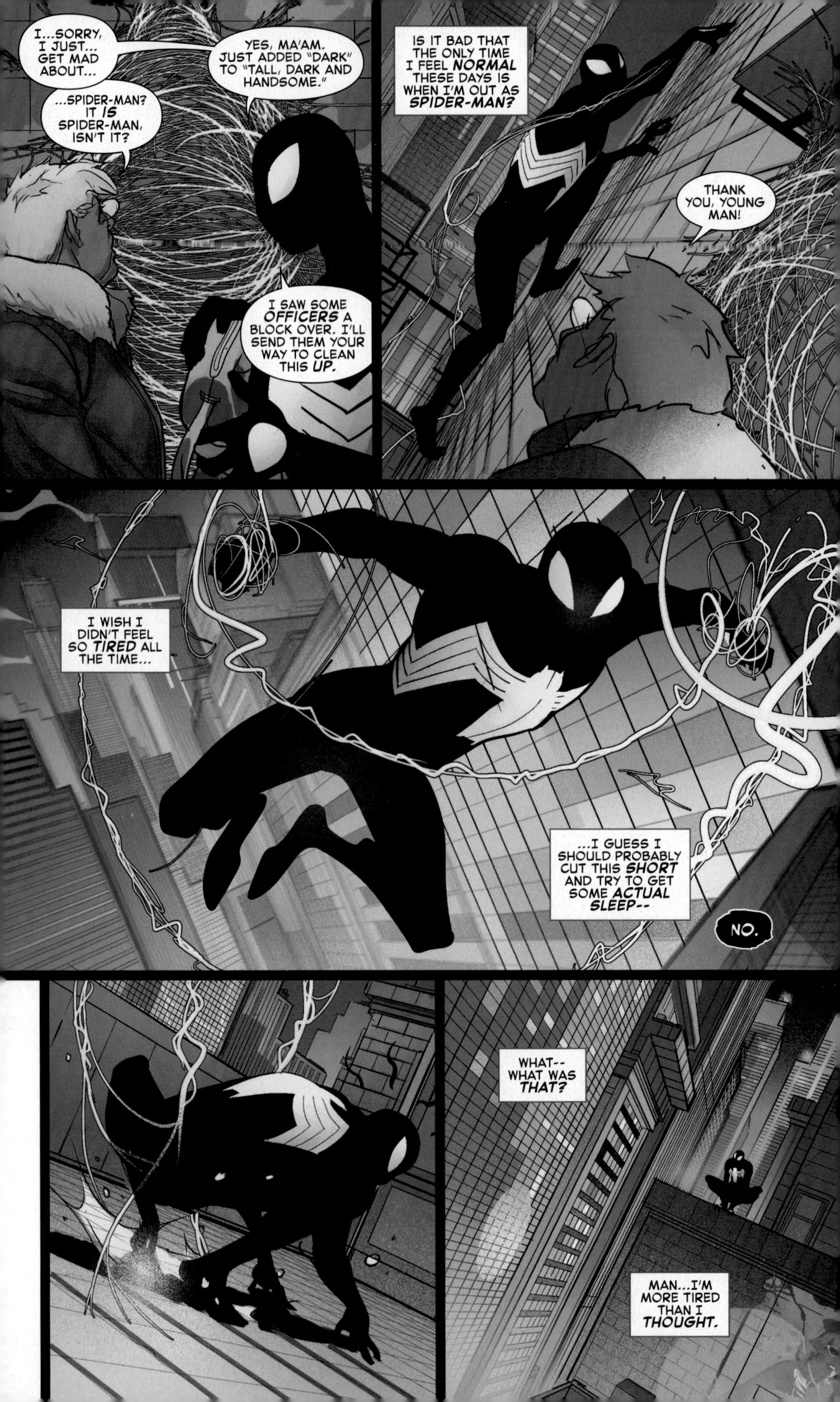
I...SORRY, I JUST... GET MAD ABOUT...
...SPIDER-MAN? IT IS SPIDER-MAN, ISN'T IT?
YES, MA'AM. JUST ADDED "DARK" TO "TALL, DARK AND HANDSOME."
I SAW SOME OFFICERS A BLOCK OVER. I'LL SEND THEM YOUR WAY TO CLEAN THIS UP.
IS IT BAD THAT THE ONLY TIME I FEEL NORMAL THESE DAYS IS WHEN I'M OUT AS SPIDER-MAN?
THANK YOU, YOUNG MAN!
I WISH I DIDN'T FEEL SO TIRED ALL THE TIME...
...I GUESS I SHOULD PROBABLY CUT THIS SHORT AND TRY TO GET SOME ACTUAL SLEEP--
NO.
WHAT-- WHAT WAS THAT?
MAN...I'M MORE TIRED THAN I THOUGHT.

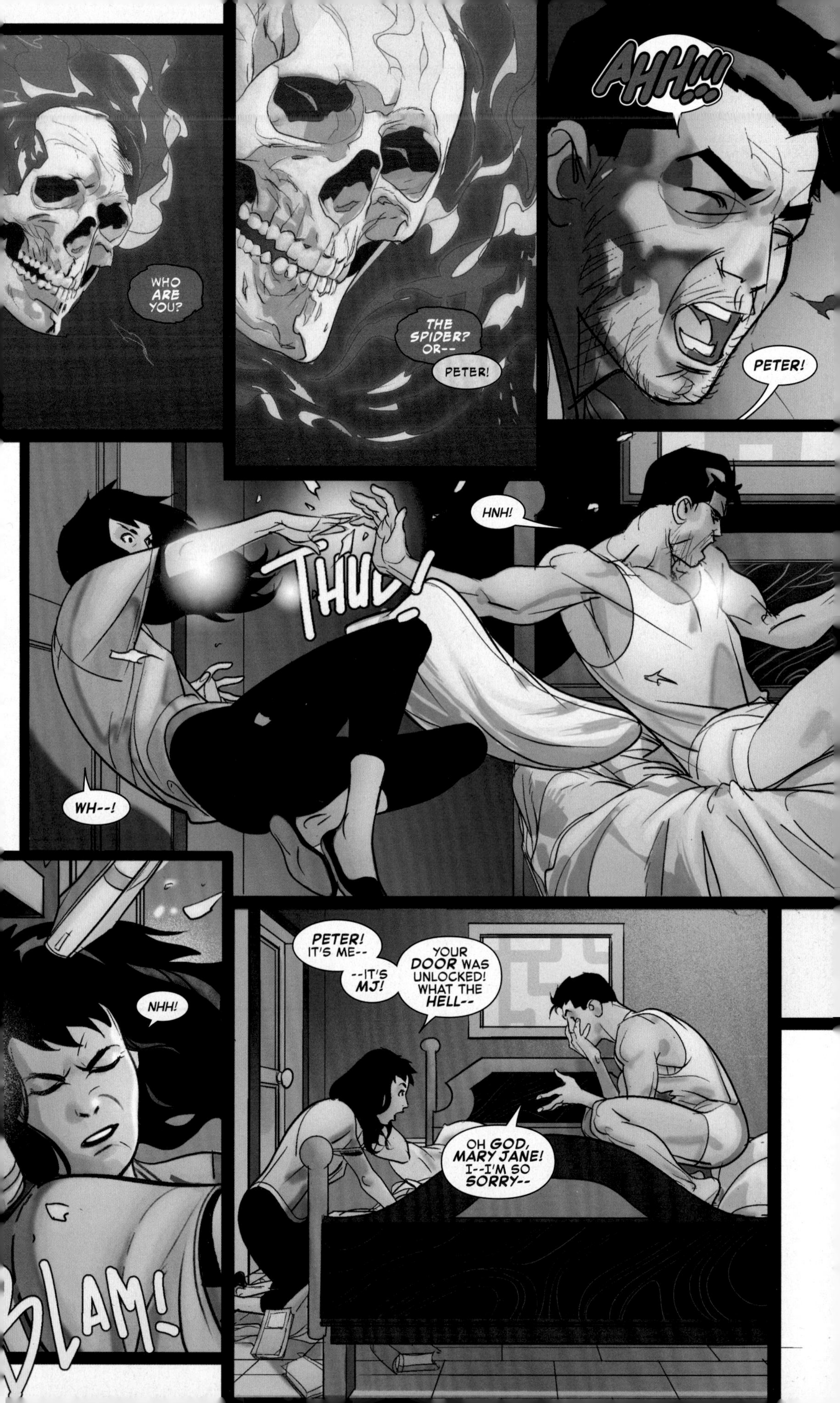
WHO ARE YOU?
THE SPIDER? OR--
PETER!
AHH!!!
PETER!
HNH!
THUD!
WH--!
NHH!
BLAM!
PETER! IT'S ME--
--IT'S MJ!
YOUR DOOR WAS UNLOCKED! WHAT THE HELL--
OH GOD, MARY JANE! I--I'M SO SORRY--

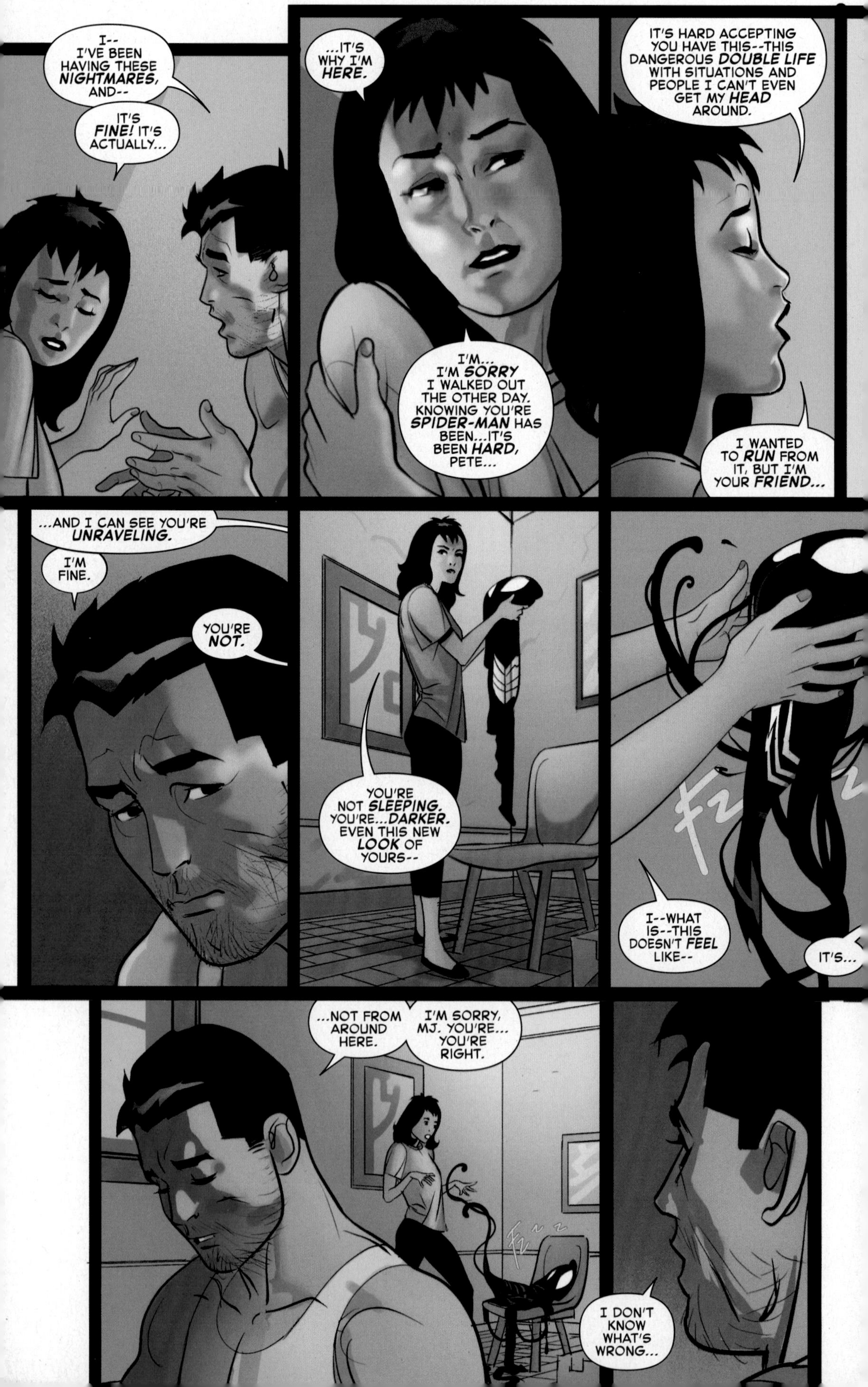

I-- I'VE BEEN HAVING THESE NIGHTMARES, AND--
IT'S FINE! IT'S ACTUALLY...
...IT'S WHY I'M HERE.
I'M... I'M SORRY I WALKED OUT THE OTHER DAY. KNOWING YOU'RE SPIDER-MAN HAS BEEN...IT'S BEEN HARD, PETE...
IT'S HARD ACCEPTING YOU HAVE THIS--THIS DANGEROUS DOUBLE LIFE WITH SITUATIONS AND PEOPLE I CAN'T EVEN GET MY HEAD AROUND.
I WANTED TO RUN FROM IT, BUT I'M YOUR FRIEND...
...AND I CAN SEE YOU'RE UNRAVELING.
I'M FINE.
YOU'RE NOT.
YOU'RE NOT SLEEPING. YOU'RE...DARKER. EVEN THIS NEW LOOK OF YOURS--
I--WHAT IS--THIS DOESN'T FEEL LIKE--
IT'S...
...NOT FROM AROUND HERE.
I'M SORRY, MJ. YOU'RE... YOU'RE RIGHT.
I DON'T KNOW WHAT'S WRONG...

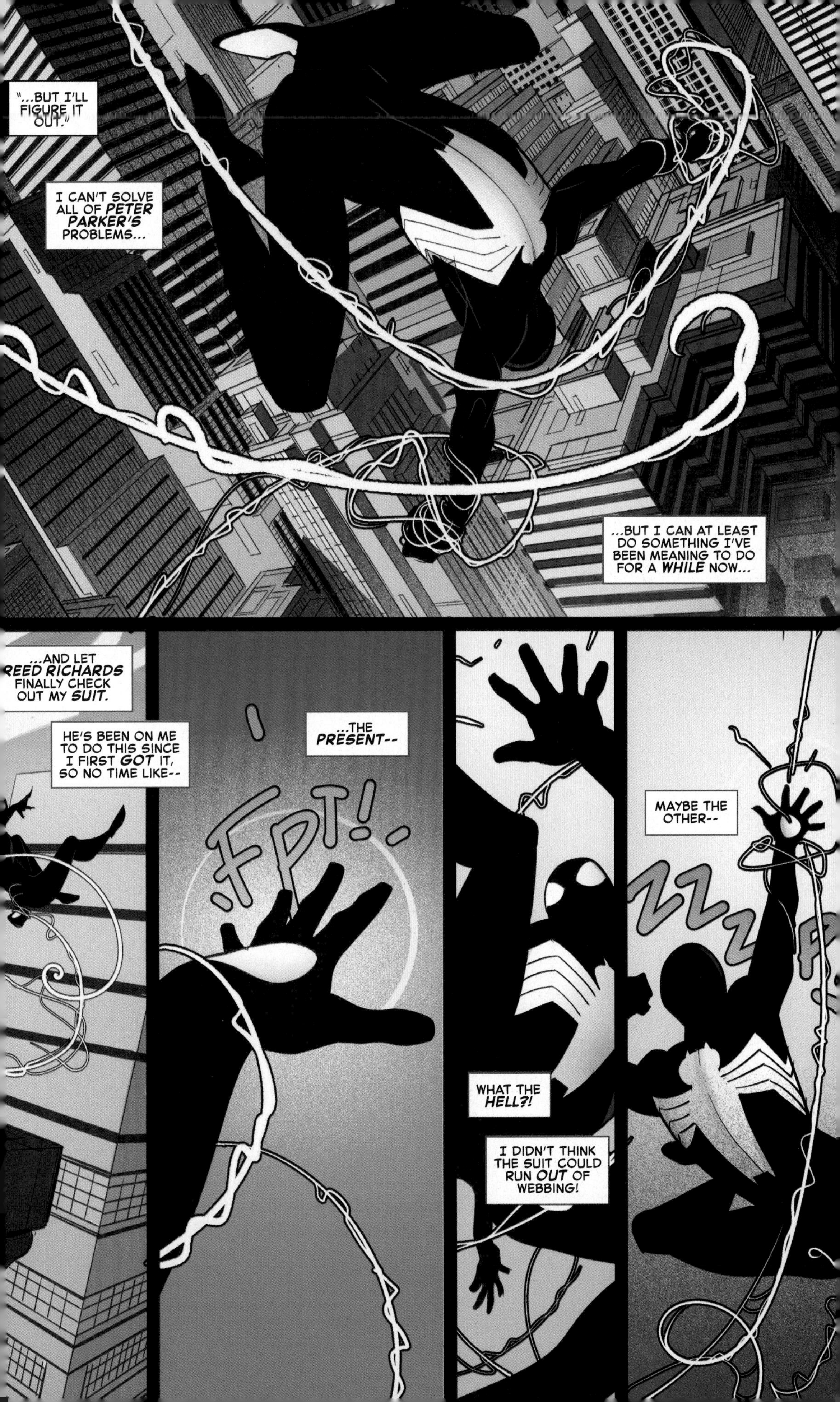
"...BUT I'LL FIGURE IT OUT."
I CAN'T SOLVE ALL OF PETER PARKER'S PROBLEMS...
...BUT I CAN AT LEAST DO SOMETHING I'VE BEEN MEANING TO DO FOR A WHILE NOW...
...AND LET REED RICHARDS FINALLY CHECK OUT MY SUIT.
HE'S BEEN ON ME TO DO THIS SINCE I FIRST GOT IT, SO NO TIME LIKE--
...THE PRESENT--
FPT!
WHAT THE HELL?!
I DIDN'T THINK THE SUIT COULD RUN OUT OF WEBBING!
MAYBE THE OTHER--
ZZZ

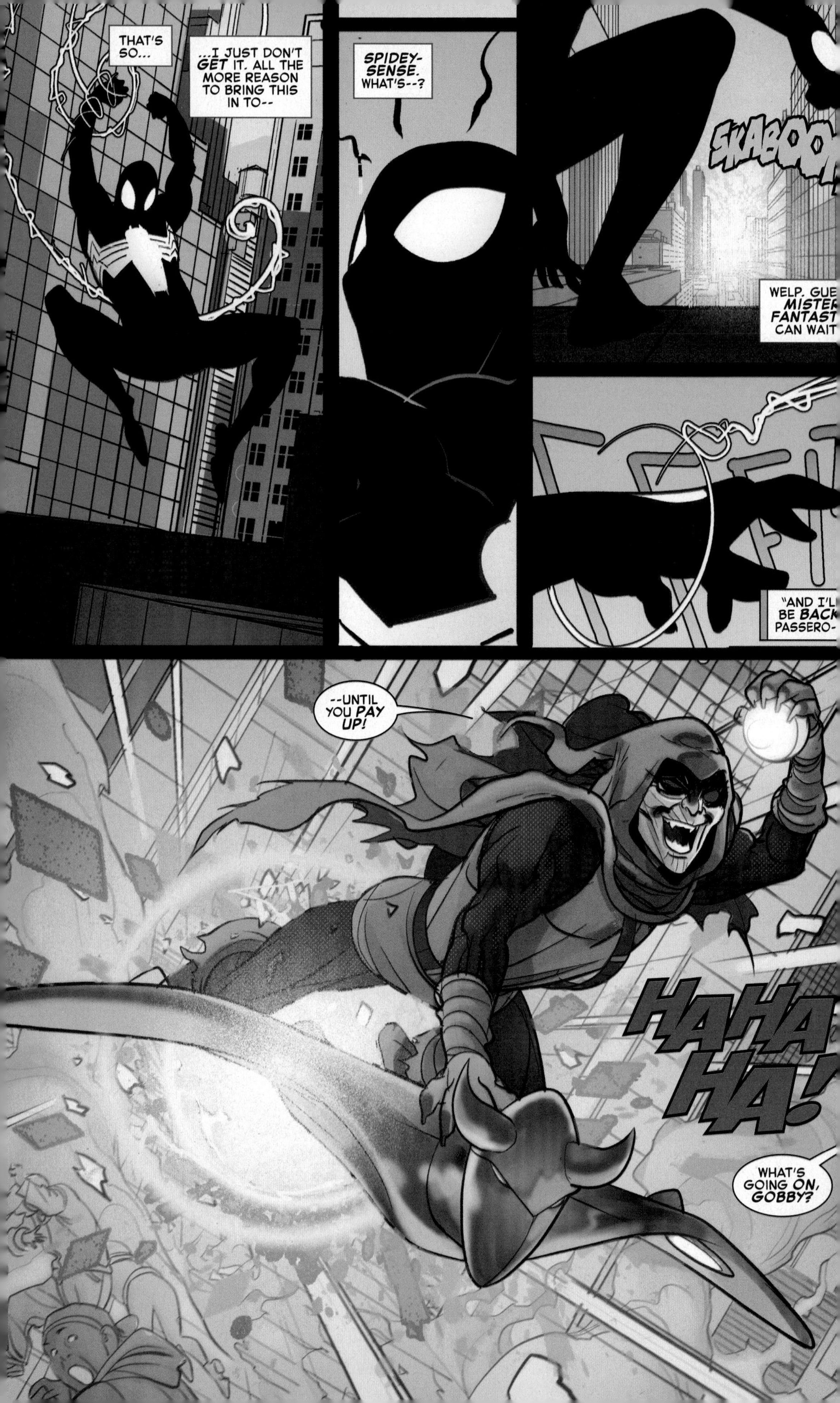
THAT'S SO...
...I JUST DON'T GET IT. ALL THE MORE REASON TO BRING THIS IN TO--
SPIDEY-SENSE. WHAT'S--?
SKABOO
WELP. GUE MISTER FANTAST CAN WAIT
"AND I'L BE BACK PASSERO-
--UNTIL YOU PAY UP!
HAHA HA!
WHAT'S GOING ON, GOBBY?

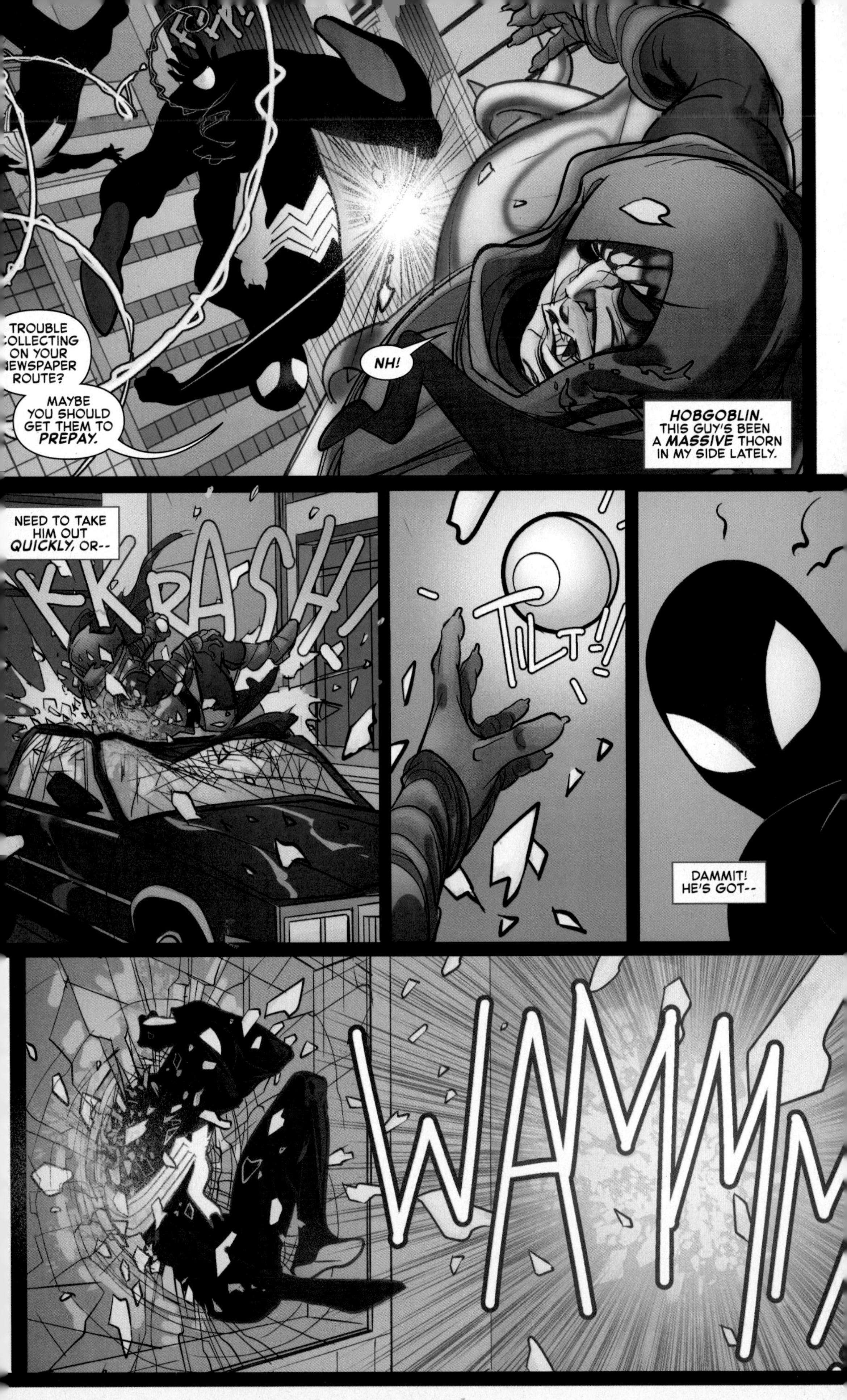
TROUBLE COLLECTING ON YOUR NEWSPAPER ROUTE?
MAYBE YOU SHOULD GET THEM TO PREPAY.
NH!
HOBGOBLIN. THIS GUY'S BEEN A MASSIVE THORN IN MY SIDE LATELY.
NEED TO TAKE HIM OUT QUICKLY, OR--
KKRASH!
TILT!!
DAMMIT! HE'S GOT--
WAMM

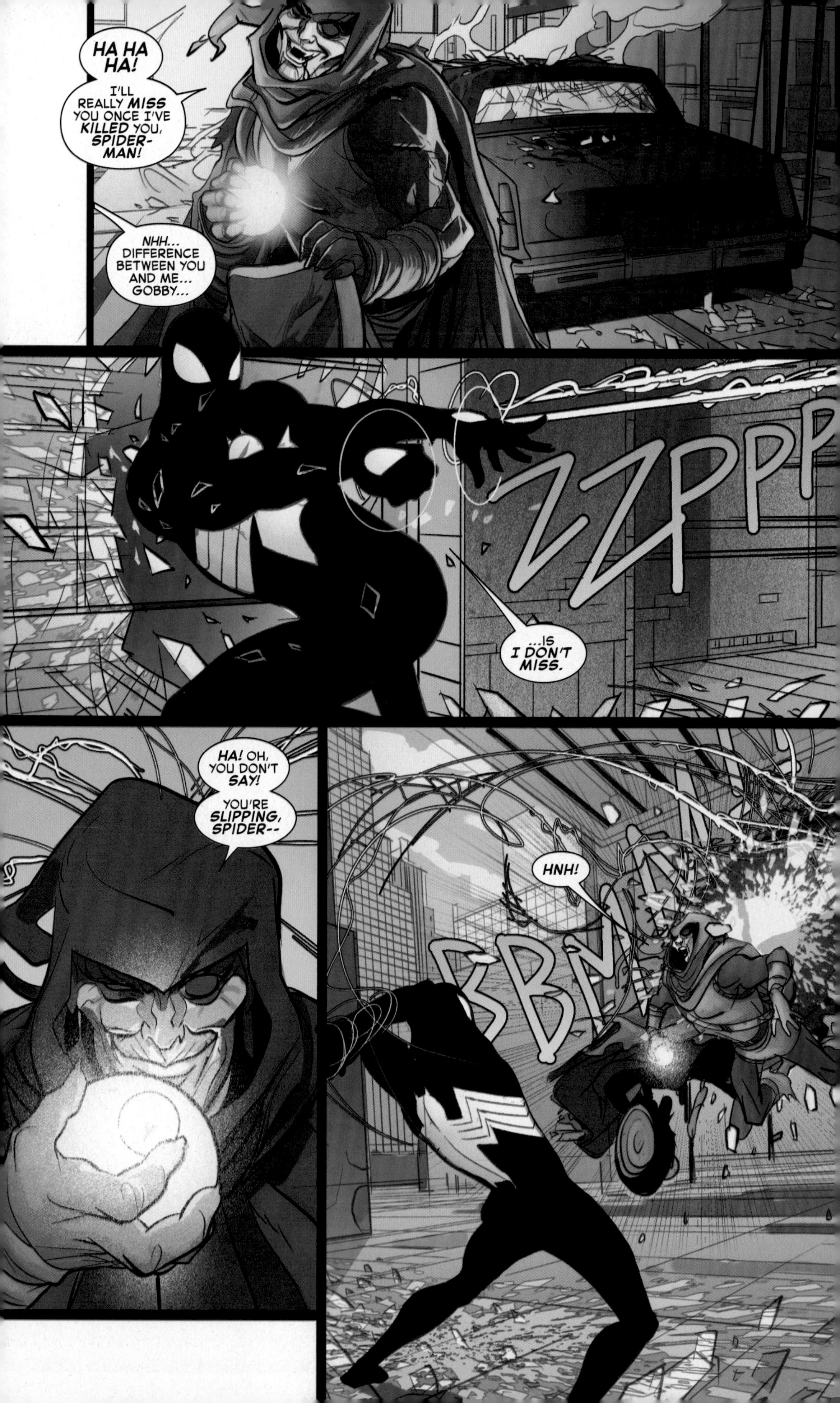
HA HA HA!
I'LL REALLY MISS YOU ONCE I'VE KILLED YOU, SPIDER-MAN!
NHH... DIFFERENCE BETWEEN YOU AND ME... GOBBY...
ZZPPP
...IS I DON'T MISS.
HA! OH, YOU DON'T SAY!
YOU'RE SLIPPING, SPIDER--
HNH!
BBM

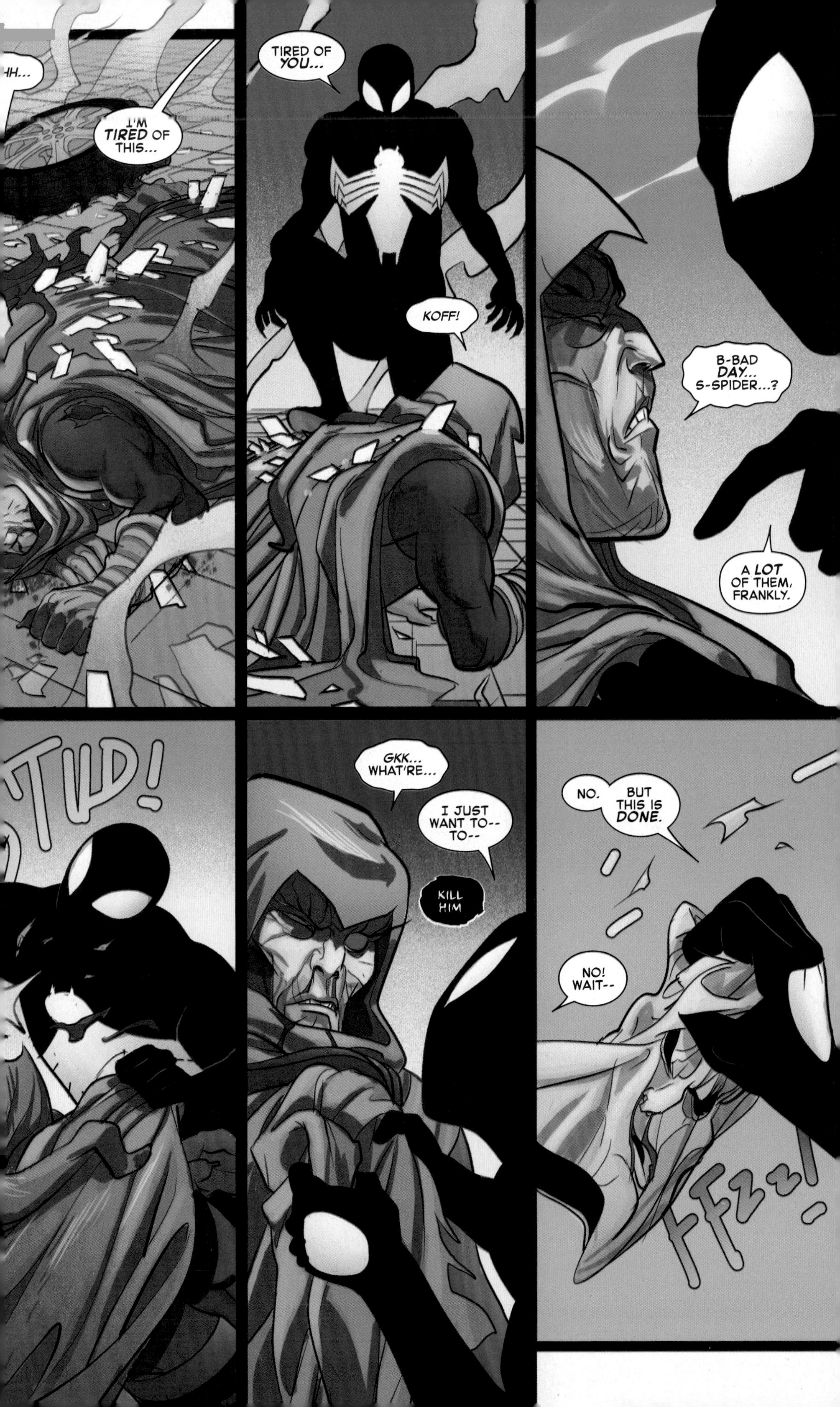

HH...
I'M TIRED OF THIS...
TIRED OF YOU...
KOFF!
B-BAD DAY... S-SPIDER...?
A LOT OF THEM, FRANKLY.
TUD!
GKK... WHAT'RE...
I JUST WANT TO-- TO--
KILL HIM
NO.
BUT THIS IS DONE.
NO! WAIT--
FFZZ

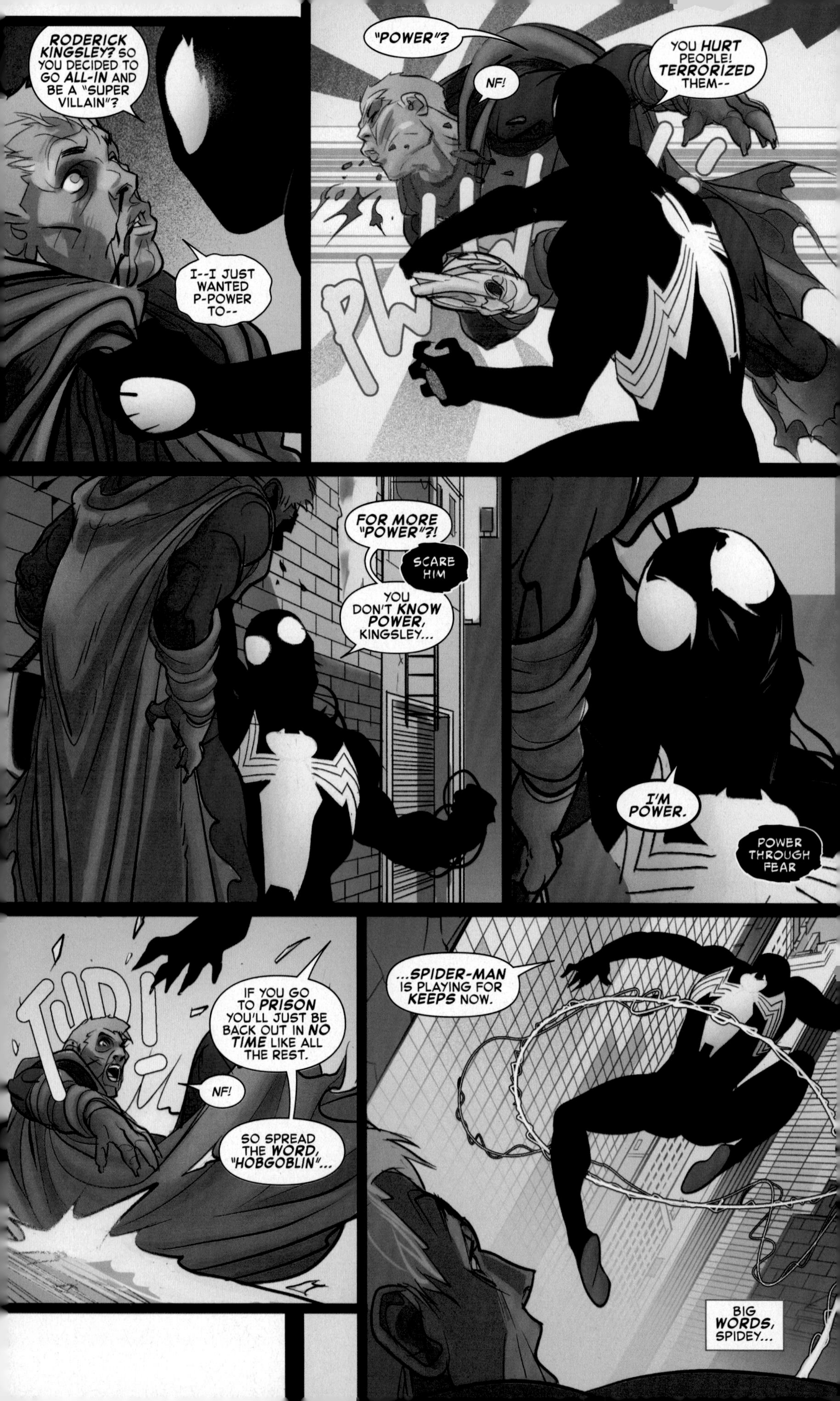
RODERICK KINGSLEY? SO YOU DECIDED TO GO ALL-IN AND BE A "SUPER VILLAIN"?
I--I JUST WANTED P-POWER TO--
"POWER"?
NF!
YOU HURT PEOPLE! TERRORIZED THEM--
PWUD
FOR MORE "POWER"?!
SCARE HIM
YOU DON'T KNOW POWER, KINGSLEY...
I'M POWER.
POWER THROUGH FEAR
THUD
IF YOU GO TO PRISON YOU'LL JUST BE BACK OUT IN NO TIME LIKE ALL THE REST.
NF!
SO SPREAD THE WORD, "HOBGOBLIN"...
...SPIDER-MAN IS PLAYING FOR KEEPS NOW.
BIG WORDS, SPIDEY...

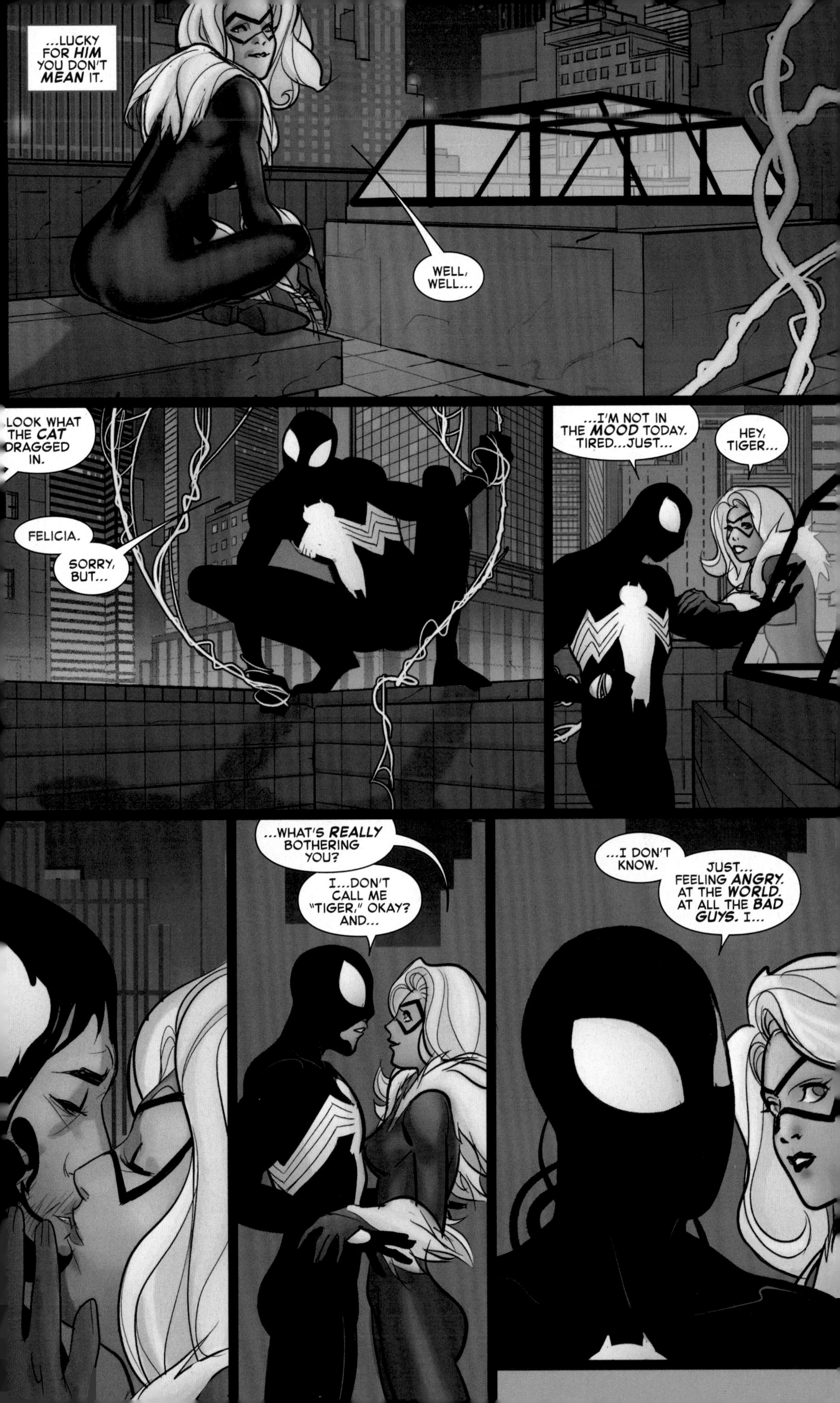

...LUCKY FOR HIM YOU DON'T MEAN IT.
WELL, WELL...
LOOK WHAT THE CAT DRAGGED IN.
FELICIA.
SORRY, BUT...
...I'M NOT IN THE MOOD TODAY. TIRED...JUST...
HEY, TIGER...
...WHAT'S REALLY BOTHERING YOU?
I...DON'T CALL ME "TIGER," OKAY? AND...
...I DON'T KNOW.
JUST... FEELING ANGRY. AT THE WORLD. AT ALL THE BAD GUYS. I...

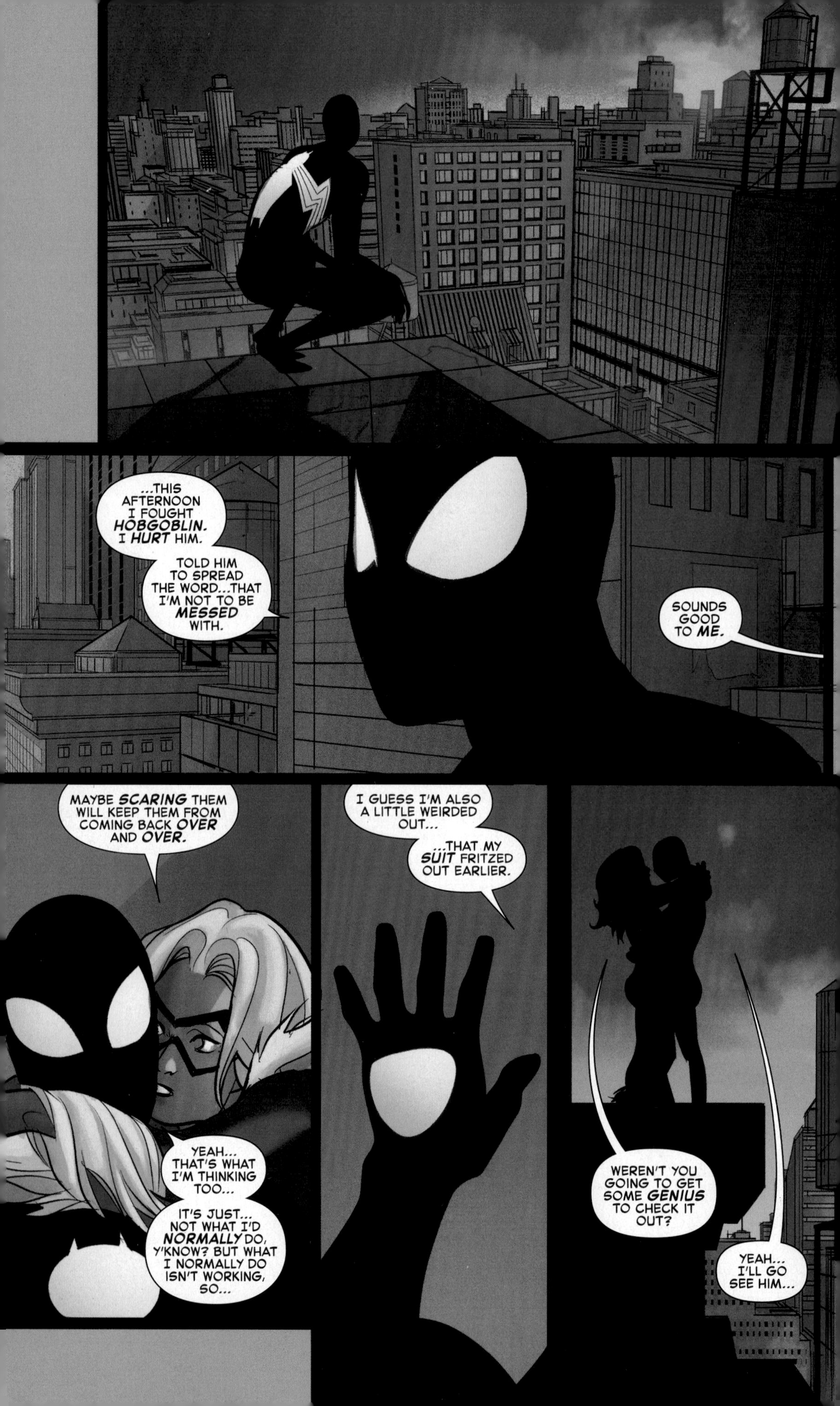
...THIS AFTERNOON I FOUGHT HOBGOBLIN. I HURT HIM.
TOLD HIM TO SPREAD THE WORD...THAT I'M NOT TO BE MESSED WITH.
SOUNDS GOOD TO ME.
MAYBE SCARING THEM WILL KEEP THEM FROM COMING BACK OVER AND OVER.
YEAH... THAT'S WHAT I'M THINKING TOO...
IT'S JUST... NOT WHAT I'D NORMALLY DO, Y'KNOW? BUT WHAT I NORMALLY DO ISN'T WORKING, SO...
I GUESS I'M ALSO A LITTLE WEIRDED OUT...
...THAT MY SUIT FRITZED OUT EARLIER.
WEREN'T YOU GOING TO GET SOME GENIUS TO CHECK IT OUT?
YEAH... I'LL GO SEE HIM...

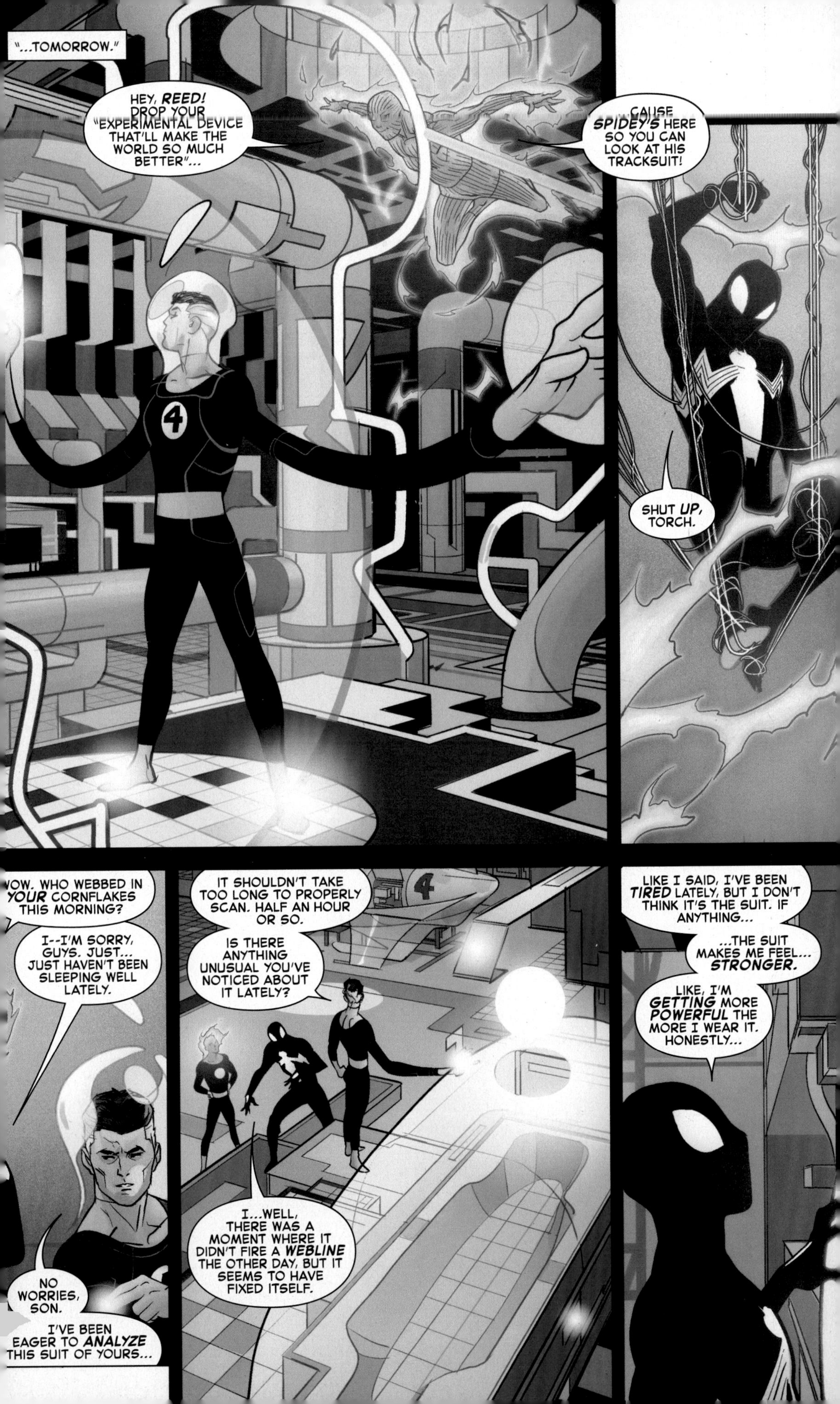
"...TOMORROW."
HEY, REED! DROP YOUR "EXPERIMENTAL DEVICE THAT'LL MAKE THE WORLD SO MUCH BETTER"...
CAUSE SPIDEY'S HERE SO YOU CAN LOOK AT HIS TRACKSUIT!
SHUT UP, TORCH.
WOW. WHO WEBBED IN YOUR CORNFLAKES THIS MORNING?
I--I'M SORRY, GUYS. JUST... JUST HAVEN'T BEEN SLEEPING WELL LATELY.
NO WORRIES, SON.
I'VE BEEN EAGER TO ANALYZE THIS SUIT OF YOURS...
IT SHOULDN'T TAKE TOO LONG TO PROPERLY SCAN. HALF AN HOUR OR SO.
IS THERE ANYTHING UNUSUAL YOU'VE NOTICED ABOUT IT LATELY?
I...WELL, THERE WAS A MOMENT WHERE IT DIDN'T FIRE A WEBLINE THE OTHER DAY, BUT IT SEEMS TO HAVE FIXED ITSELF.
LIKE I SAID, I'VE BEEN TIRED LATELY, BUT I DON'T THINK IT'S THE SUIT. IF ANYTHING...
...THE SUIT MAKES ME FEEL... STRONGER.
LIKE, I'M GETTING MORE POWERFUL THE MORE I WEAR IT. HONESTLY...

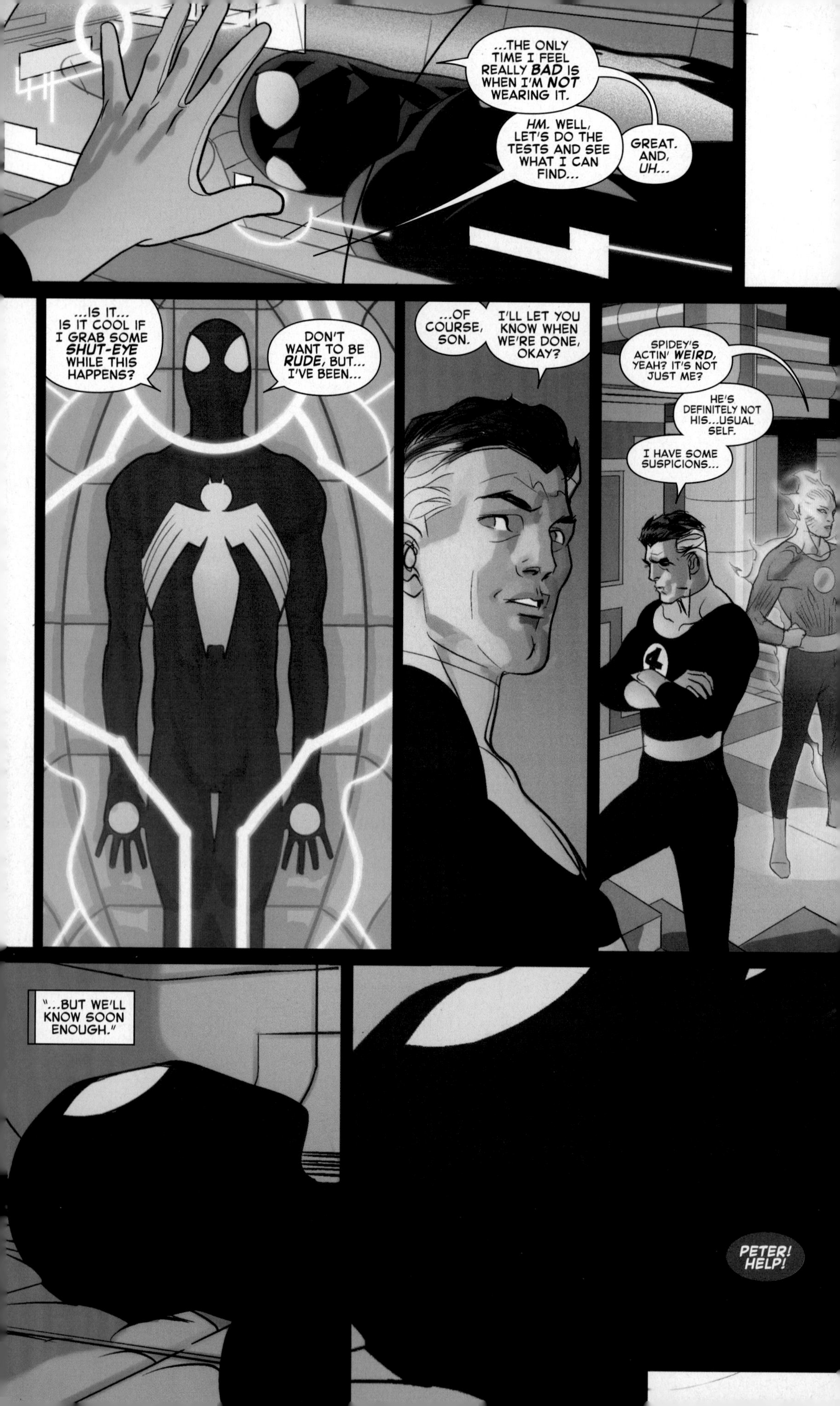

...THE ONLY TIME I FEEL REALLY BAD IS WHEN I'M NOT WEARING IT.
HM. WELL, LET'S DO THE TESTS AND SEE WHAT I CAN FIND...
GREAT. AND, UH...
...IS IT... IS IT COOL IF I GRAB SOME SHUT-EYE WHILE THIS HAPPENS?
DON'T WANT TO BE RUDE, BUT... I'VE BEEN...
...OF COURSE, SON.
I'LL LET YOU KNOW WHEN WE'RE DONE, OKAY?
SPIDEY'S ACTIN' WEIRD, YEAH? IT'S NOT JUST ME?
HE'S DEFINITELY NOT HIS...USUAL SELF.
I HAVE SOME SUSPICIONS...
"...BUT WE'LL KNOW SOON ENOUGH."
PETER! HELP!

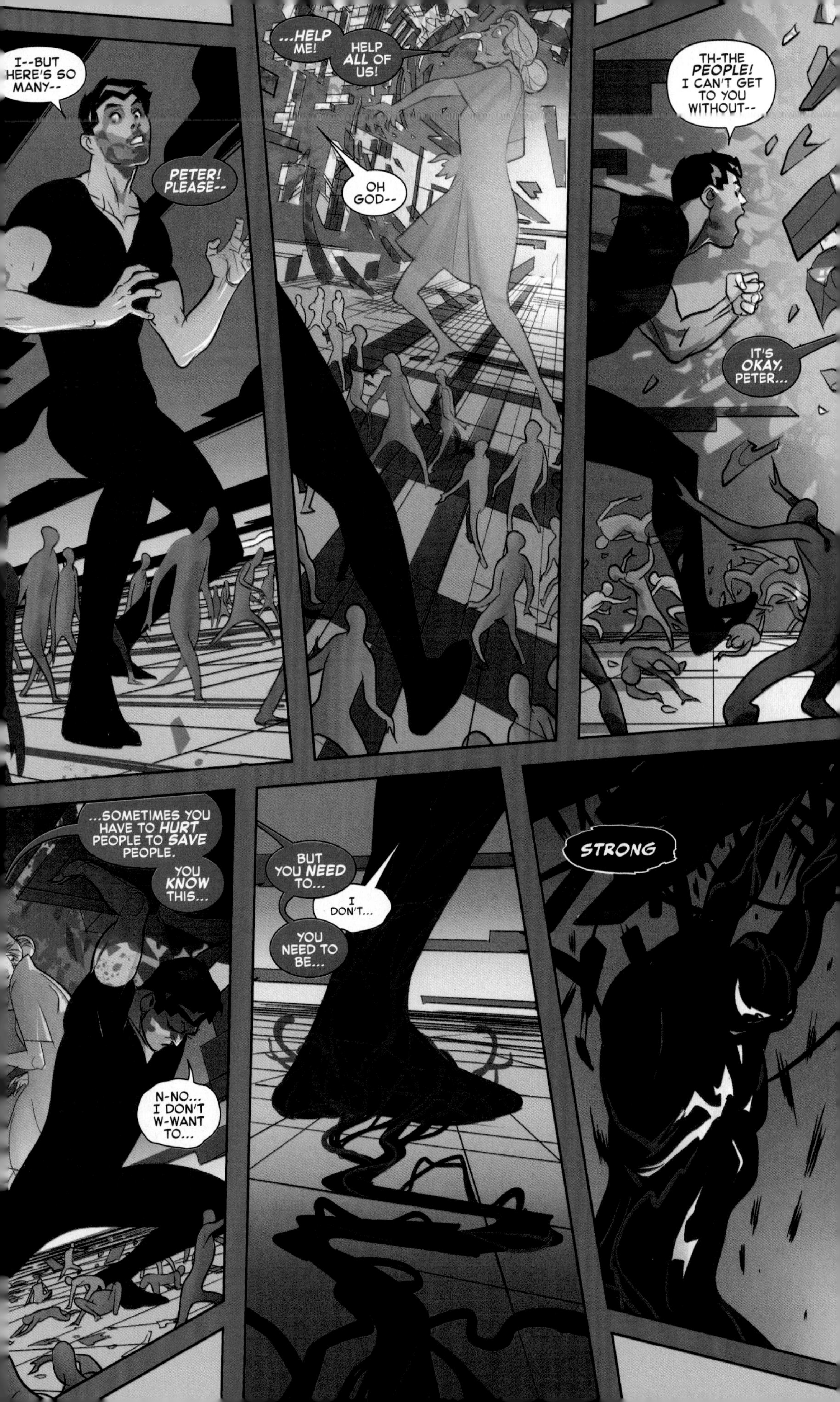
I--BUT HERE'S SO MANY--
PETER! PLEASE--
...HELP ME!
HELP ALL OF US!
OH GOD--
TH-THE PEOPLE! I CAN'T GET TO YOU WITHOUT--
IT'S OKAY, PETER...
...SOMETIMES YOU HAVE TO HURT PEOPLE TO SAVE PEOPLE.
YOU KNOW THIS...
N-NO... I DON'T W-WANT TO...
BUT YOU NEED TO...
I DON'T...
YOU NEED TO BE...
STRONG

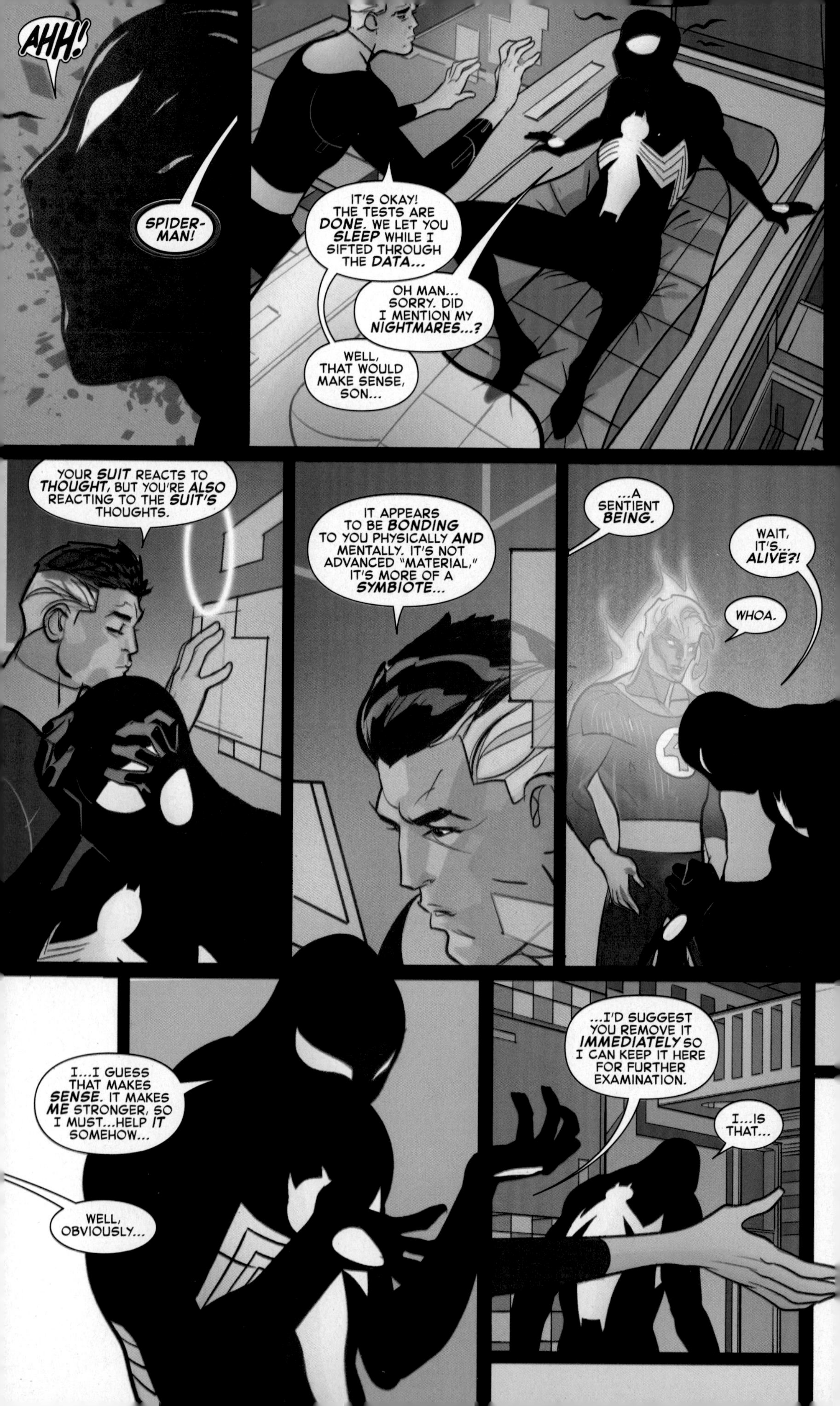
AHH!
SPIDER-MAN!
IT'S OKAY! THE TESTS ARE DONE. WE LET YOU SLEEP WHILE I SIFTED THROUGH THE DATA...
OH MAN... SORRY. DID I MENTION MY NIGHTMARES...?
WELL, THAT WOULD MAKE SENSE, SON...
YOUR SUIT REACTS TO THOUGHT, BUT YOU'RE ALSO REACTING TO THE SUIT'S THOUGHTS.
IT APPEARS TO BE BONDING TO YOU PHYSICALLY AND MENTALLY. IT'S NOT ADVANCED "MATERIAL," IT'S MORE OF A SYMBIOTE...
...A SENTIENT BEING.
WAIT, IT'S... ALIVE?!
WHOA.
I...I GUESS THAT MAKES SENSE. IT MAKES ME STRONGER, SO I MUST...HELP IT SOMEHOW...
WELL, OBVIOUSLY...
...I'D SUGGEST YOU REMOVE IT IMMEDIATELY SO I CAN KEEP IT HERE FOR FURTHER EXAMINATION.
I...IS THAT...

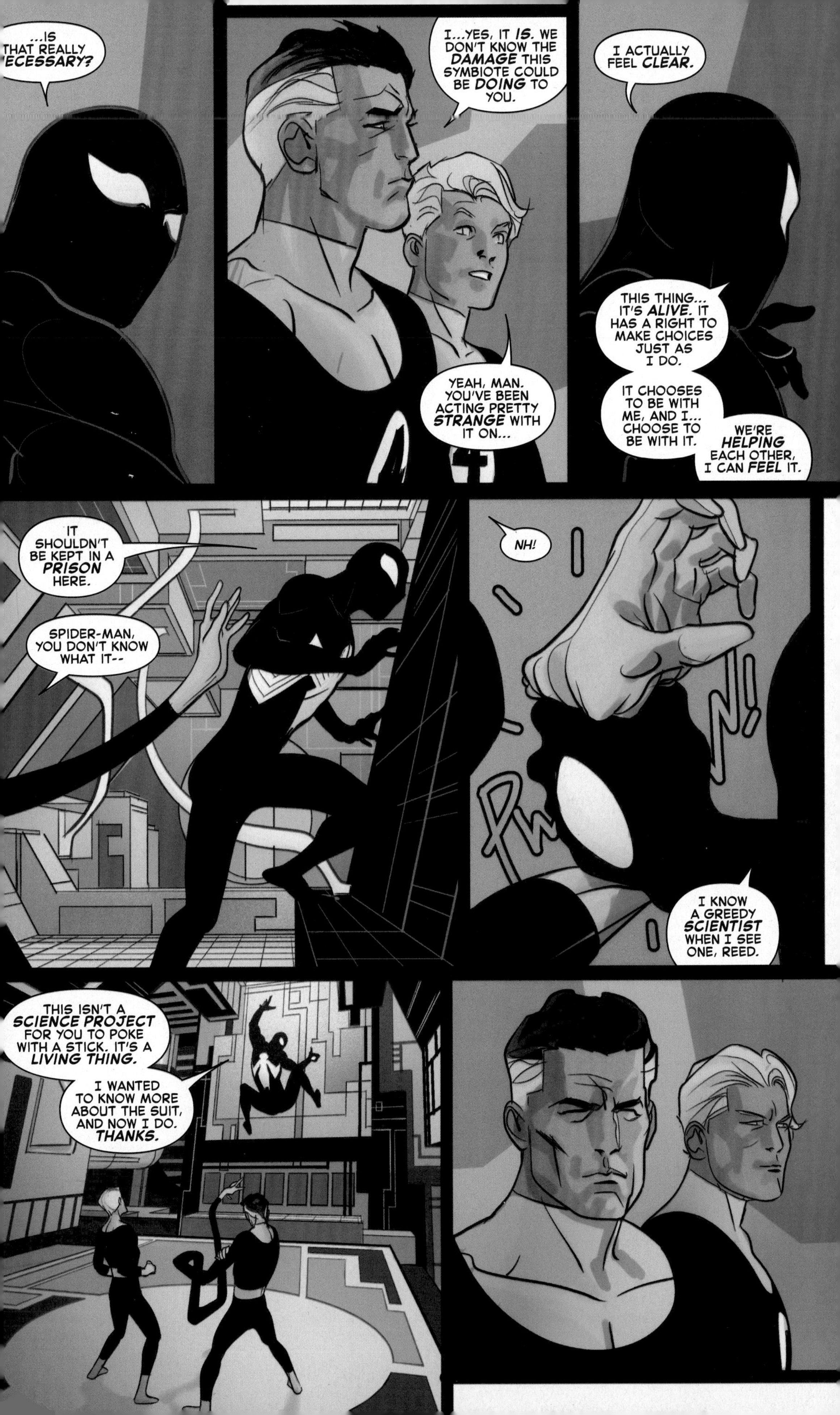

...IS THAT REALLY NECESSARY?
I...YES, IT IS. WE DON'T KNOW THE DAMAGE THIS SYMBIOTE COULD BE DOING TO YOU.
YEAH, MAN. YOU'VE BEEN ACTING PRETTY STRANGE WITH IT ON...
I ACTUALLY FEEL CLEAR.
THIS THING... IT'S ALIVE. IT HAS A RIGHT TO MAKE CHOICES JUST AS I DO.
IT CHOOSES TO BE WITH ME, AND I... CHOOSE TO BE WITH IT.
WE'RE HELPING EACH OTHER, I CAN FEEL IT.
IT SHOULDN'T BE KEPT IN A PRISON HERE.
SPIDER-MAN, YOU DON'T KNOW WHAT IT--
NH!
I KNOW A GREEDY SCIENTIST WHEN I SEE ONE, REED.
THIS ISN'T A SCIENCE PROJECT FOR YOU TO POKE WITH A STICK. IT'S A LIVING THING.
I WANTED TO KNOW MORE ABOUT THE SUIT, AND NOW I DO. THANKS.

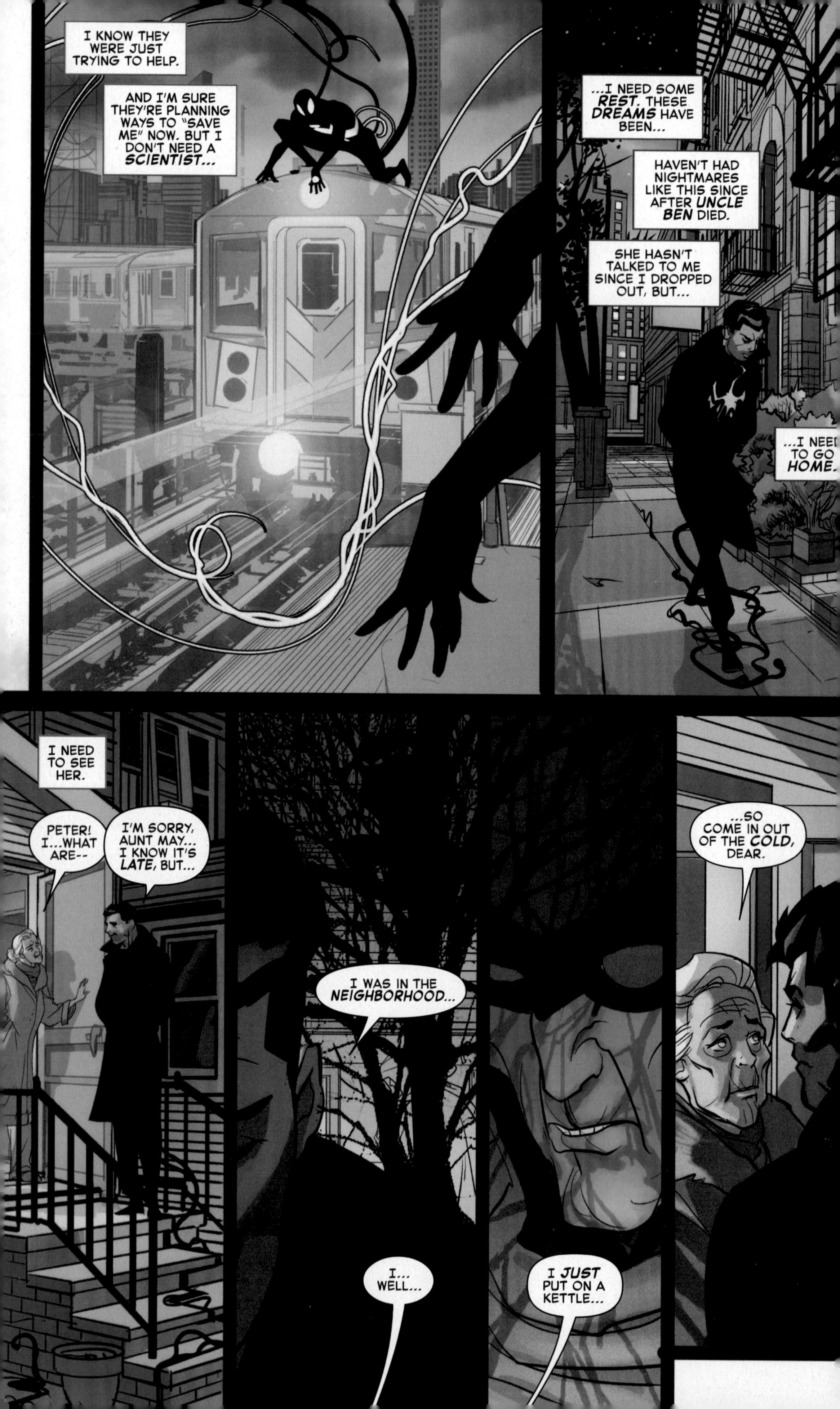
I KNOW THEY WERE JUST TRYING TO HELP.
AND I'M SURE THEY'RE PLANNING WAYS TO "SAVE ME" NOW. BUT I DON'T NEED A SCIENTIST...
...I NEED SOME REST. THESE DREAMS HAVE BEEN...
HAVEN'T HAD NIGHTMARES LIKE THIS SINCE AFTER UNCLE BEN DIED.
SHE HASN'T TALKED TO ME SINCE I DROPPED OUT, BUT...
...I NEED TO GO HOME.
I NEED TO SEE HER.
PETER! I...WHAT ARE--
I'M SORRY, AUNT MAY... I KNOW IT'S LATE, BUT...
I WAS IN THE NEIGHBORHOOD...
I... WELL...
I JUST PUT ON A KETTLE...
...SO COME IN OUT OF THE COLD, DEAR.

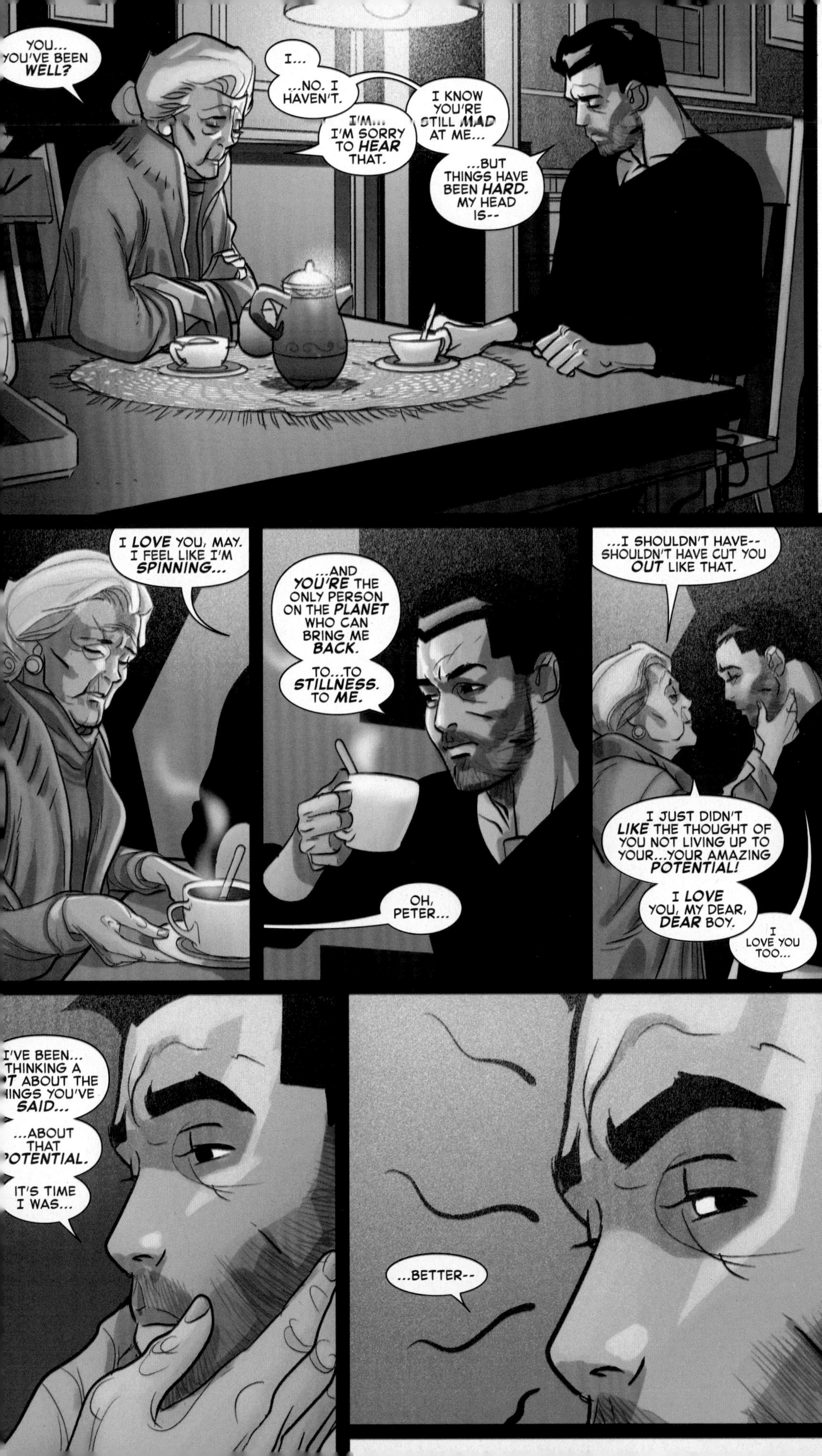
YOU... YOU'VE BEEN WELL?
I...
...NO. I HAVEN'T.
I'M... I'M SORRY TO HEAR THAT.
I KNOW YOU'RE STILL MAD AT ME...
...BUT THINGS HAVE BEEN HARD. MY HEAD IS--
I LOVE YOU, MAY. I FEEL LIKE I'M SPINNING...
...AND YOU'RE THE ONLY PERSON ON THE PLANET WHO CAN BRING ME BACK.
TO...TO STILLNESS. TO ME.
OH, PETER...
...I SHOULDN'T HAVE-- SHOULDN'T HAVE CUT YOU OUT LIKE THAT.
I JUST DIDN'T LIKE THE THOUGHT OF YOU NOT LIVING UP TO YOUR...YOUR AMAZING POTENTIAL!
I LOVE YOU, MY DEAR, DEAR BOY.
I LOVE YOU TOO...
I'VE BEEN... THINKING A
ABOUT THE
INGS YOU'VE SAID...
...ABOUT THAT
OTENTIAL.
IT'S TIME I WAS...
...BETTER--

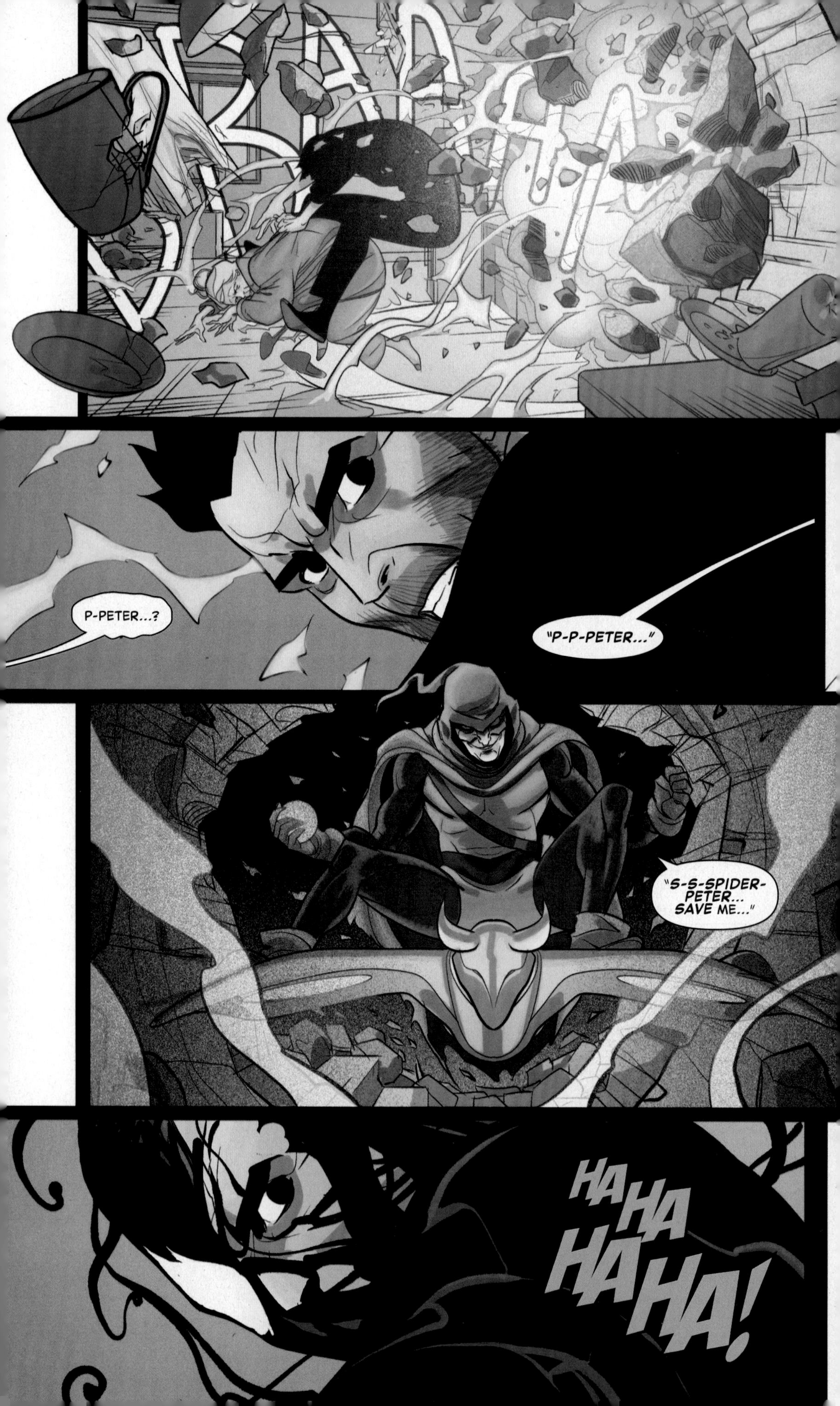
P-PETER...?
"P-P-PETER..."
"S-S-SPIDER-PETER... SAVE ME..."
HA HA HA HA!

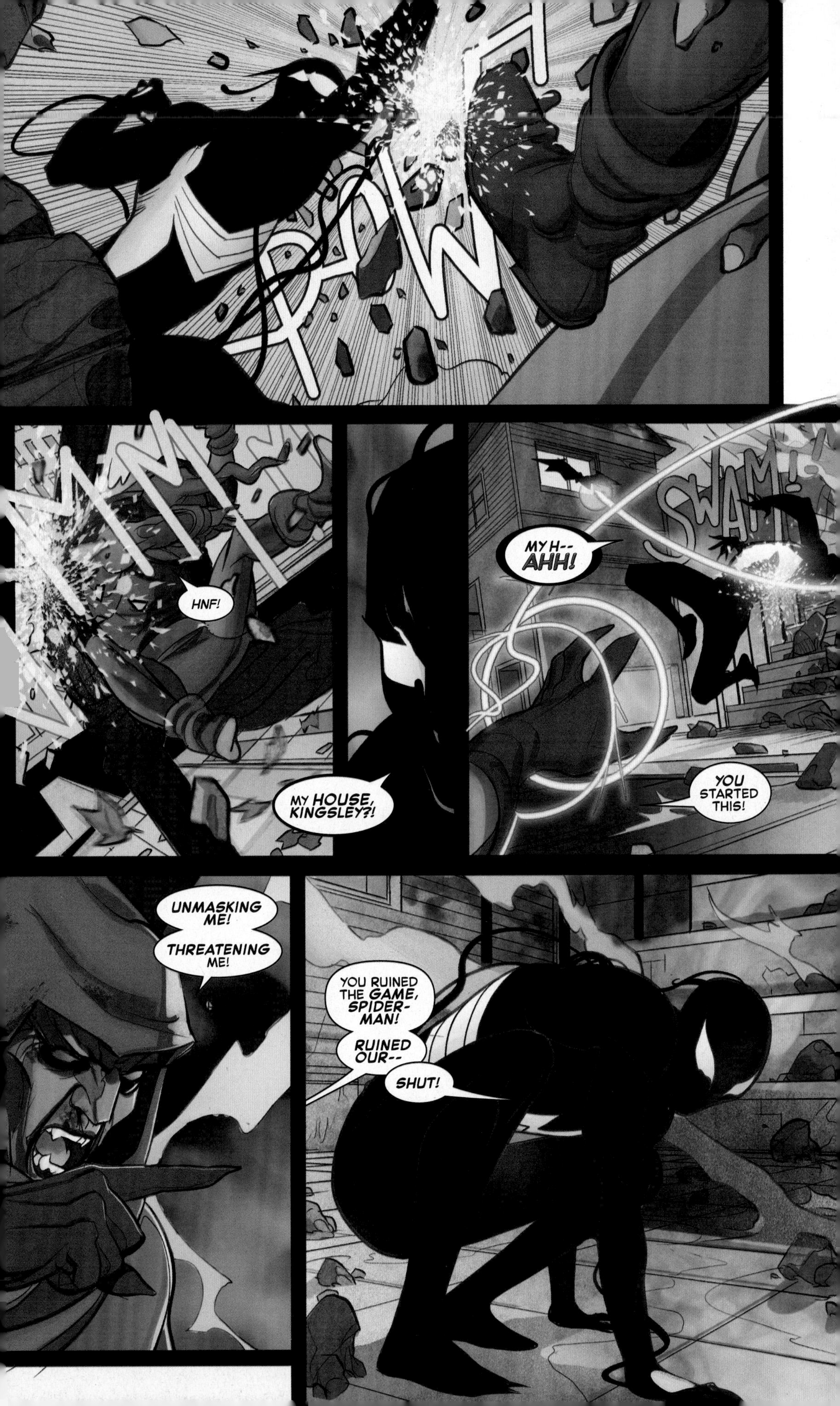
POW
SWAM
HNF!
MY HOUSE, KINGSLEY?!
MY H-- AHH!
SWAM!
YOU STARTED THIS!
UNMASKING ME!
THREATENING ME!
YOU RUINED THE GAME, SPIDER-MAN!
RUINED OUR--
SHUT!

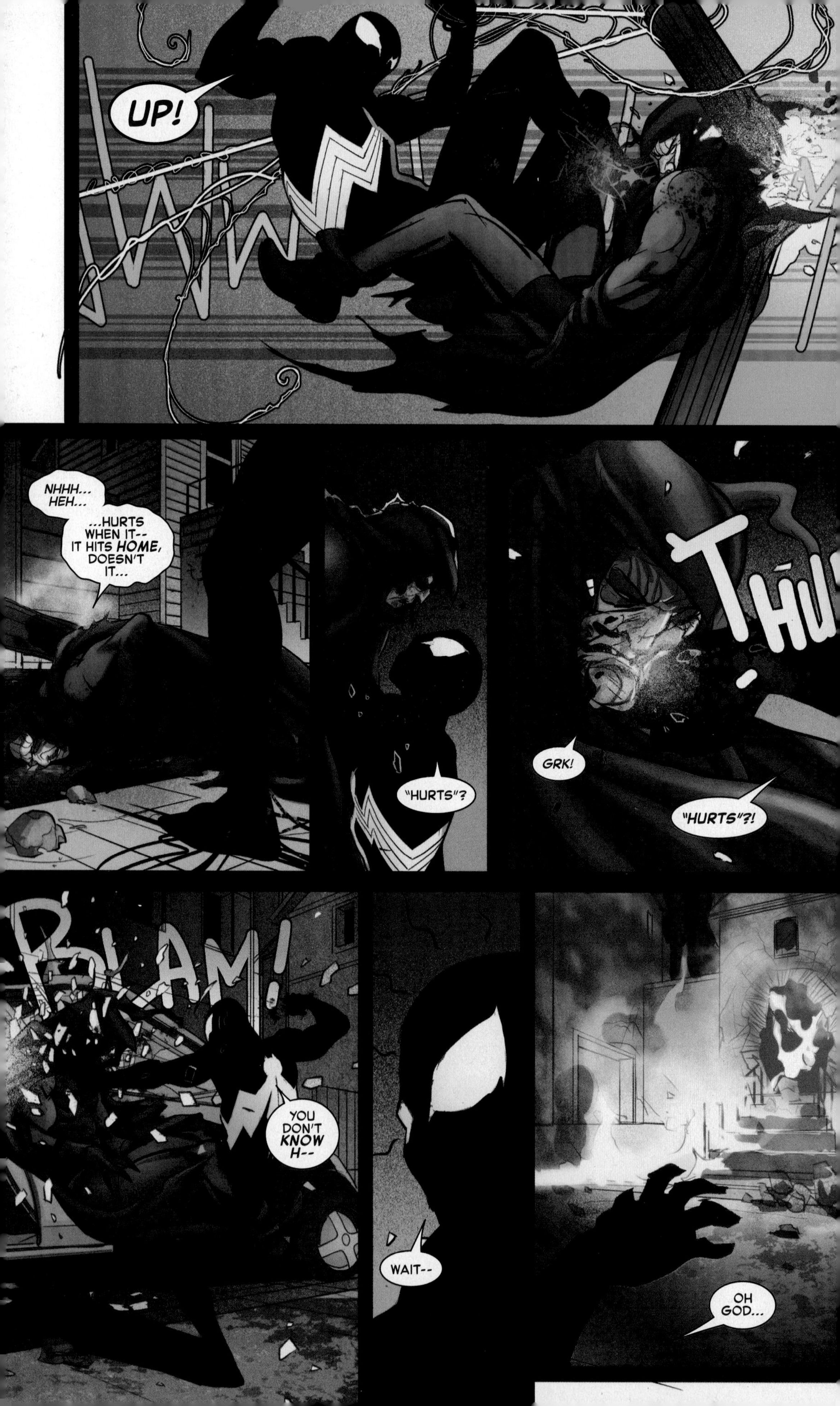
UP!
NHHH... HEH...
...HURTS WHEN IT-- IT HITS HOME, DOESN'T IT...
"HURTS"?
GRK!
"HURTS"?!
BLAM!
YOU DON'T KNOW H--
WAIT--
OH GOD...

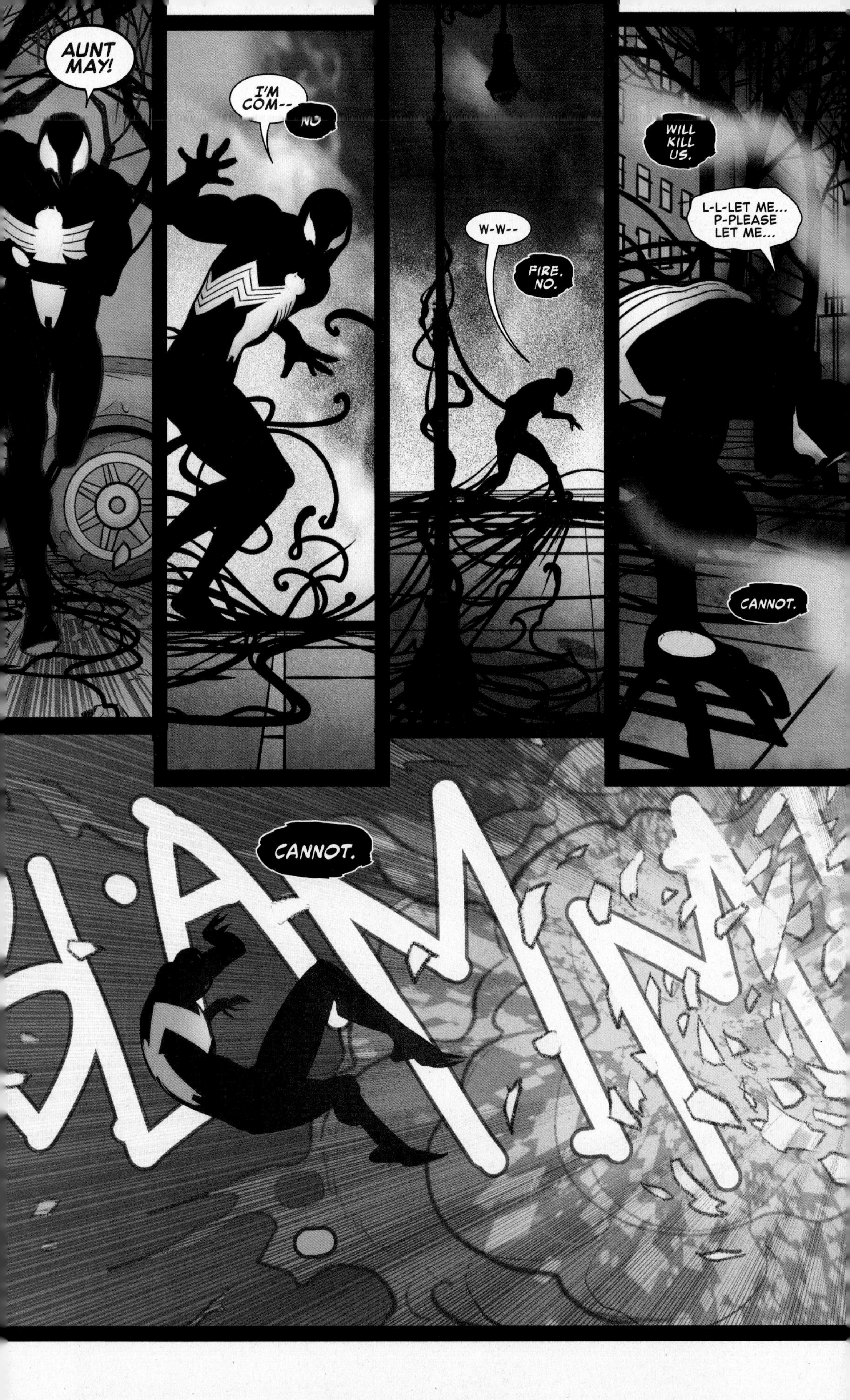
AUNT MAY!
I'M COM--
NO
W-W--
FIRE. NO.
WILL KILL US.
L-L-LET ME... P-PLEASE LET ME...
CANNOT.
CANNOT.

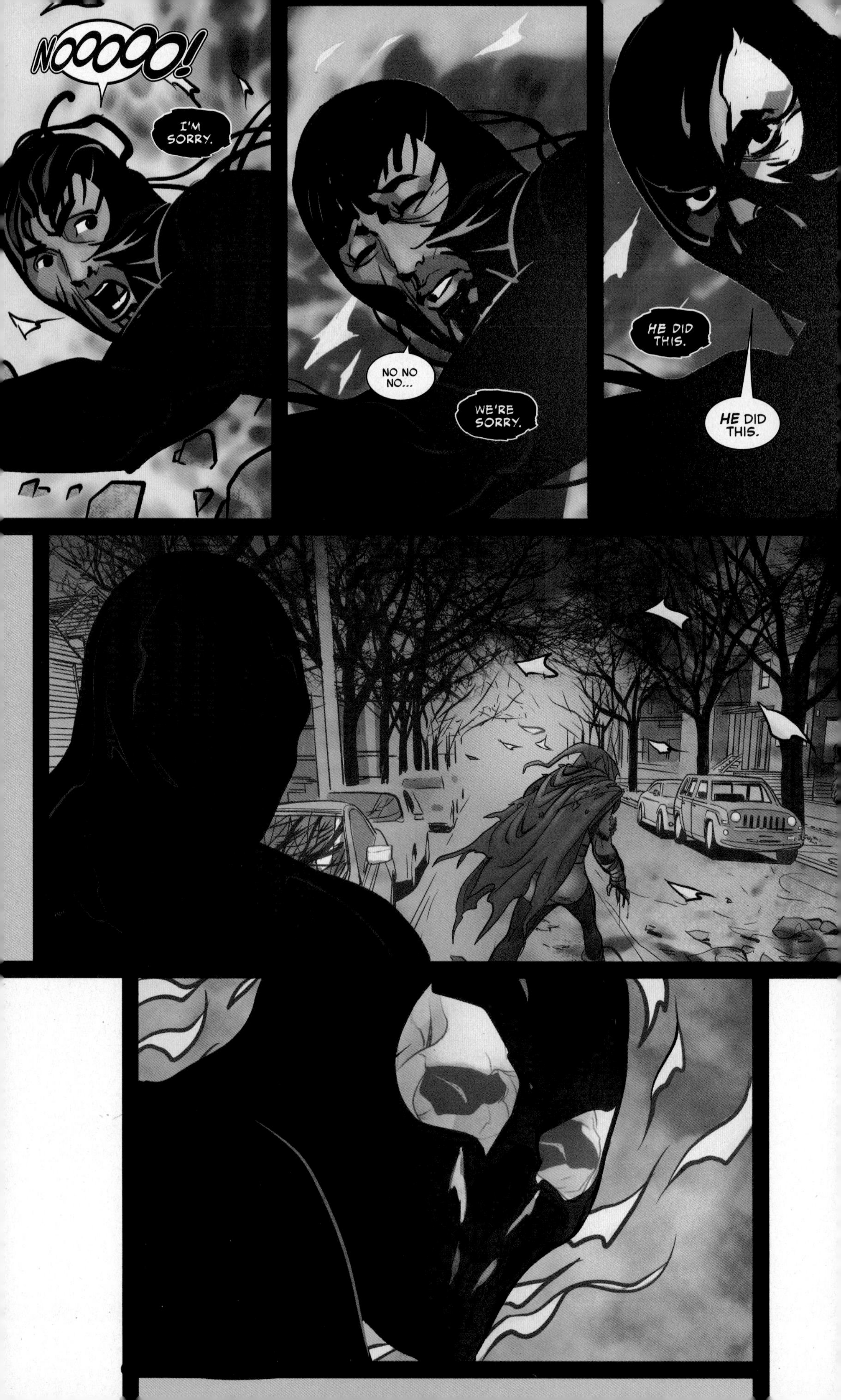
NOOOOO!
I'M SORRY.
NO NO NO...
WE'RE SORRY.
HE DID THIS.
HE DID THIS.

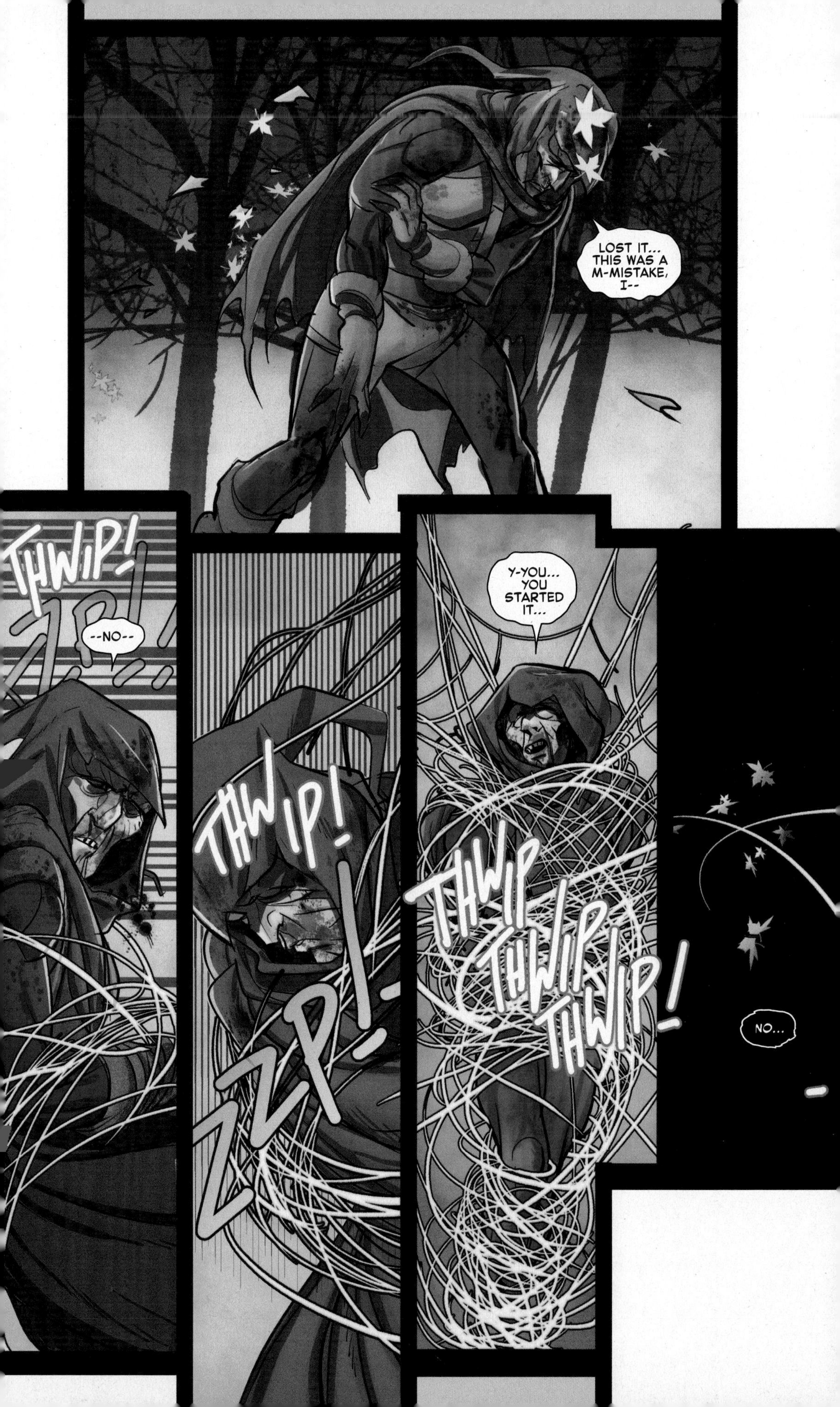
LOST IT... THIS WAS A M-MISTAKE, I--
THWIP!
ZIP!
--NO--
THWIP!
ZZP!
Y-YOU... YOU STARTED IT...
THWIP THWIP THWIP!
NO...

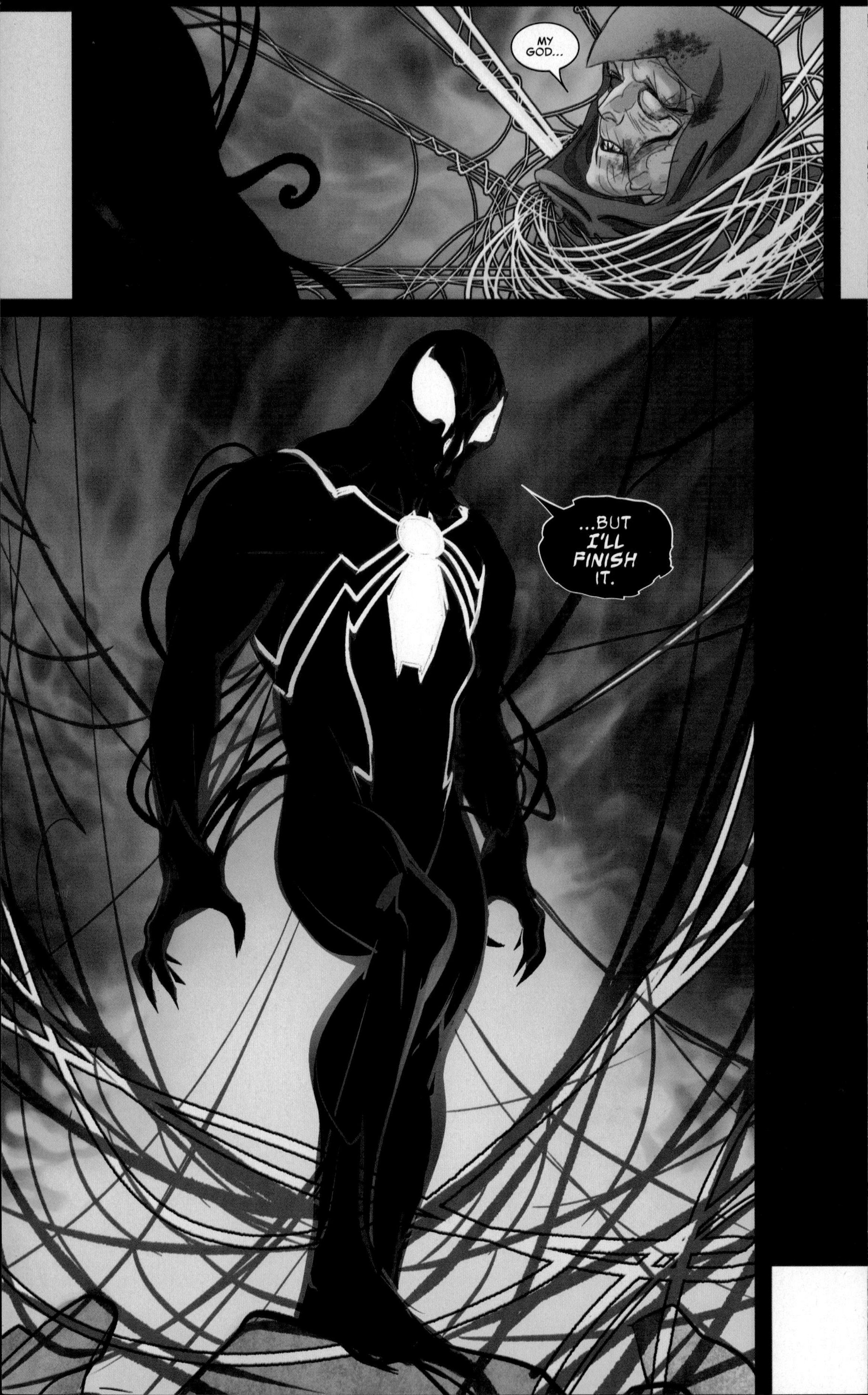
MY GOD...
...BUT I'LL FINISH IT.

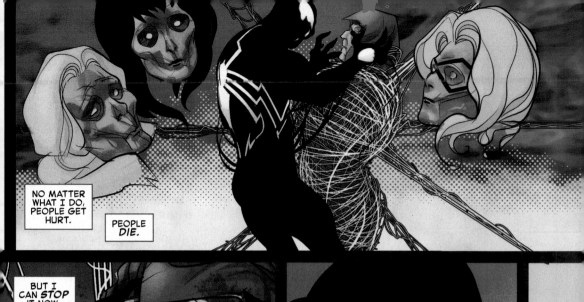

NO MATTER WHAT I DO, PEOPLE GET HURT.

PEOPLE *DIE*.

BUT I CAN *STOP* IT NOW.

I HAVE THE *POWER*.

IT'S TIME TO USE IT.

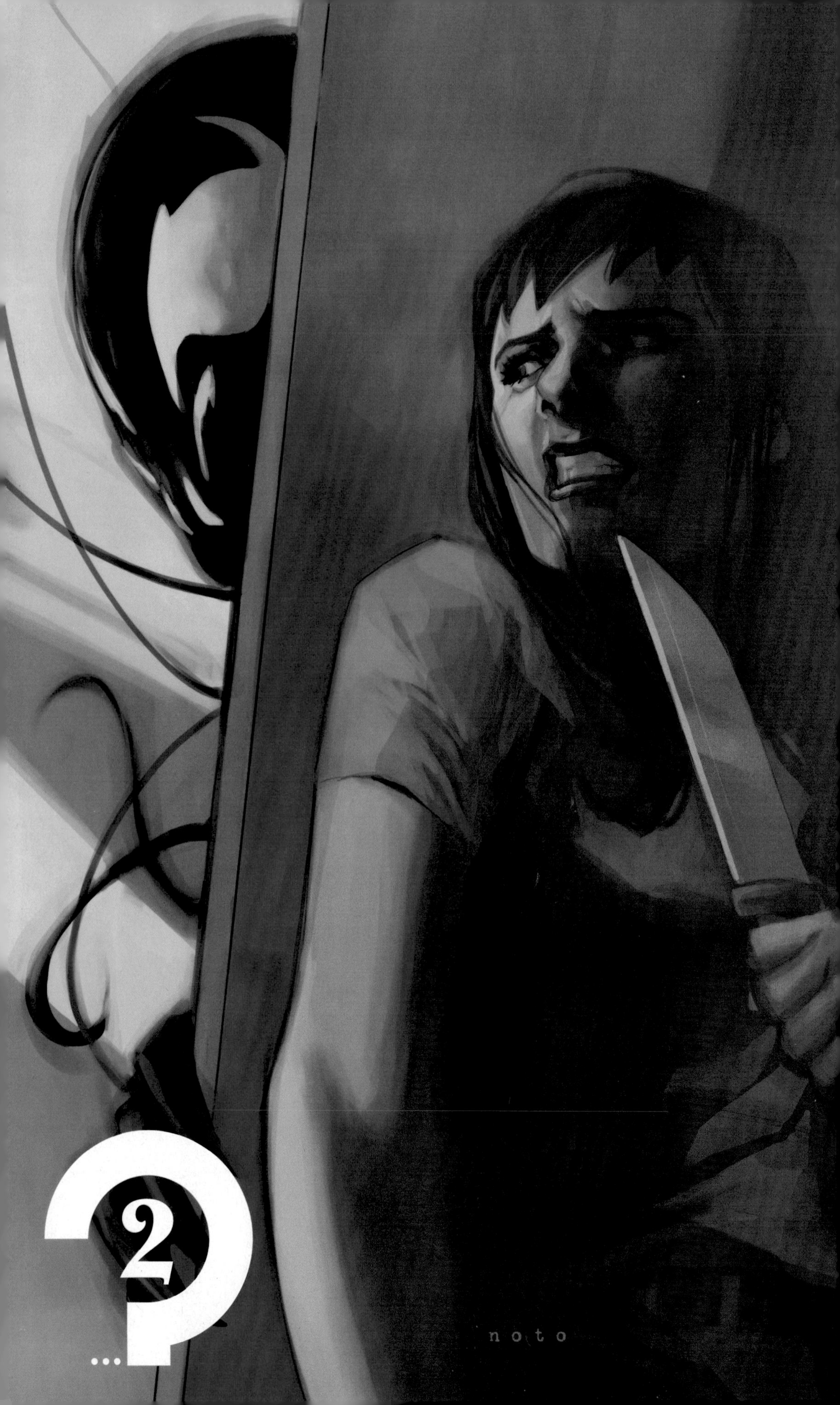
2
noto

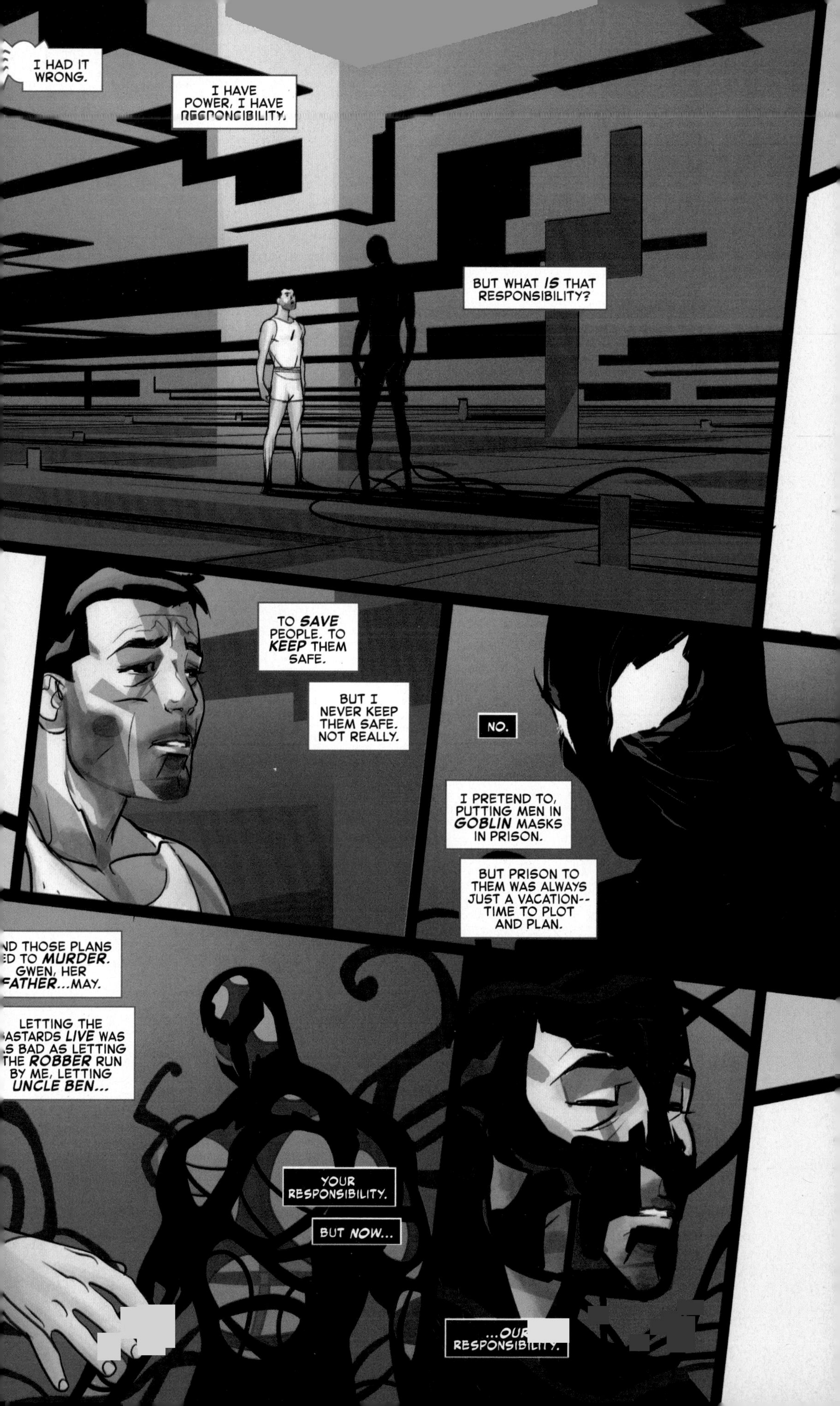

I HAD IT WRONG.
I HAVE POWER, I HAVE RESPONSIBILITY.
BUT WHAT *IS* THAT RESPONSIBILITY?
TO *SAVE* PEOPLE. TO *KEEP* THEM SAFE.
BUT I NEVER KEEP THEM SAFE. NOT REALLY.
NO.
I PRETEND TO, PUTTING MEN IN *GOBLIN* MASKS IN PRISON.
BUT PRISON TO THEM WAS ALWAYS JUST A VACATION-- TIME TO PLOT AND PLAN.
ND THOSE PLANS ED TO *MURDER*. GWEN, HER FATHER...MAY.
LETTING THE ASTARDS *LIVE* WAS S BAD AS LETTING THE *ROBBER* RUN BY ME, LETTING *UNCLE BEN...*
YOUR RESPONSIBILITY.
BUT *NOW...*
...OUR RESPONSIBILITY.

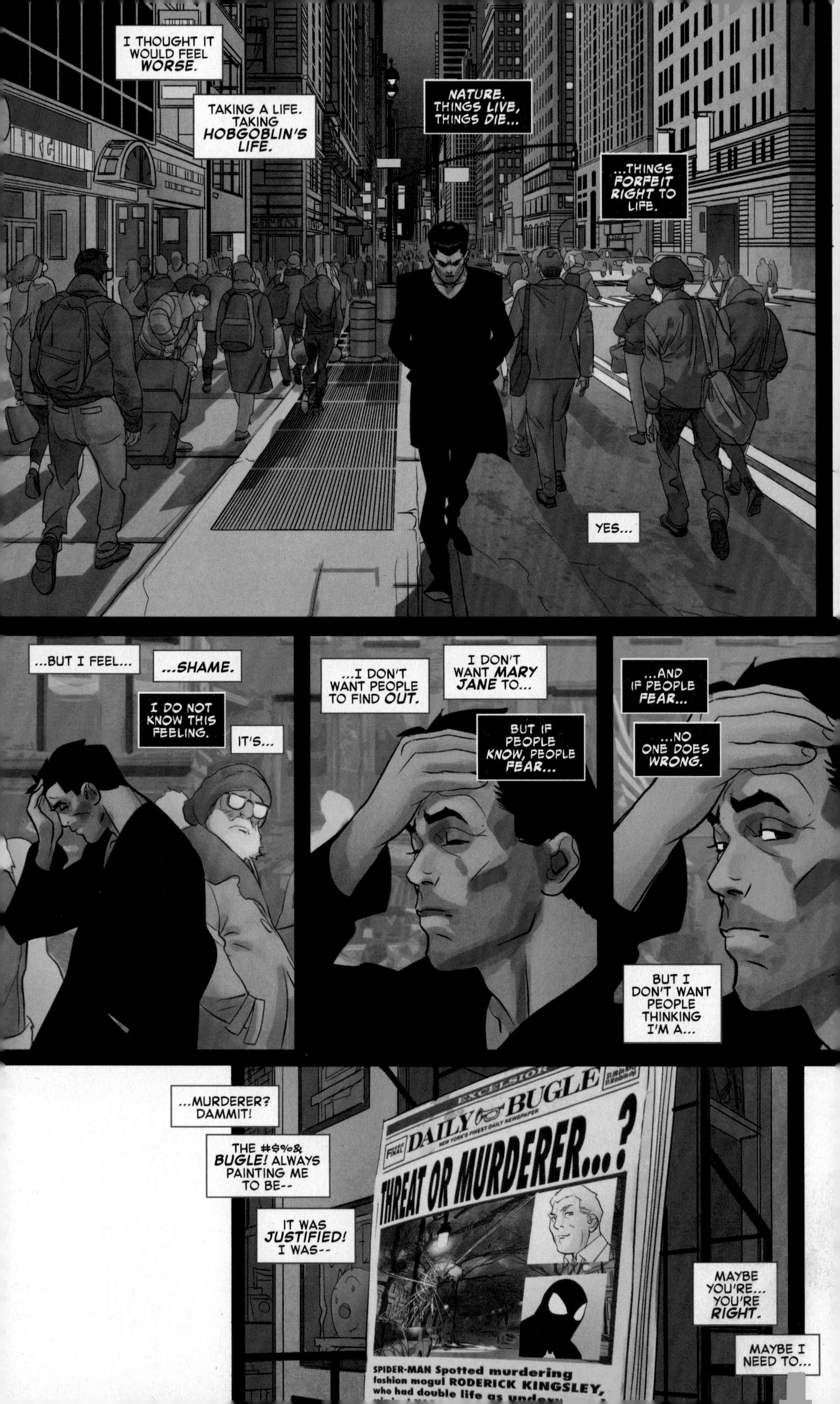

I THOUGHT IT WOULD FEEL WORSE.
TAKING A LIFE. TAKING HOBGOBLIN'S LIFE.
NATURE. THINGS LIVE, THINGS DIE...
...THINGS FORFEIT RIGHT TO LIFE.
YES...
...BUT I FEEL...
...SHAME.
I DO NOT KNOW THIS FEELING.
IT'S...
...I DON'T WANT PEOPLE TO FIND OUT.
I DON'T WANT MARY JANE TO...
BUT IF PEOPLE KNOW, PEOPLE FEAR...
...AND IF PEOPLE FEAR...
...NO ONE DOES WRONG.
BUT I DON'T WANT PEOPLE THINKING I'M A...
...MURDERER? DAMMIT!
THE #$%& BUGLE! ALWAYS PAINTING ME TO BE--
IT WAS JUSTIFIED! I WAS--
EXCELSIOR
DAILY BUGLE
NEW YORK'S FINEST DAILY NEWSPAPER
FINAL
THREAT OR MURDERER...?
SPIDER-MAN Spotted murdering fashion mogul RODERICK KINGSLEY, who had double life as
MAYBE YOU'RE... YOU'RE RIGHT.
MAYBE I NEED TO...

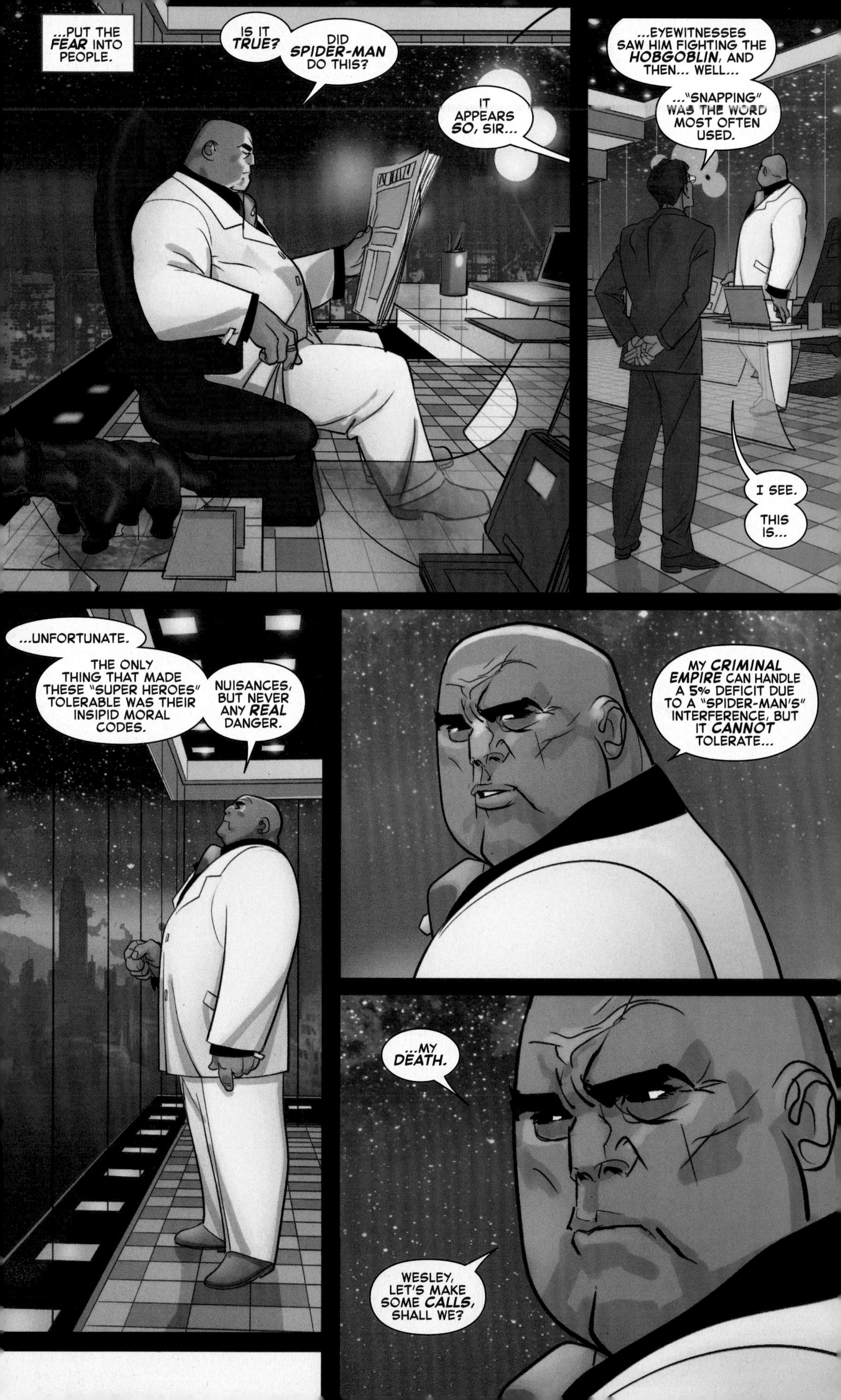
...PUT THE FEAR INTO PEOPLE.
IS IT TRUE? DID SPIDER-MAN DO THIS?
IT APPEARS SO, SIR...
...EYEWITNESSES SAW HIM FIGHTING THE HOBGOBLIN, AND THEN... WELL...
..."SNAPPING" WAS THE WORD MOST OFTEN USED.
I SEE.
THIS IS...
...UNFORTUNATE.
THE ONLY THING THAT MADE THESE "SUPER HEROES" TOLERABLE WAS THEIR INSIPID MORAL CODES.
NUISANCES, BUT NEVER ANY REAL DANGER.
MY CRIMINAL EMPIRE CAN HANDLE A 5% DEFICIT DUE TO A "SPIDER-MAN'S" INTERFERENCE, BUT IT CANNOT TOLERATE...
...MY DEATH.
WESLEY, LET'S MAKE SOME CALLS, SHALL WE?

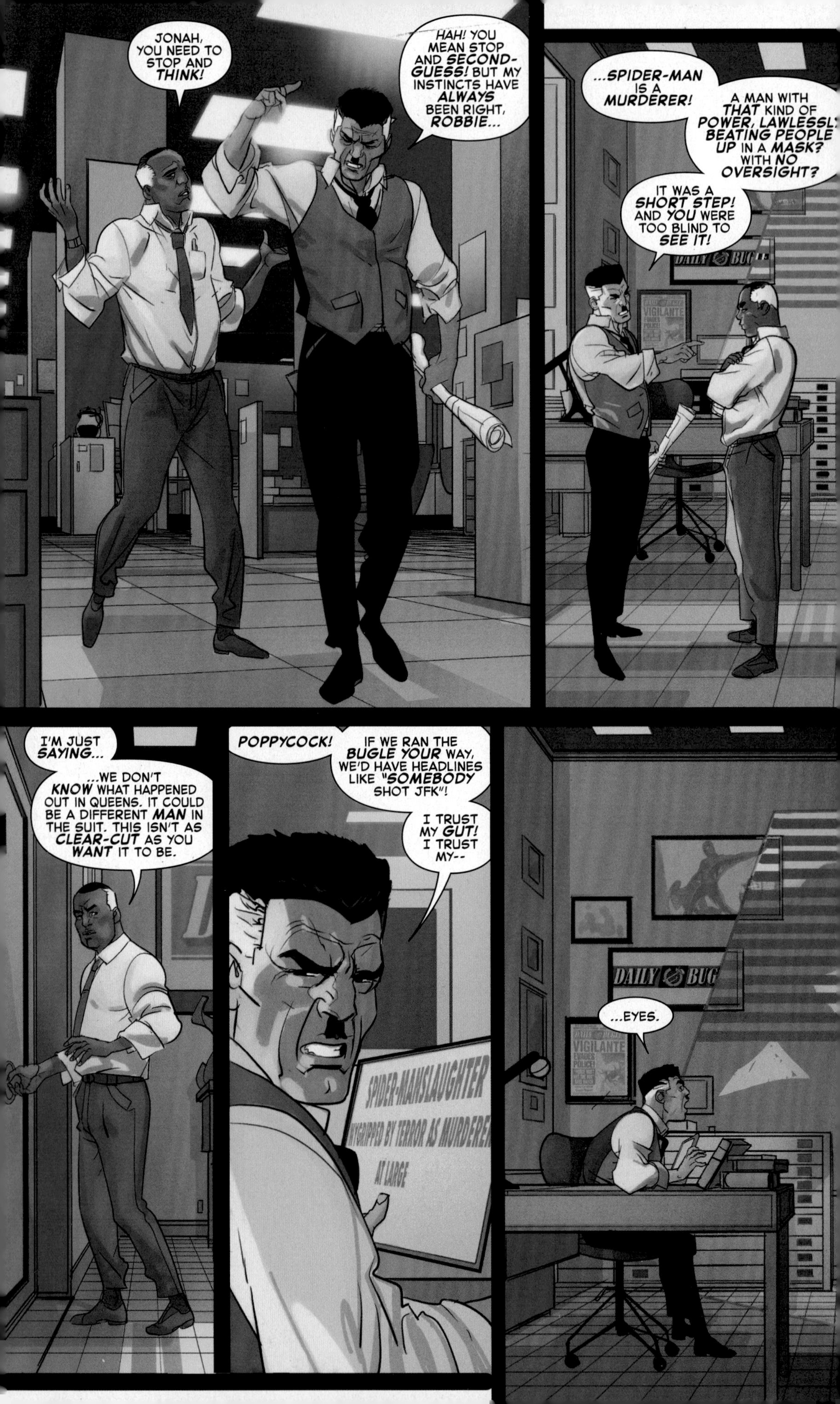

JONAH, YOU NEED TO STOP AND THINK!
HAH! YOU MEAN STOP AND SECOND-GUESS! BUT MY INSTINCTS HAVE ALWAYS BEEN RIGHT, ROBBIE...
...SPIDER-MAN IS A MURDERER!
A MAN WITH THAT KIND OF POWER, LAWLESSL BEATING PEOPLE UP IN A MASK? WITH NO OVERSIGHT?
IT WAS A SHORT STEP! AND YOU WERE TOO BLIND TO SEE IT!
VIGILANTE
I'M JUST SAYING...
...WE DON'T KNOW WHAT HAPPENED OUT IN QUEENS. IT COULD BE A DIFFERENT MAN IN THE SUIT. THIS ISN'T AS CLEAR-CUT AS YOU WANT IT TO BE.
POPPYCOCK!
IF WE RAN THE BUGLE YOUR WAY, WE'D HAVE HEADLINES LIKE "SOMEBODY SHOT JFK"!
I TRUST MY GUT! I TRUST MY--
SPIDER-MANSLAUGHTER
GRIPPED BY TERROR AS MURDERER AT LARGE
DAILY BUG
...EYES.
VIGILANTE EVADES POLICE!

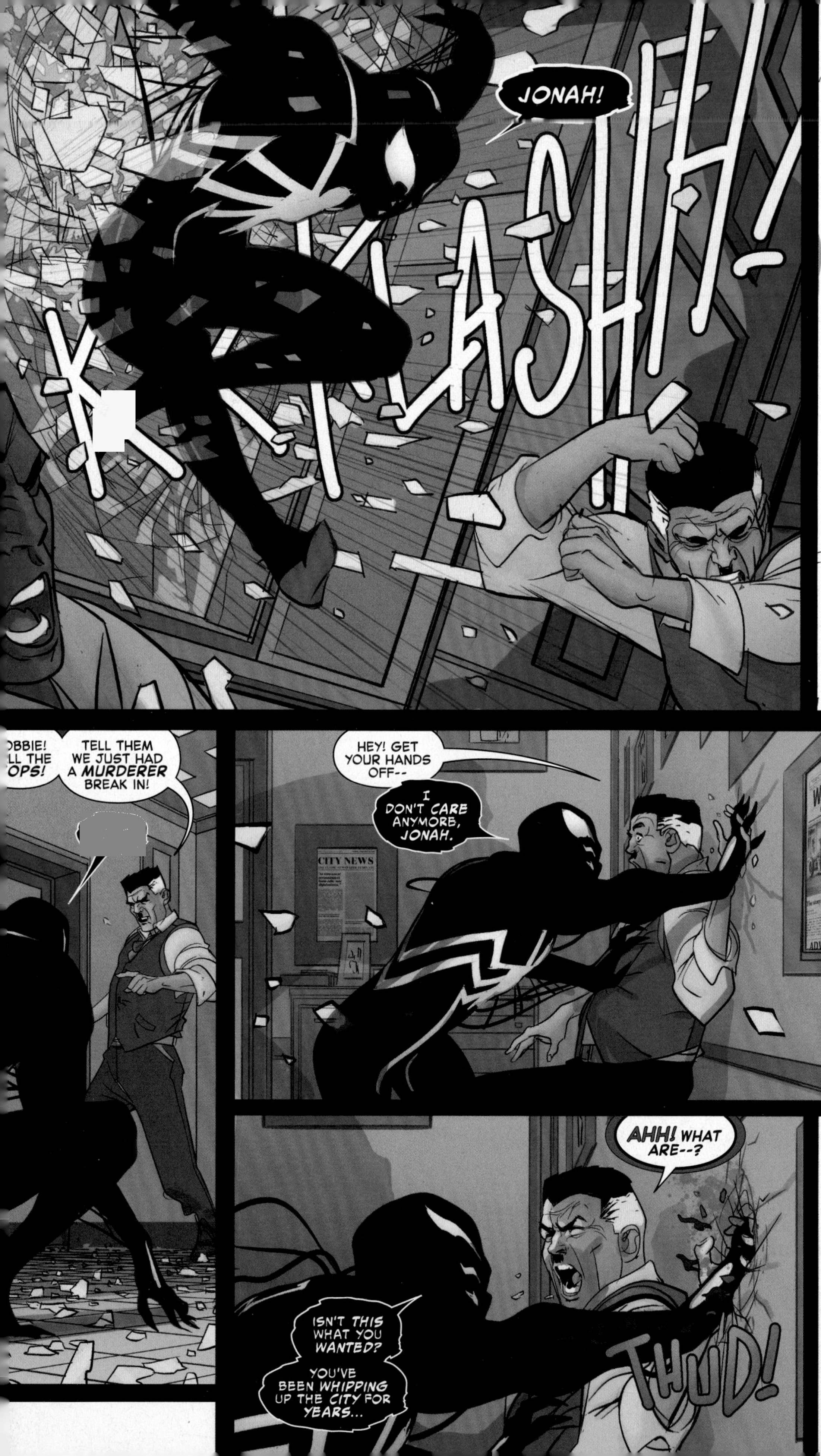

JONAH!
KLASH!
OBBIE!
LL THE
OPS!
TELL THEM WE JUST HAD A MURDERER BREAK IN!
HEY! GET YOUR HANDS OFF--
I DON'T CARE ANYMORE, JONAH.
CITY NEWS
WORD TEM
ADVERTISEMEN
AHH! WHAT ARE--?
ISN'T THIS WHAT YOU WANTED?
YOU'VE BEEN WHIPPING UP THE CITY FOR YEARS...
THUD!

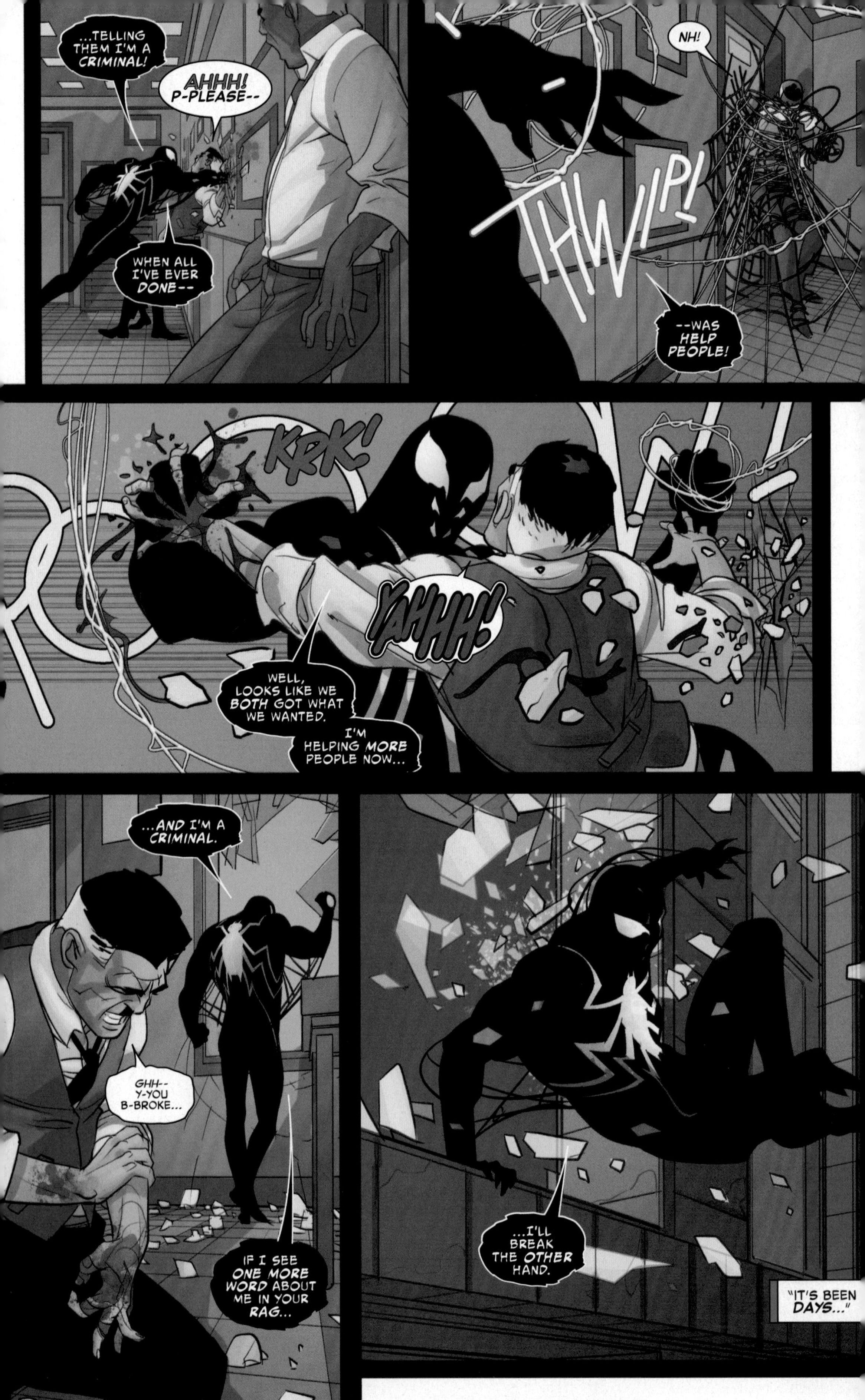

...TELLING THEM I'M A CRIMINAL!
AHHH! P-PLEASE--
WHEN ALL I'VE EVER DONE--
NH!
THWIP!
--WAS HELP PEOPLE!
KRK!
YAHHH!
WELL, LOOKS LIKE WE BOTH GOT WHAT WE WANTED.
I'M HELPING MORE PEOPLE NOW...
...AND I'M A CRIMINAL.
GHH-- Y-YOU B-BROKE...
IF I SEE ONE MORE WORD ABOUT ME IN YOUR RAG...
...I'LL BREAK THE OTHER HAND.
"IT'S BEEN DAYS..."

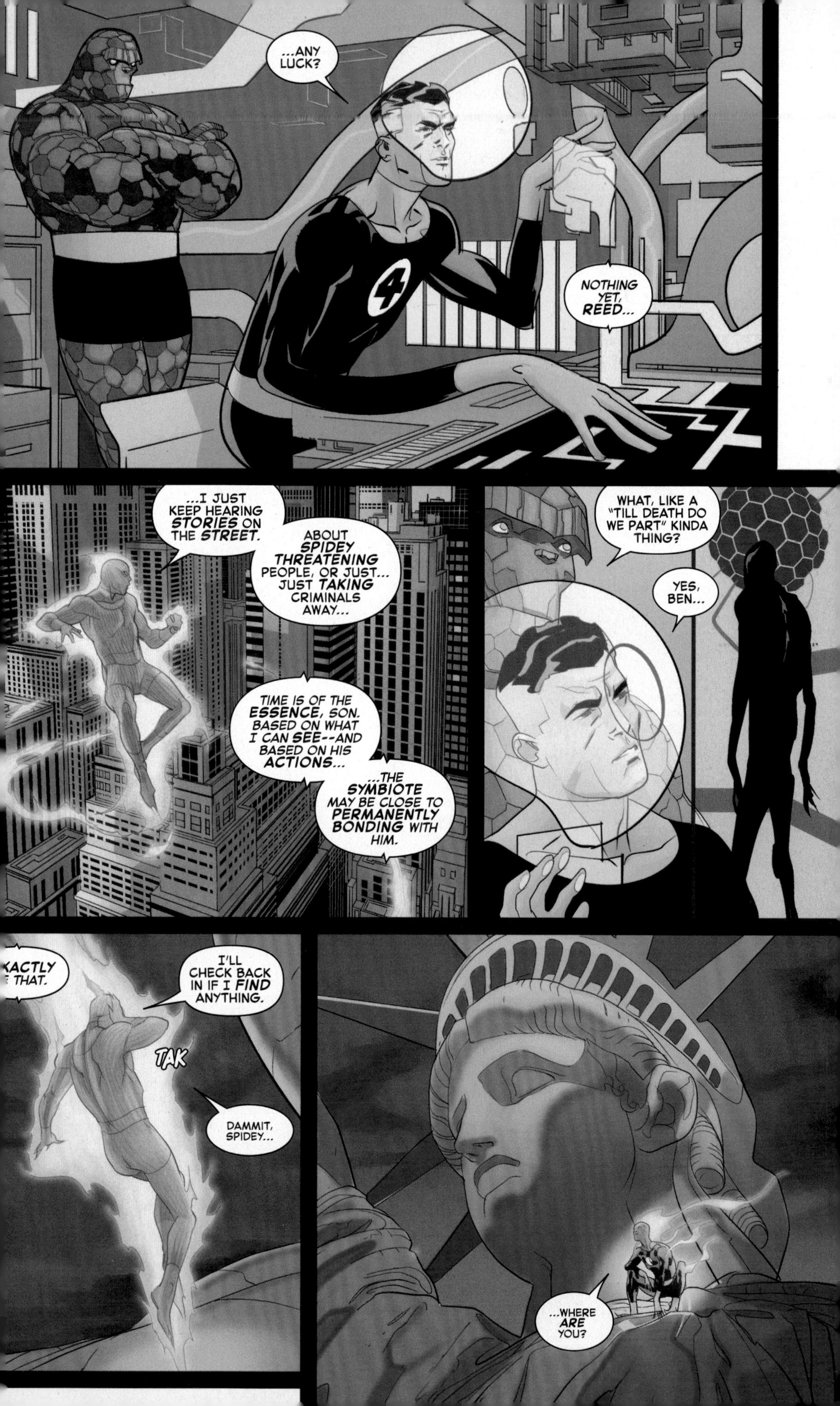

...ANY LUCK?
NOTHING YET, REED...
...I JUST KEEP HEARING STORIES ON THE STREET.
ABOUT SPIDEY THREATENING PEOPLE, OR JUST... JUST TAKING CRIMINALS AWAY...
TIME IS OF THE ESSENCE, SON. BASED ON WHAT I CAN SEE--AND BASED ON HIS ACTIONS...
...THE SYMBIOTE MAY BE CLOSE TO PERMANENTLY BONDING WITH HIM.
WHAT, LIKE A "TILL DEATH DO WE PART" KINDA THING?
YES, BEN...
I'LL CHECK BACK IN IF I FIND ANYTHING.
TAK
DAMMIT, SPIDEY...
...WHERE ARE YOU?

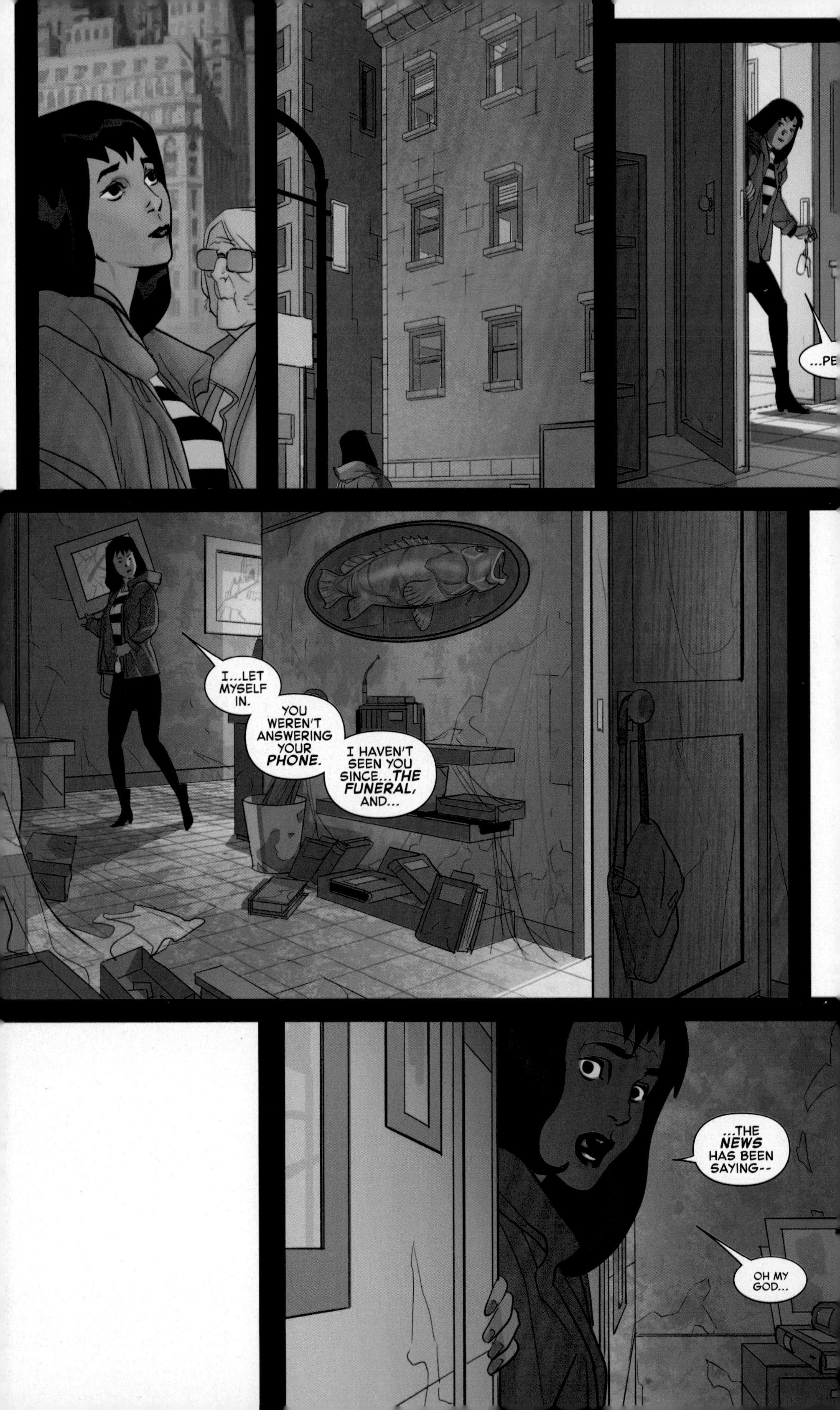
...PE
I...LET MYSELF IN.
YOU WEREN'T ANSWERING YOUR PHONE.
I HAVEN'T SEEN YOU SINCE...THE FUNERAL, AND...
...THE NEWS HAS BEEN SAYING--
OH MY GOD...

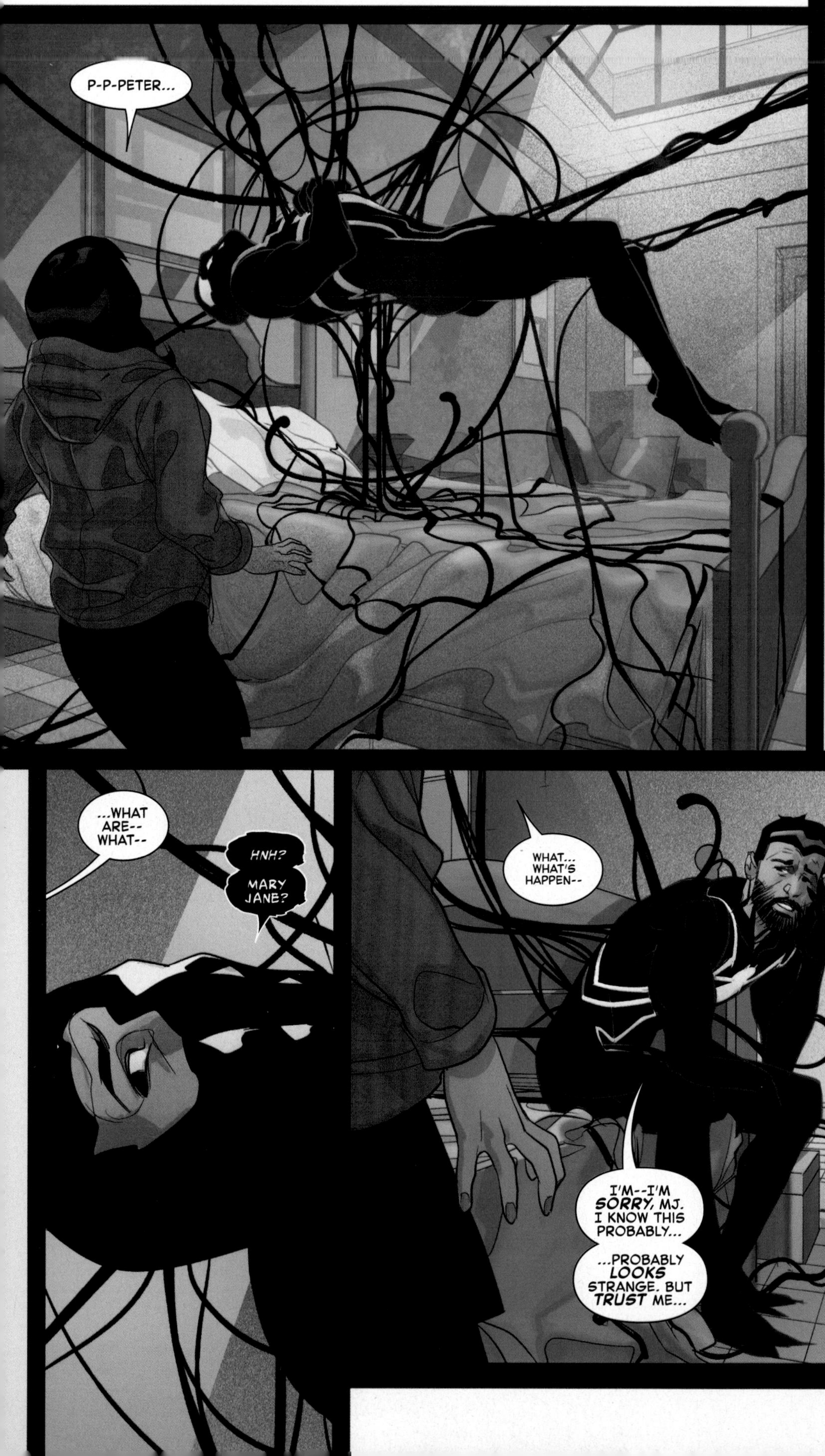
P-P-PETER...
...WHAT ARE-- WHAT--
HNH?
MARY JANE?
WHAT... WHAT'S HAPPEN--
I'M--I'M SORRY, MJ. I KNOW THIS PROBABLY...
...PROBABLY LOOKS STRANGE. BUT TRUST ME...

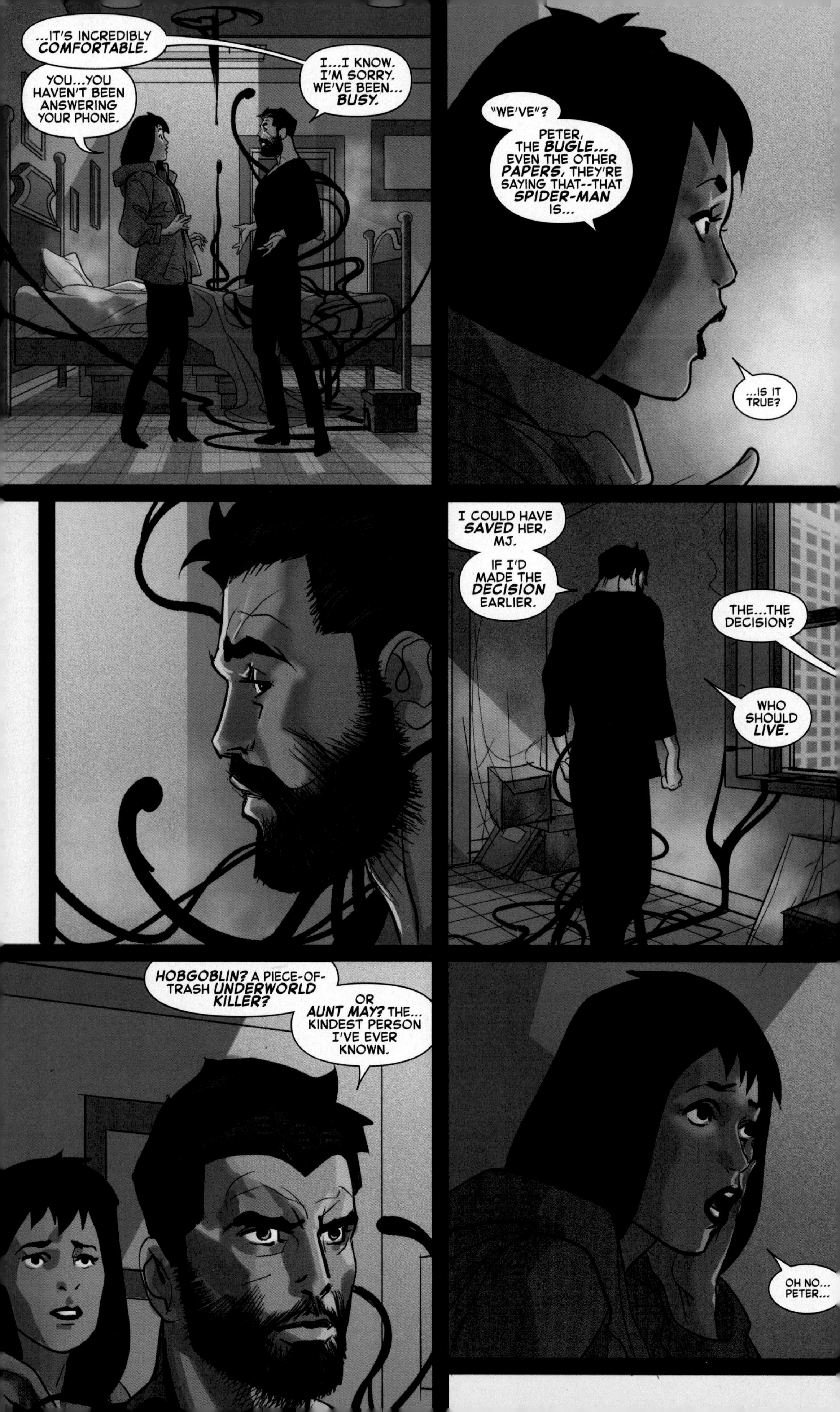
...IT'S INCREDIBLY COMFORTABLE.
YOU...YOU HAVEN'T BEEN ANSWERING YOUR PHONE.
I...I KNOW. I'M SORRY. WE'VE BEEN... BUSY.
"WE'VE"?
PETER, THE BUGLE... EVEN THE OTHER PAPERS, THEY'RE SAYING THAT--THAT SPIDER-MAN IS...
...IS IT TRUE?
I COULD HAVE SAVED HER, MJ.
IF I'D MADE THE DECISION EARLIER.
THE...THE DECISION?
WHO SHOULD LIVE.
HOBGOBLIN? A PIECE-OF-TRASH UNDERWORLD KILLER?
OR AUNT MAY? THE... KINDEST PERSON I'VE EVER KNOWN.
OH NO... PETER...

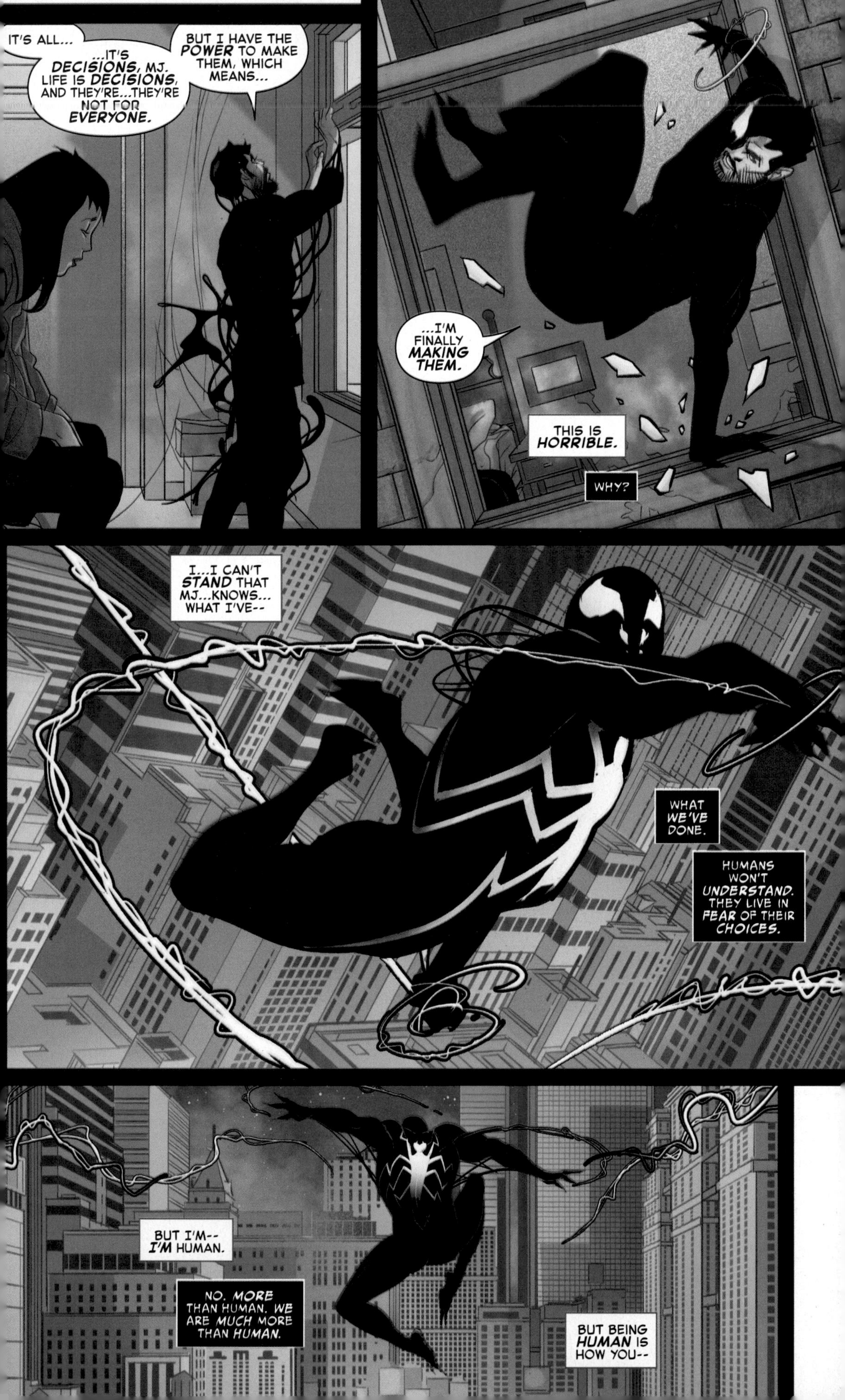
IT'S ALL...
...IT'S DECISIONS, MJ. LIFE IS DECISIONS, AND THEY'RE...THEY'RE NOT FOR EVERYONE.
BUT I HAVE THE POWER TO MAKE THEM, WHICH MEANS...
...I'M FINALLY MAKING THEM.
THIS IS HORRIBLE.
WHY?
I...I CAN'T STAND THAT MJ...KNOWS... WHAT I'VE--
WHAT WE'VE DONE.
HUMANS WON'T UNDERSTAND. THEY LIVE IN FEAR OF THEIR CHOICES.
BUT I'M-- I'M HUMAN.
NO. MORE THAN HUMAN. WE ARE MUCH MORE THAN HUMAN.
BUT BEING HUMAN IS HOW YOU--

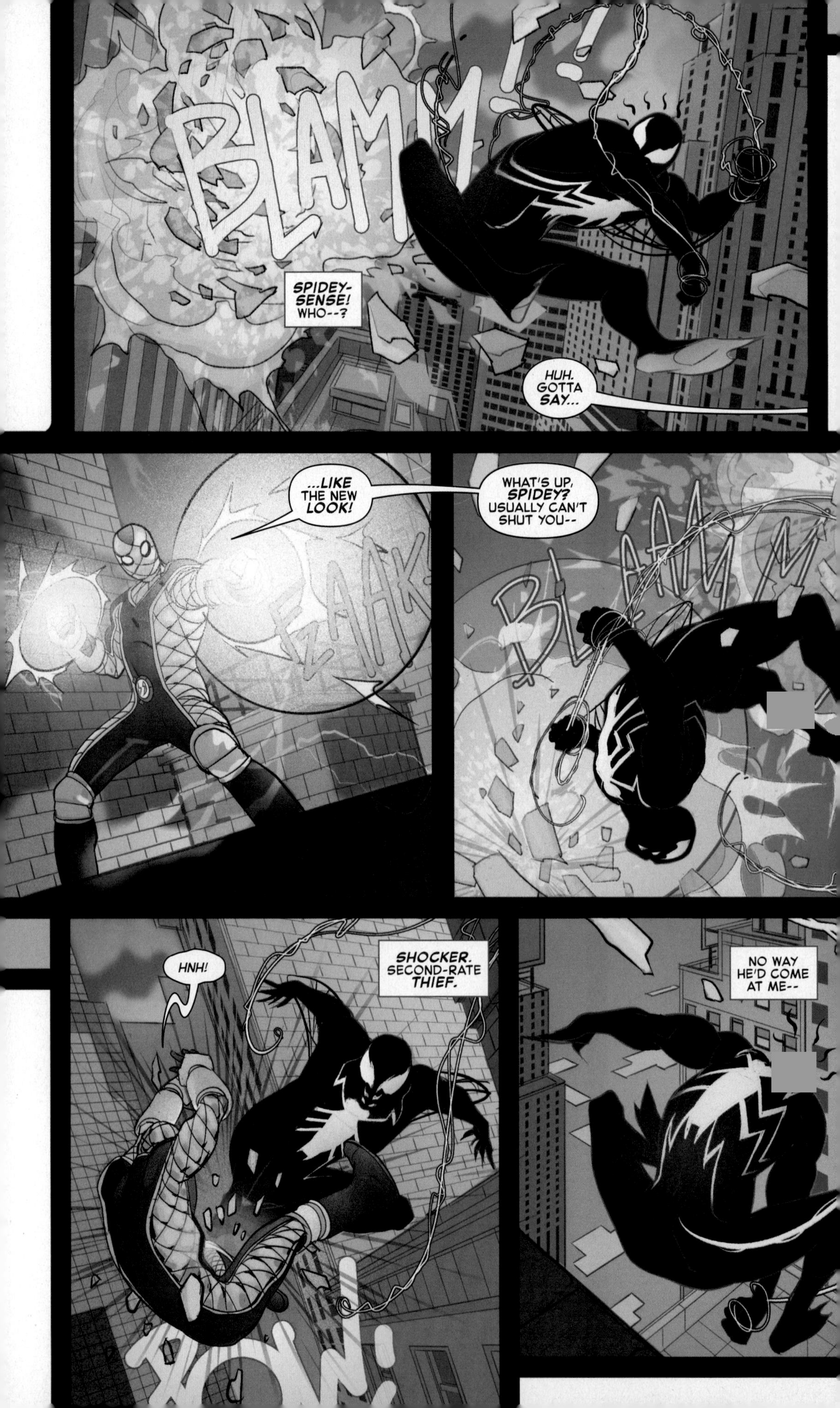
BLAMM!!
SPIDEY-SENSE! WHO--?
HUH. GOTTA SAY...
...LIKE THE NEW LOOK!
FZAAK!
WHAT'S UP, SPIDEY? USUALLY CAN'T SHUT YOU--
BLAAMM
HNH!
SHOCKER. SECOND-RATE THIEF.
NO WAY HE'D COME AT ME--

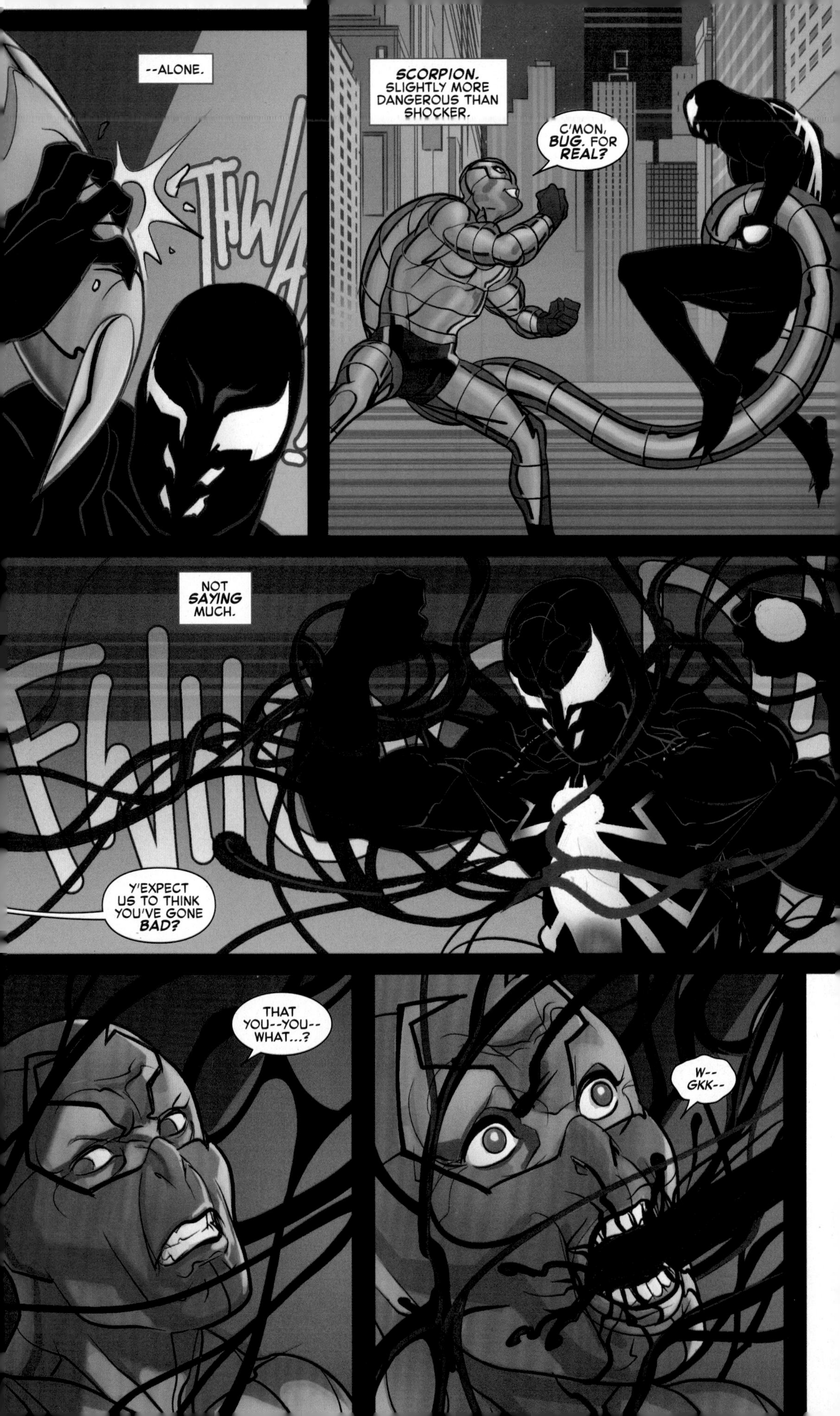
--ALONE.
THWAK!
SCORPION. SLIGHTLY MORE DANGEROUS THAN SHOCKER.
C'MON, BUG. FOR REAL?
NOT SAYING MUCH.
Y'EXPECT US TO THINK YOU'VE GONE BAD?
THAT YOU--YOU-- WHAT...?
W-- GKK--

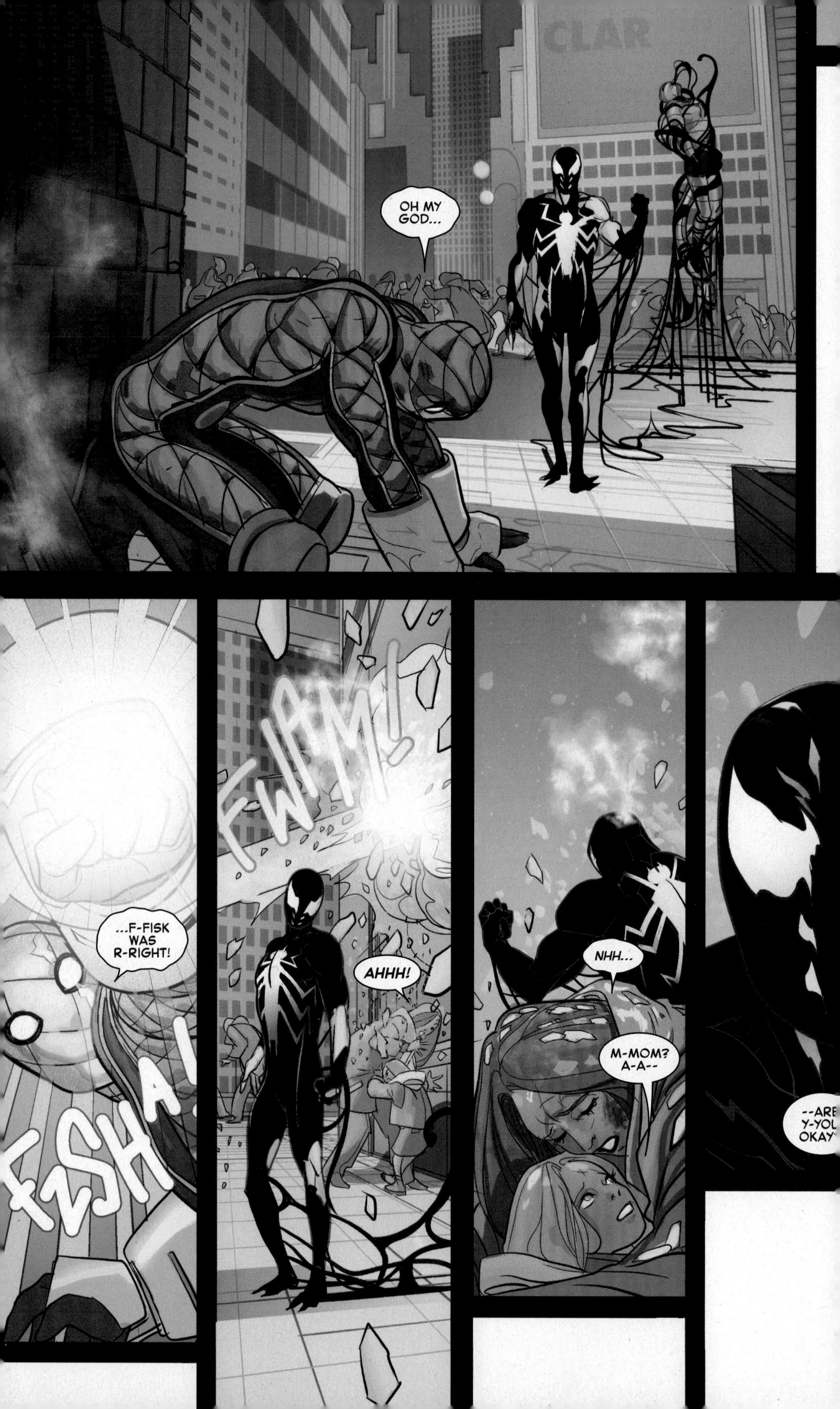
OH MY GOD...
...F-FISK WAS R-RIGHT!
FSHAA!
FWAM!
AHHH!
NHH...
M-MOM? A-A--
--ARE Y-YOU OKAY

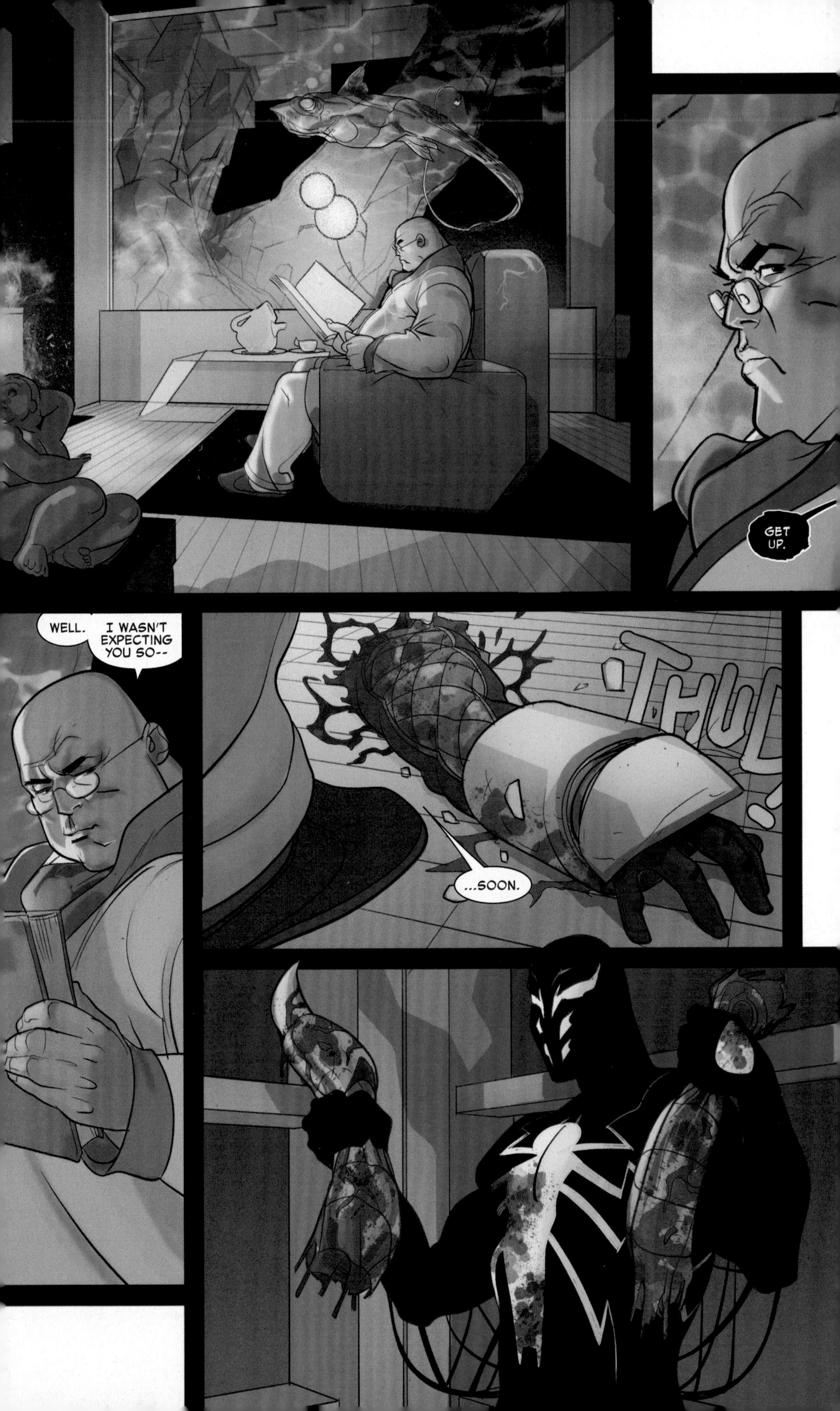
GET UP.
WELL. I WASN'T EXPECTING YOU SO--
THUD!
...SOON.

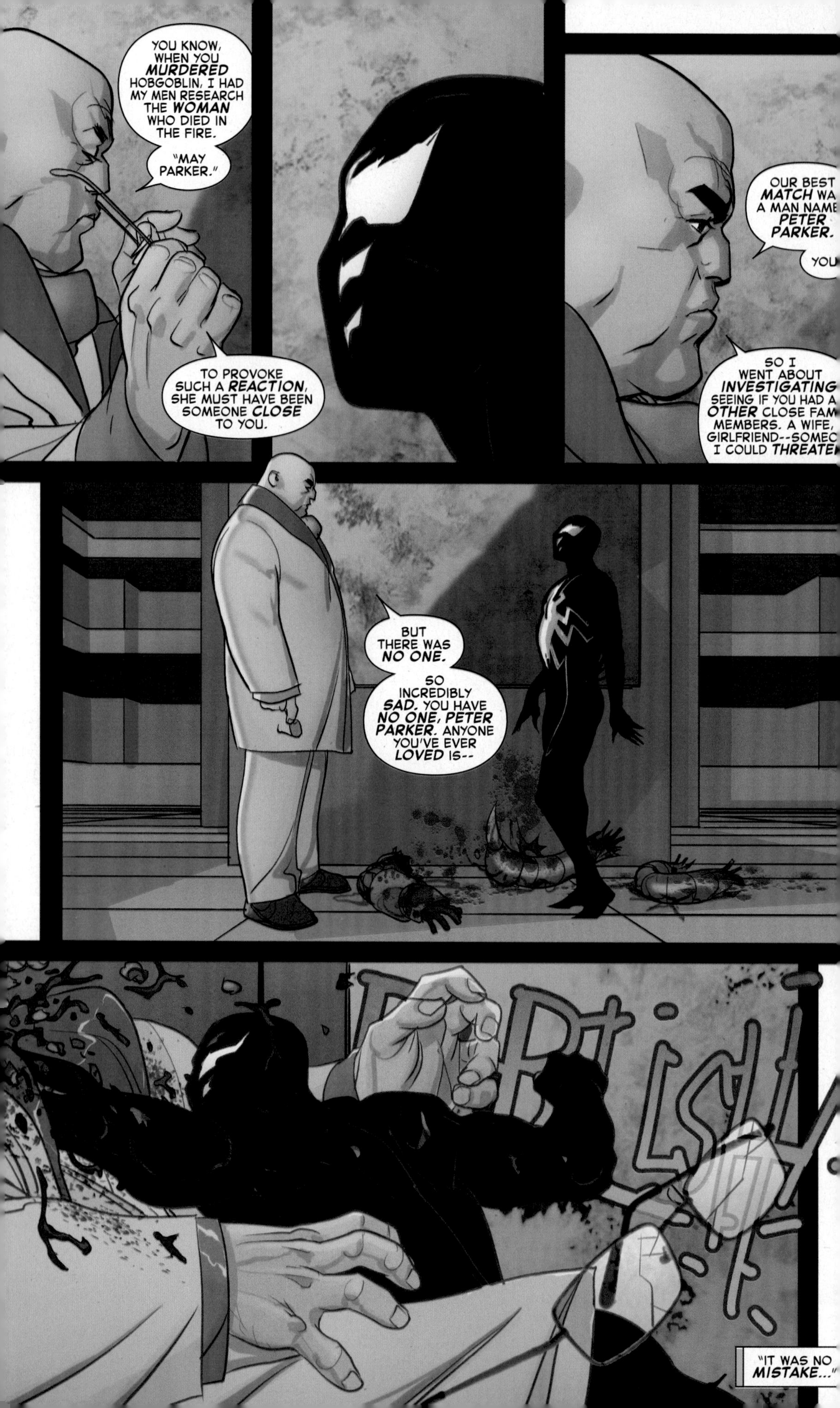

YOU KNOW, WHEN YOU MURDERED HOBGOBLIN, I HAD MY MEN RESEARCH THE WOMAN WHO DIED IN THE FIRE.
"MAY PARKER."
TO PROVOKE SUCH A REACTION, SHE MUST HAVE BEEN SOMEONE CLOSE TO YOU.
OUR BEST MATCH WA A MAN NAME PETER PARKER.
YOU
SO I WENT ABOUT INVESTIGATING SEEING IF YOU HAD A OTHER CLOSE FAM MEMBERS. A WIFE, GIRLFRIEND--SOMEC I COULD THREATE
BUT THERE WAS NO ONE.
SO INCREDIBLY SAD. YOU HAVE NO ONE, PETER PARKER. ANYONE YOU'VE EVER LOVED IS--
"IT WAS NO MISTAKE..."

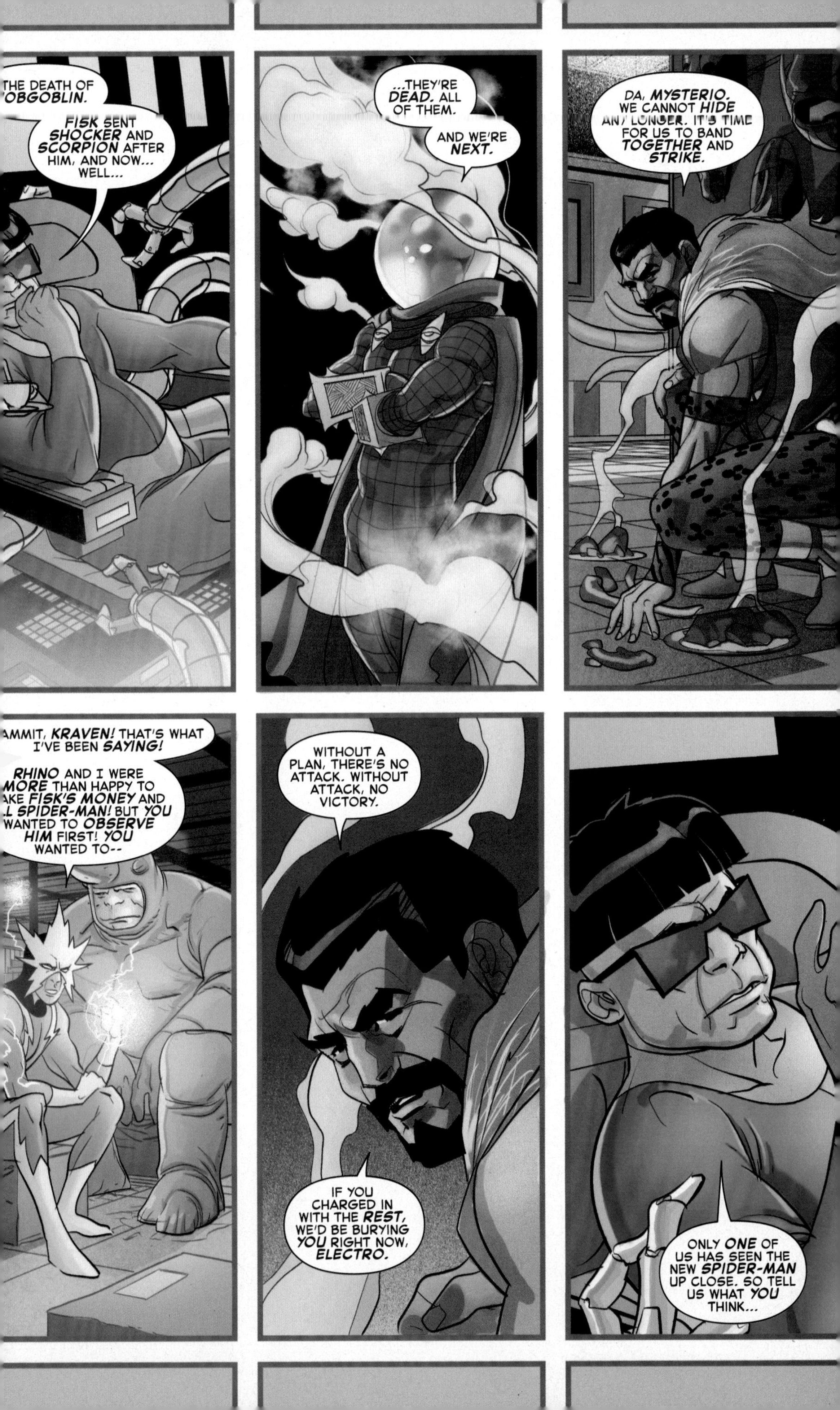
THE DEATH OF 'OBGOBLIN.
FISK SENT SHOCKER AND SCORPION AFTER HIM, AND NOW... WELL...
...THEY'RE DEAD. ALL OF THEM.
AND WE'RE NEXT.
DA, MYSTERIO. WE CANNOT HIDE ANY LONGER. IT'S TIME FOR US TO BAND TOGETHER AND STRIKE.
AMMIT, KRAVEN! THAT'S WHAT I'VE BEEN SAYING!
RHINO AND I WERE MORE THAN HAPPY TO AKE FISK'S MONEY AND L SPIDER-MAN! BUT YOU WANTED TO OBSERVE HIM FIRST! YOU WANTED TO--
WITHOUT A PLAN, THERE'S NO ATTACK. WITHOUT ATTACK, NO VICTORY.
IF YOU CHARGED IN WITH THE REST, WE'D BE BURYING YOU RIGHT NOW, ELECTRO.
ONLY ONE OF US HAS SEEN THE NEW SPIDER-MAN UP CLOSE. SO TELL US WHAT YOU THINK...

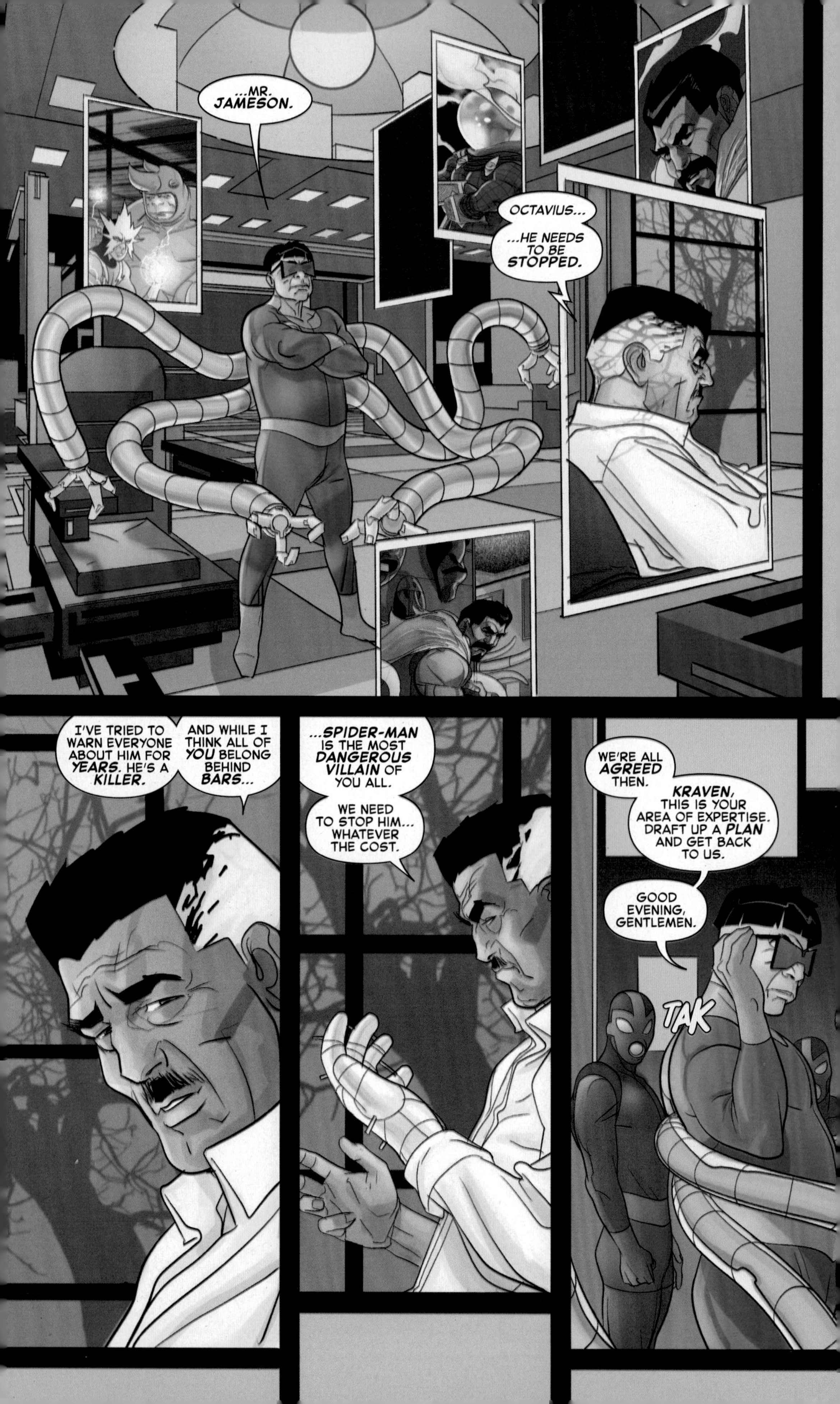

...MR. JAMESON.
OCTAVIUS...
...HE NEEDS TO BE STOPPED.
I'VE TRIED TO WARN EVERYONE ABOUT HIM FOR YEARS. HE'S A KILLER.
AND WHILE I THINK ALL OF YOU BELONG BEHIND BARS...
...SPIDER-MAN IS THE MOST DANGEROUS VILLAIN OF YOU ALL.
WE NEED TO STOP HIM... WHATEVER THE COST.
WE'RE ALL AGREED THEN.
KRAVEN, THIS IS YOUR AREA OF EXPERTISE. DRAFT UP A PLAN AND GET BACK TO US.
GOOD EVENING, GENTLEMEN.
TAK

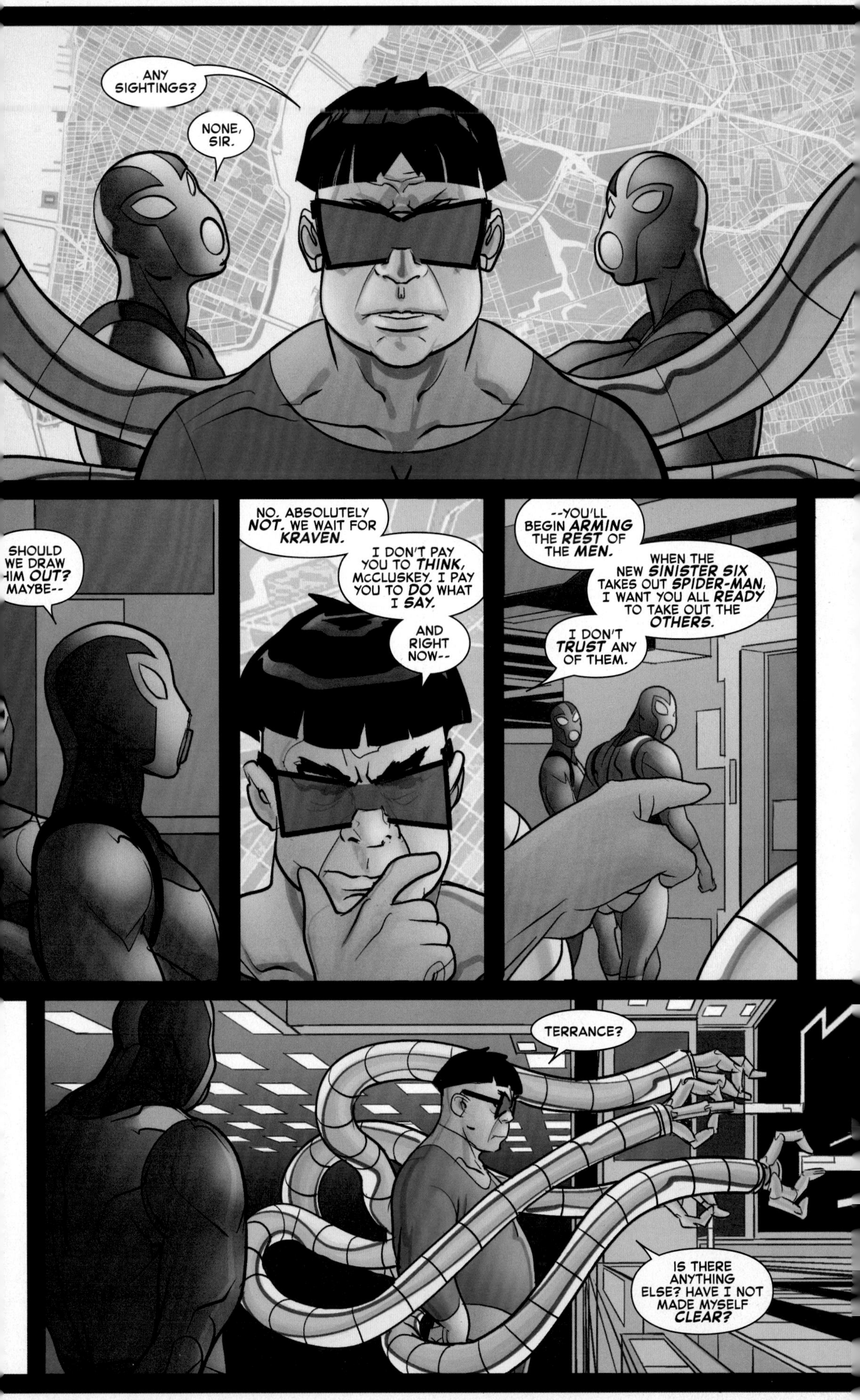
ANY SIGHTINGS?
NONE, SIR.
SHOULD WE DRAW HIM OUT? MAYBE--
NO. ABSOLUTELY NOT. WE WAIT FOR KRAVEN.
I DON'T PAY YOU TO THINK, McCLUSKEY. I PAY YOU TO DO WHAT I SAY.
AND RIGHT NOW--
--YOU'LL BEGIN ARMING THE REST OF THE MEN.
WHEN THE NEW SINISTER SIX TAKES OUT SPIDER-MAN, I WANT YOU ALL READY TO TAKE OUT THE OTHERS.
I DON'T TRUST ANY OF THEM.
TERRANCE?
IS THERE ANYTHING ELSE? HAVE I NOT MADE MYSELF CLEAR?

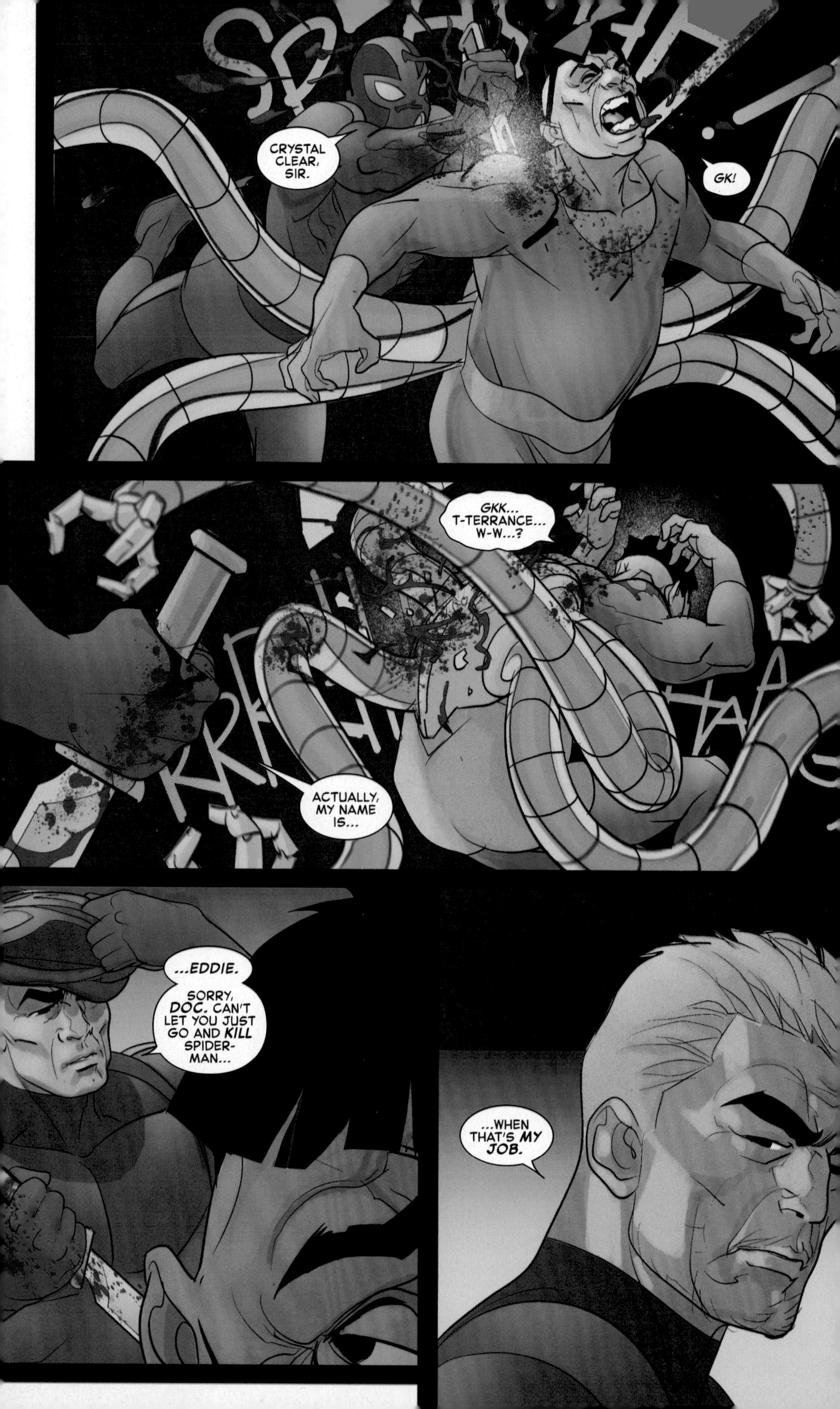
CRYSTAL CLEAR, SIR.
GK!
GKK... T-TERRANCE... W-W...?
ACTUALLY, MY NAME IS...
...EDDIE.
SORRY, DOC. CAN'T LET YOU JUST GO AND KILL SPIDER-MAN...
...WHEN THAT'S MY JOB.

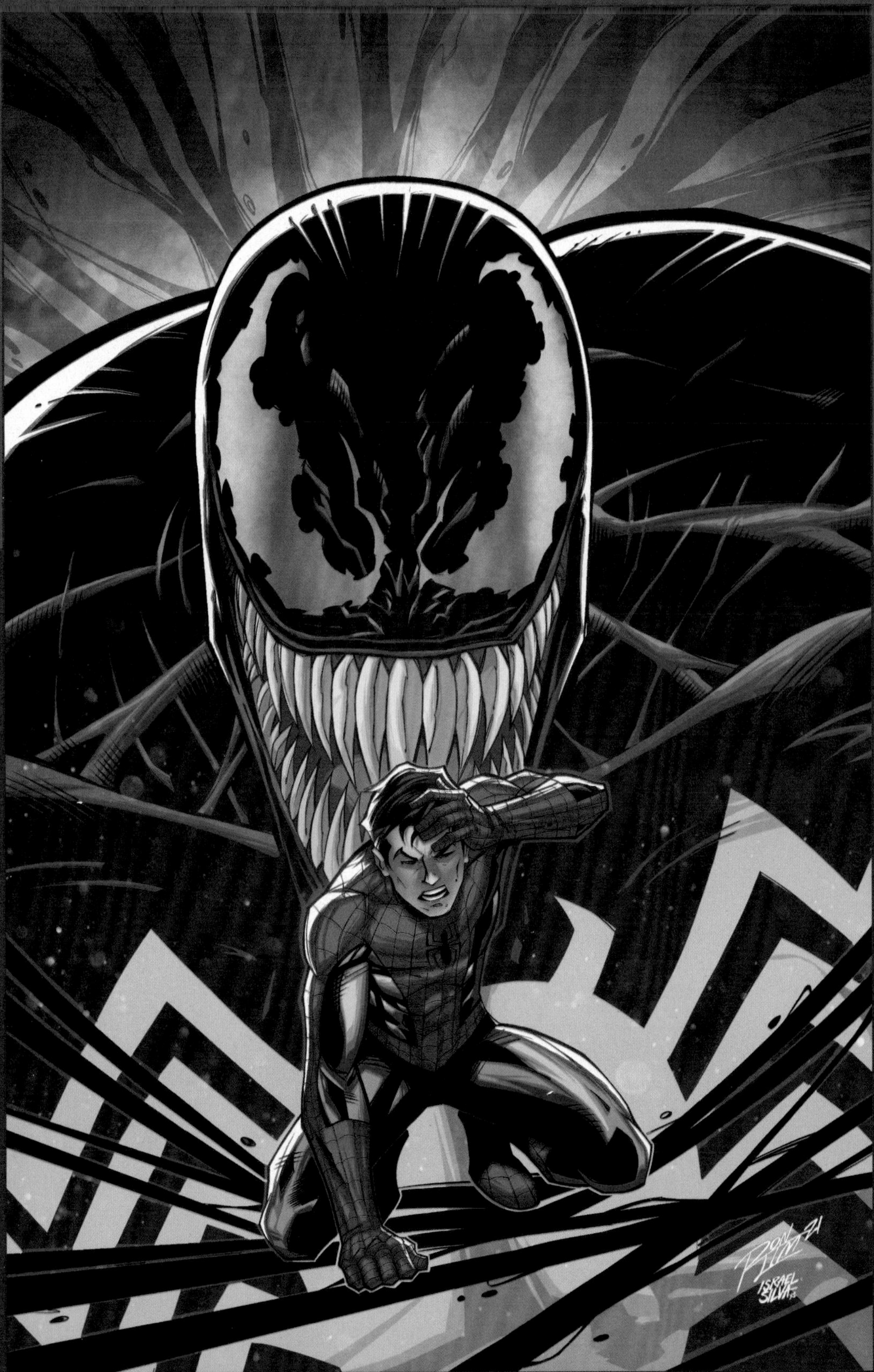

ISRAEL SILVA

#1 VARIANT BY RON LIM & ISRAEL SILVA

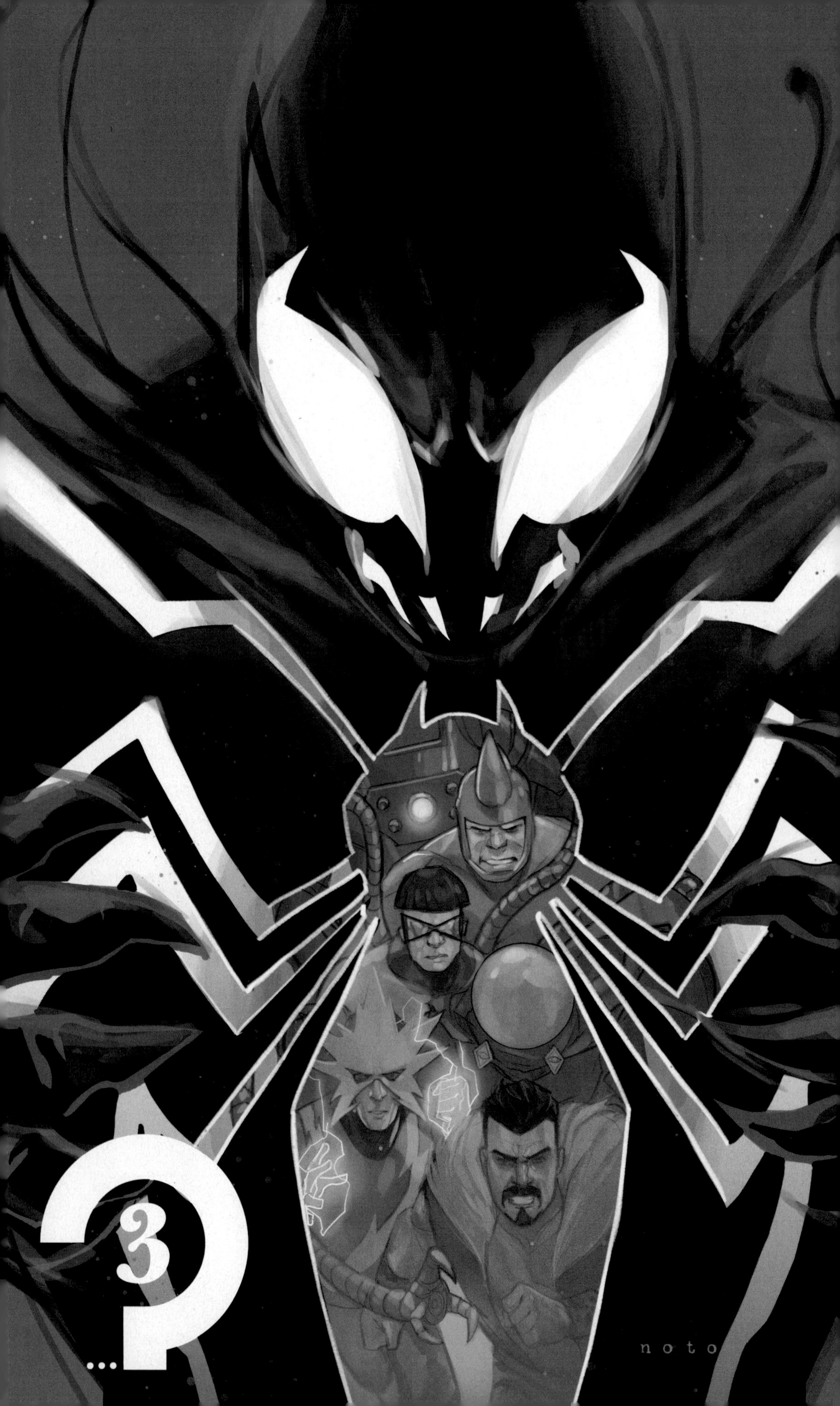

...3
noto

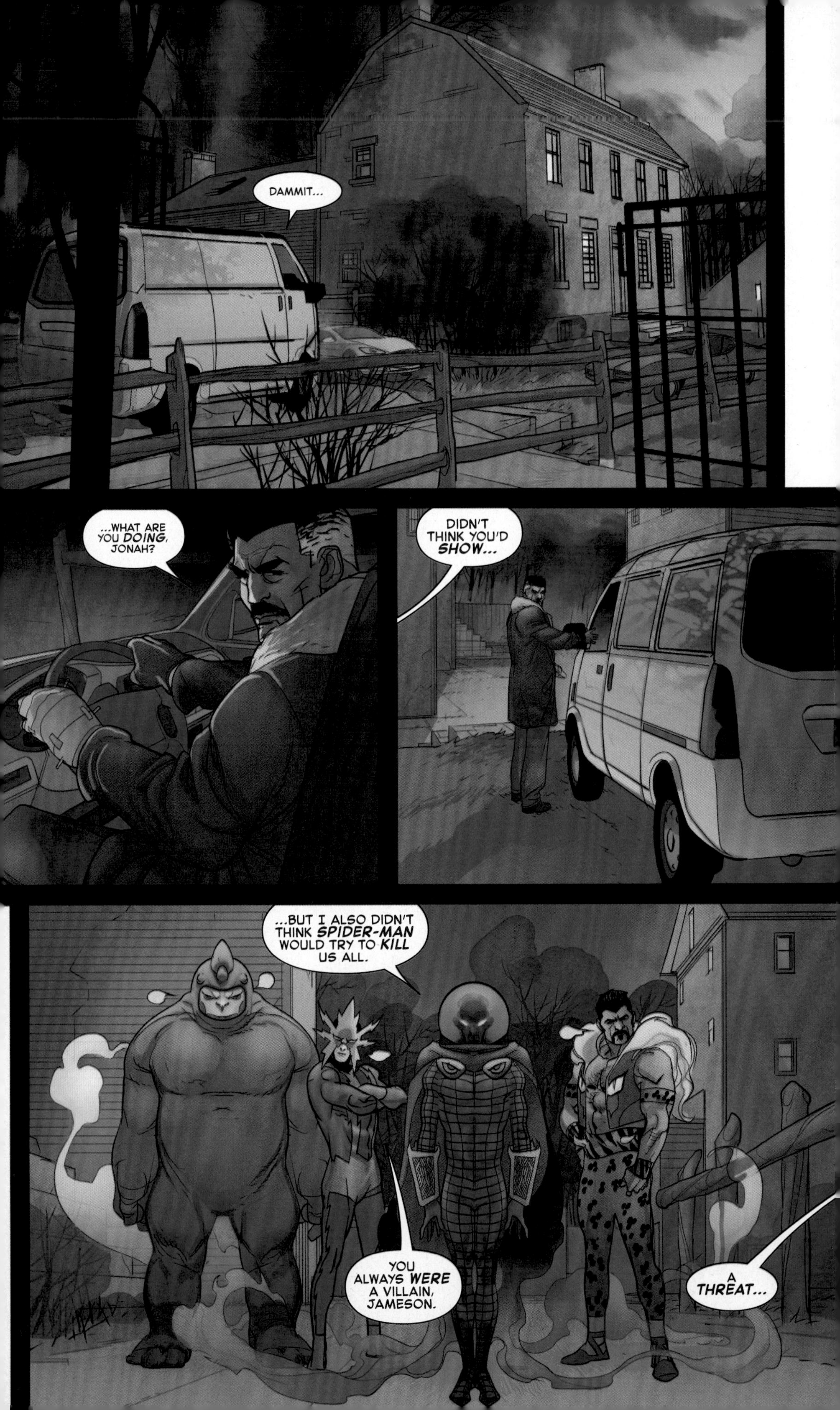
DAMMIT...
...WHAT ARE YOU DOING, JONAH?
DIDN'T THINK YOU'D SHOW...
...BUT I ALSO DIDN'T THINK SPIDER-MAN WOULD TRY TO KILL US ALL.
YOU ALWAYS WERE A VILLAIN, JAMESON.
A THREAT...

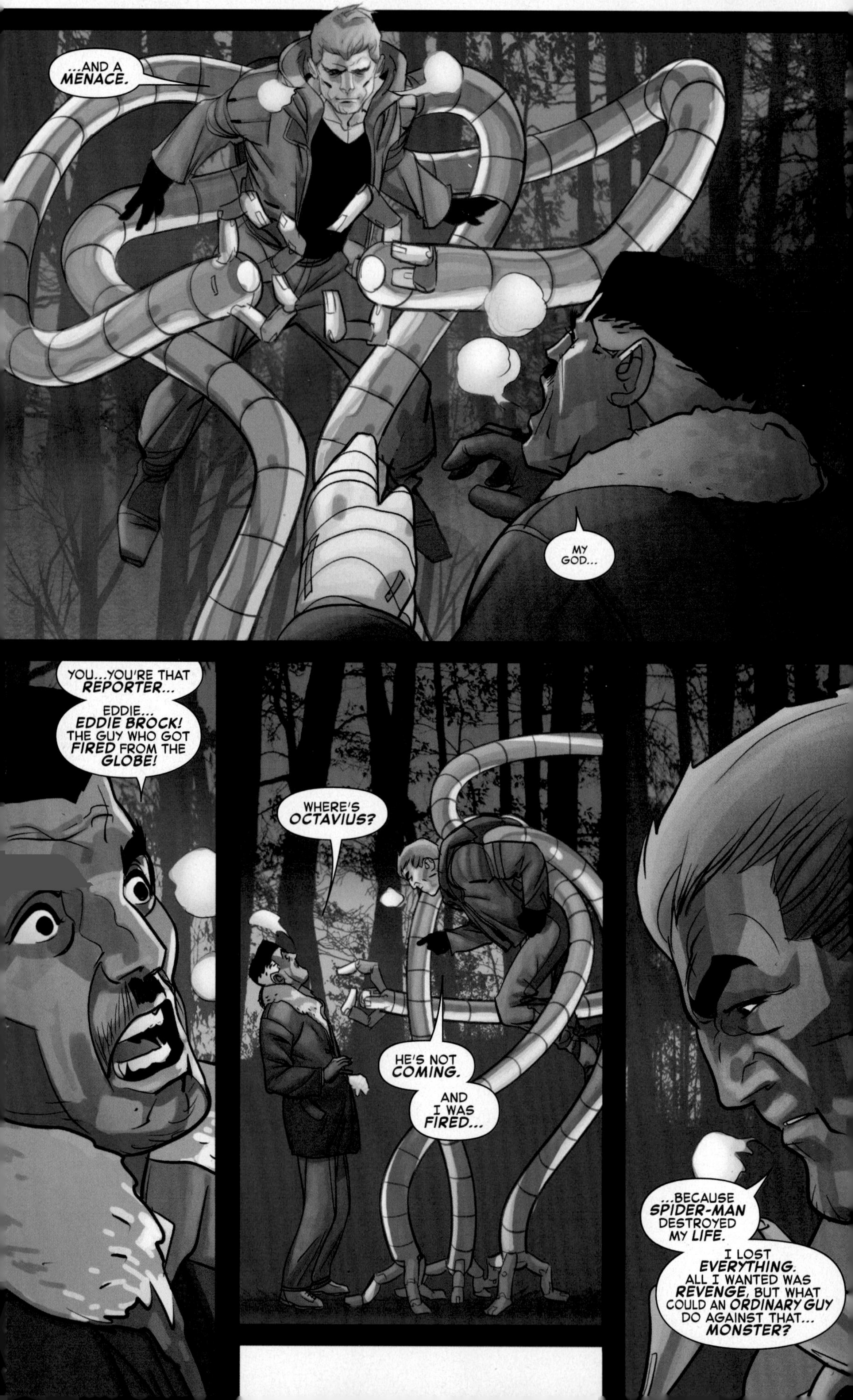
...AND A MENACE.
MY GOD...
YOU...YOU'RE THAT REPORTER...
EDDIE... EDDIE BROCK! THE GUY WHO GOT FIRED FROM THE GLOBE!
WHERE'S OCTAVIUS?
HE'S NOT COMING.
AND I WAS FIRED...
...BECAUSE SPIDER-MAN DESTROYED MY LIFE.
I LOST EVERYTHING. ALL I WANTED WAS REVENGE, BUT WHAT COULD AN ORDINARY GUY DO AGAINST THAT... MONSTER?

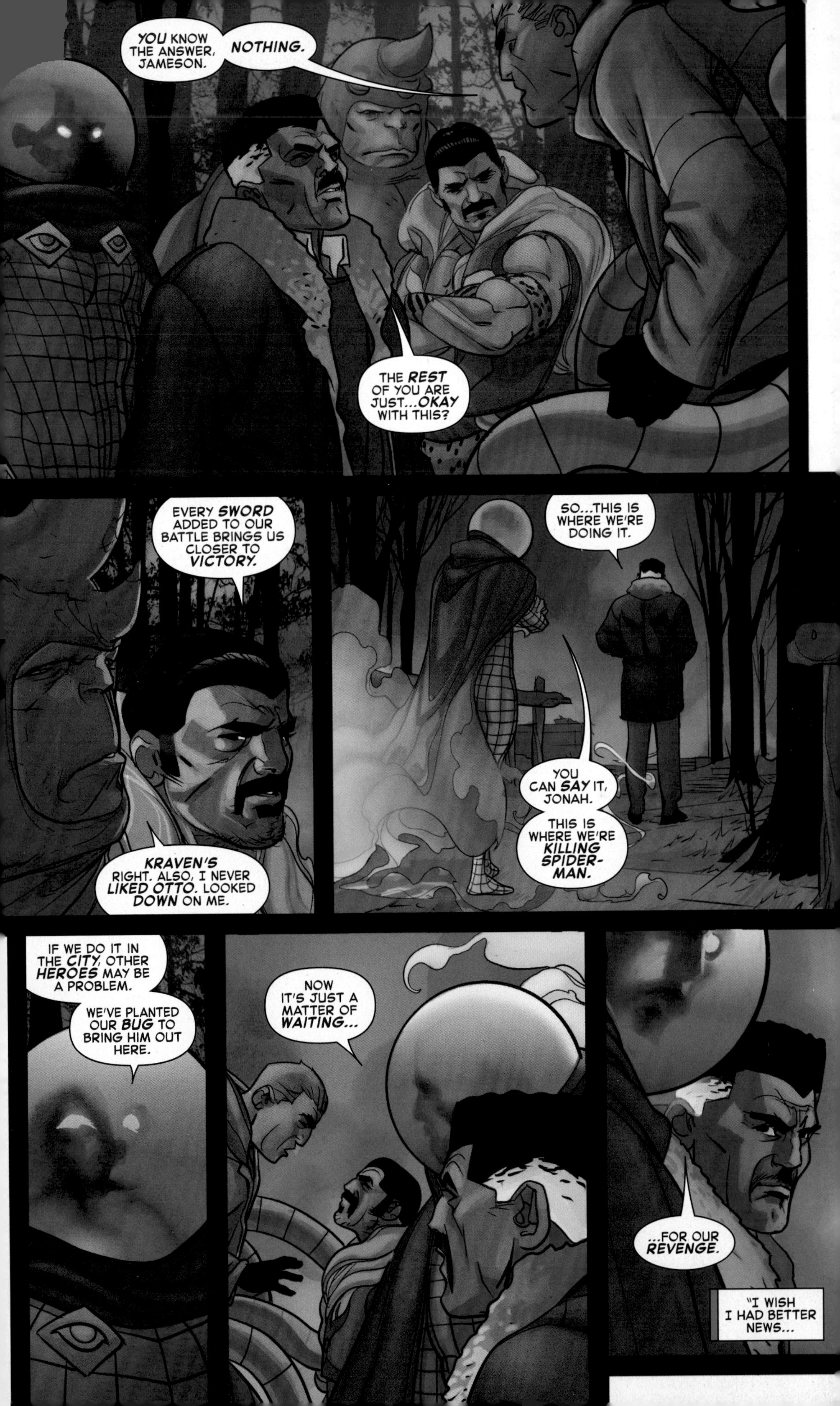
YOU KNOW THE ANSWER, JAMESON.
NOTHING.
THE REST OF YOU ARE JUST...OKAY WITH THIS?
EVERY SWORD ADDED TO OUR BATTLE BRINGS US CLOSER TO VICTORY.
KRAVEN'S RIGHT. ALSO, I NEVER LIKED OTTO. LOOKED DOWN ON ME.
SO...THIS IS WHERE WE'RE DOING IT.
YOU CAN SAY IT, JONAH.
THIS IS WHERE WE'RE KILLING SPIDER-MAN.
IF WE DO IT IN THE CITY, OTHER HEROES MAY BE A PROBLEM.
WE'VE PLANTED OUR BUG TO BRING HIM OUT HERE.
NOW IT'S JUST A MATTER OF WAITING...
...FOR OUR REVENGE.
"I WISH I HAD BETTER NEWS...

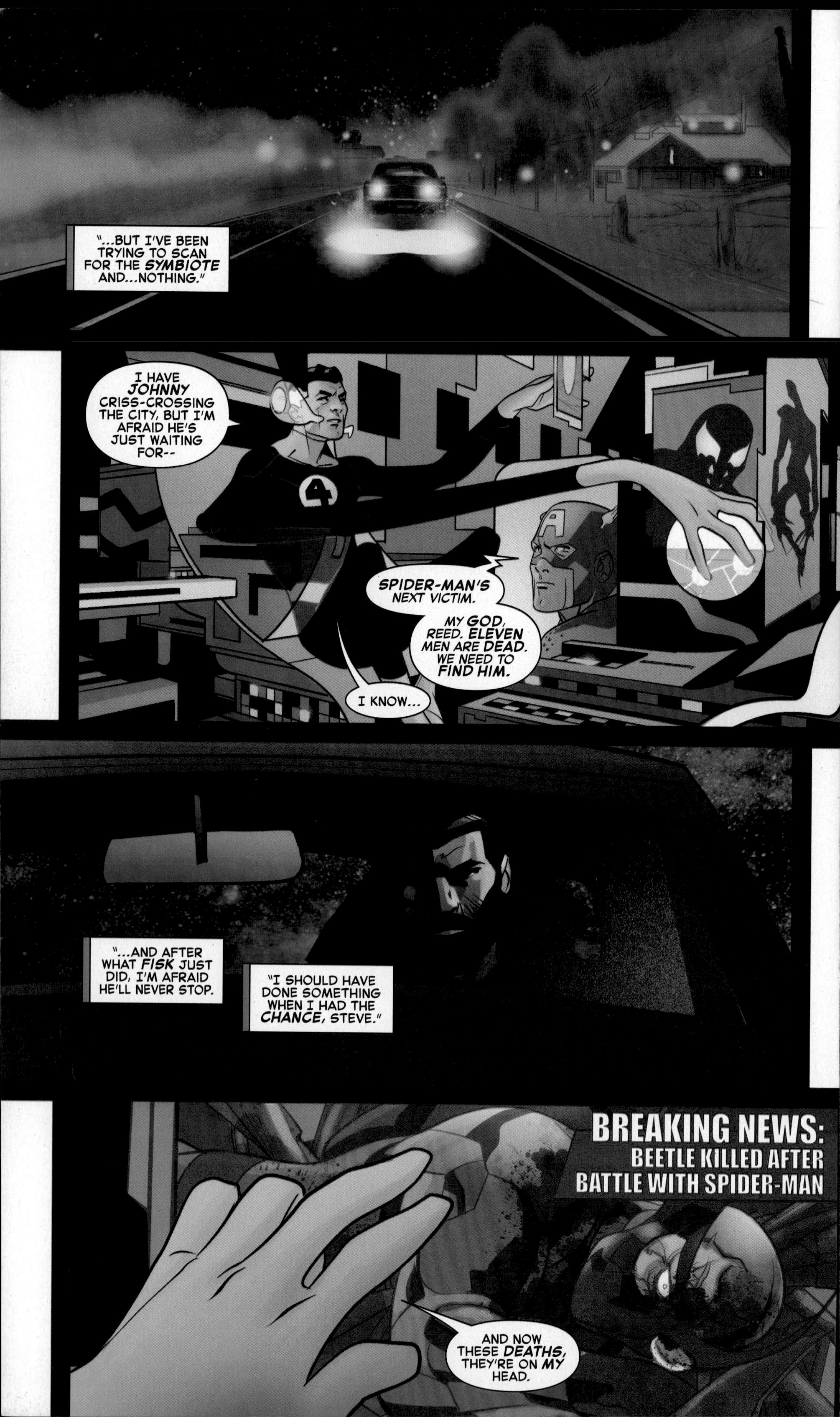
"...BUT I'VE BEEN TRYING TO SCAN FOR THE SYMBIOTE AND...NOTHING."
I HAVE JOHNNY CRISS-CROSSING THE CITY, BUT I'M AFRAID HE'S JUST WAITING FOR--
SPIDER-MAN'S NEXT VICTIM.
MY GOD, REED. ELEVEN MEN ARE DEAD. WE NEED TO FIND HIM.
I KNOW...
"...AND AFTER WHAT FISK JUST DID, I'M AFRAID HE'LL NEVER STOP.
"I SHOULD HAVE DONE SOMETHING WHEN I HAD THE CHANCE, STEVE."
BREAKING NEWS:
BEETLE KILLED AFTER BATTLE WITH SPIDER-MAN
AND NOW THESE DEATHS, THEY'RE ON MY HEAD.

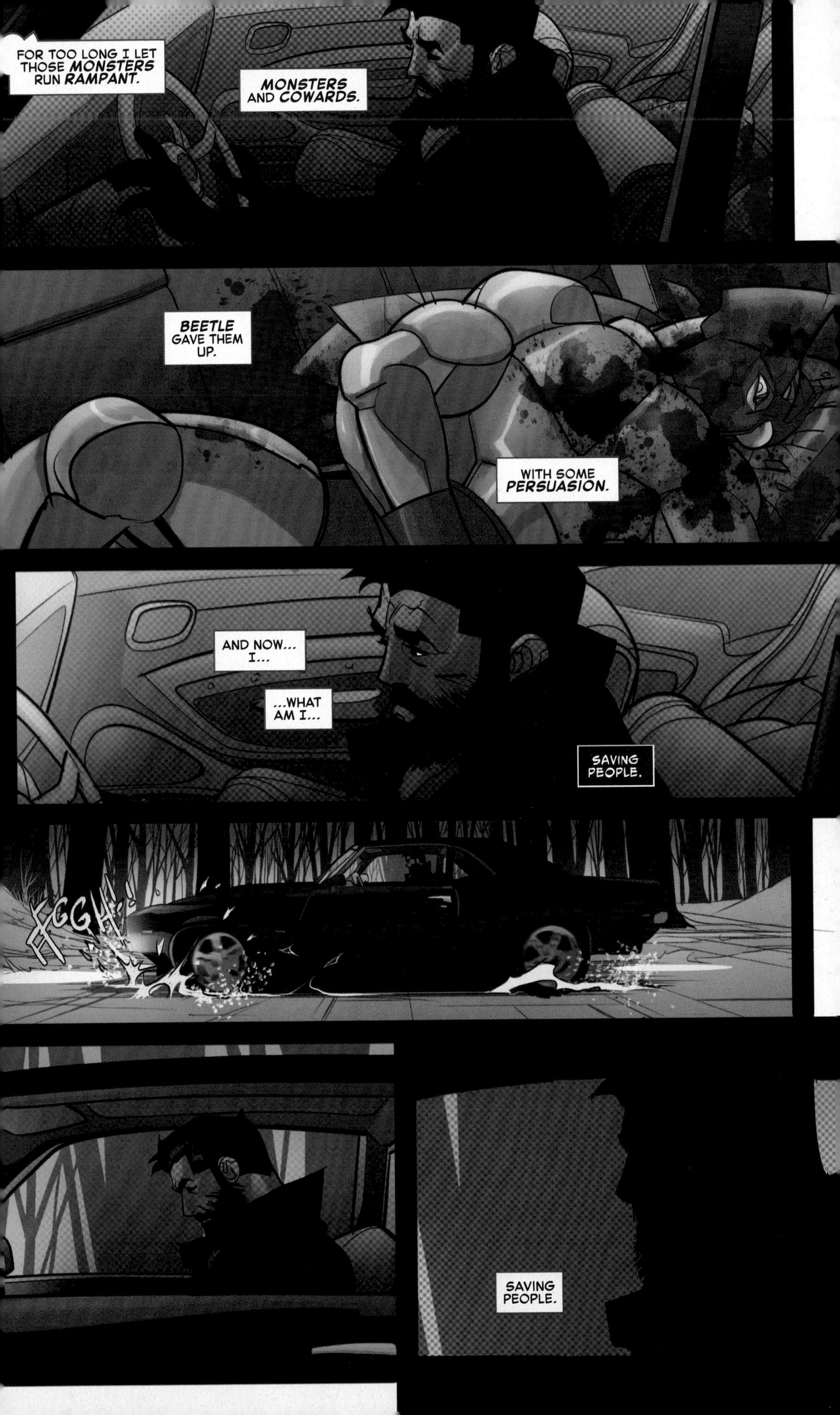
FOR TOO LONG I LET THOSE MONSTERS RUN RAMPANT.
MONSTERS AND COWARDS.
BEETLE GAVE THEM UP.
WITH SOME PERSUASION.
AND NOW... I...
...WHAT AM I...
SAVING PEOPLE.
FGGH!
SAVING PEOPLE.

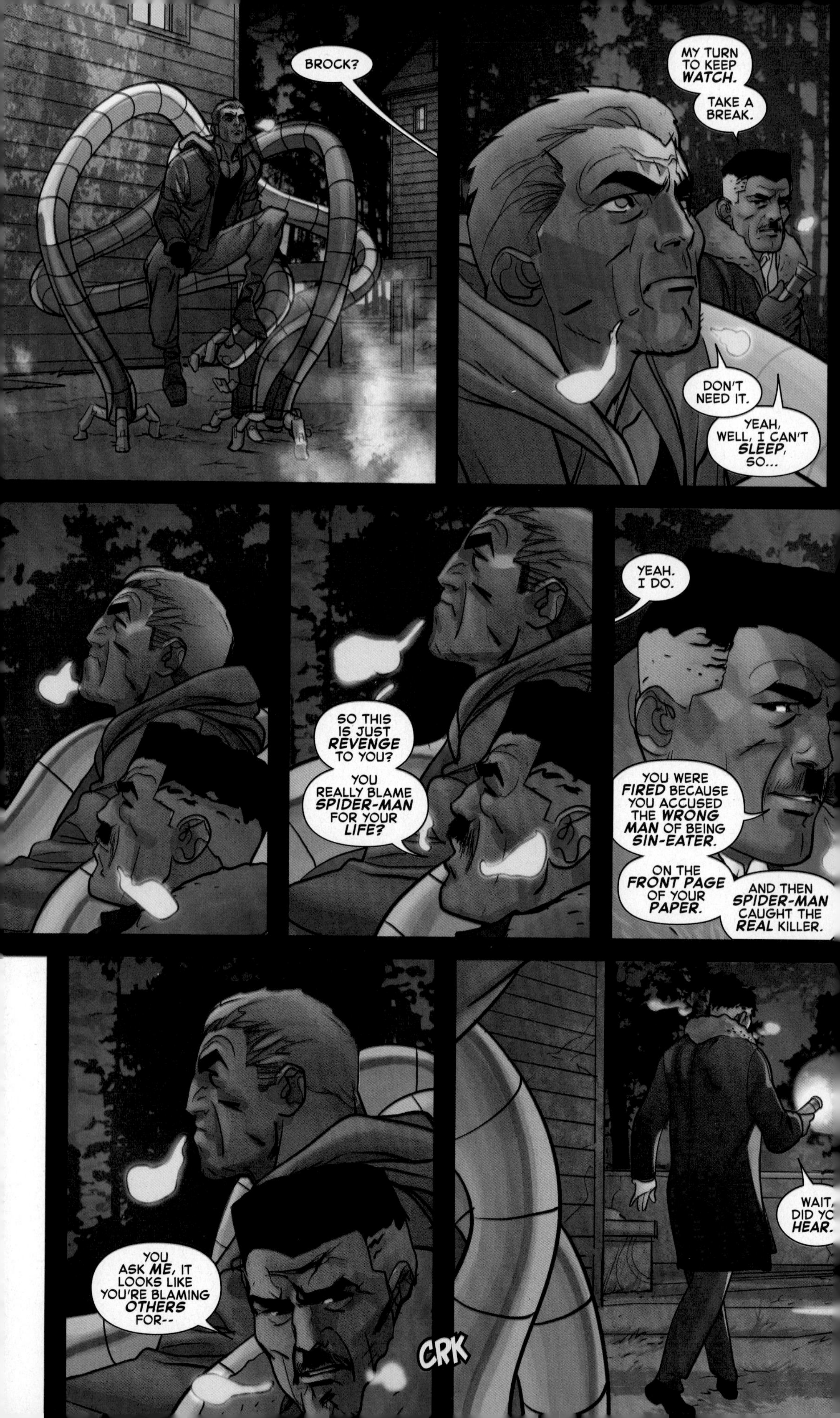
BROCK?
MY TURN TO KEEP WATCH.
TAKE A BREAK.
DON'T NEED IT.
YEAH, WELL, I CAN'T SLEEP, SO...
SO THIS IS JUST REVENGE TO YOU?
YOU REALLY BLAME SPIDER-MAN FOR YOUR LIFE?
YEAH. I DO.
YOU WERE FIRED BECAUSE YOU ACCUSED THE WRONG MAN OF BEING SIN-EATER.
ON THE FRONT PAGE OF YOUR PAPER.
AND THEN SPIDER-MAN CAUGHT THE REAL KILLER.
YOU ASK ME, IT LOOKS LIKE YOU'RE BLAMING OTHERS FOR--
CRK
WAIT, DID YO HEAR.

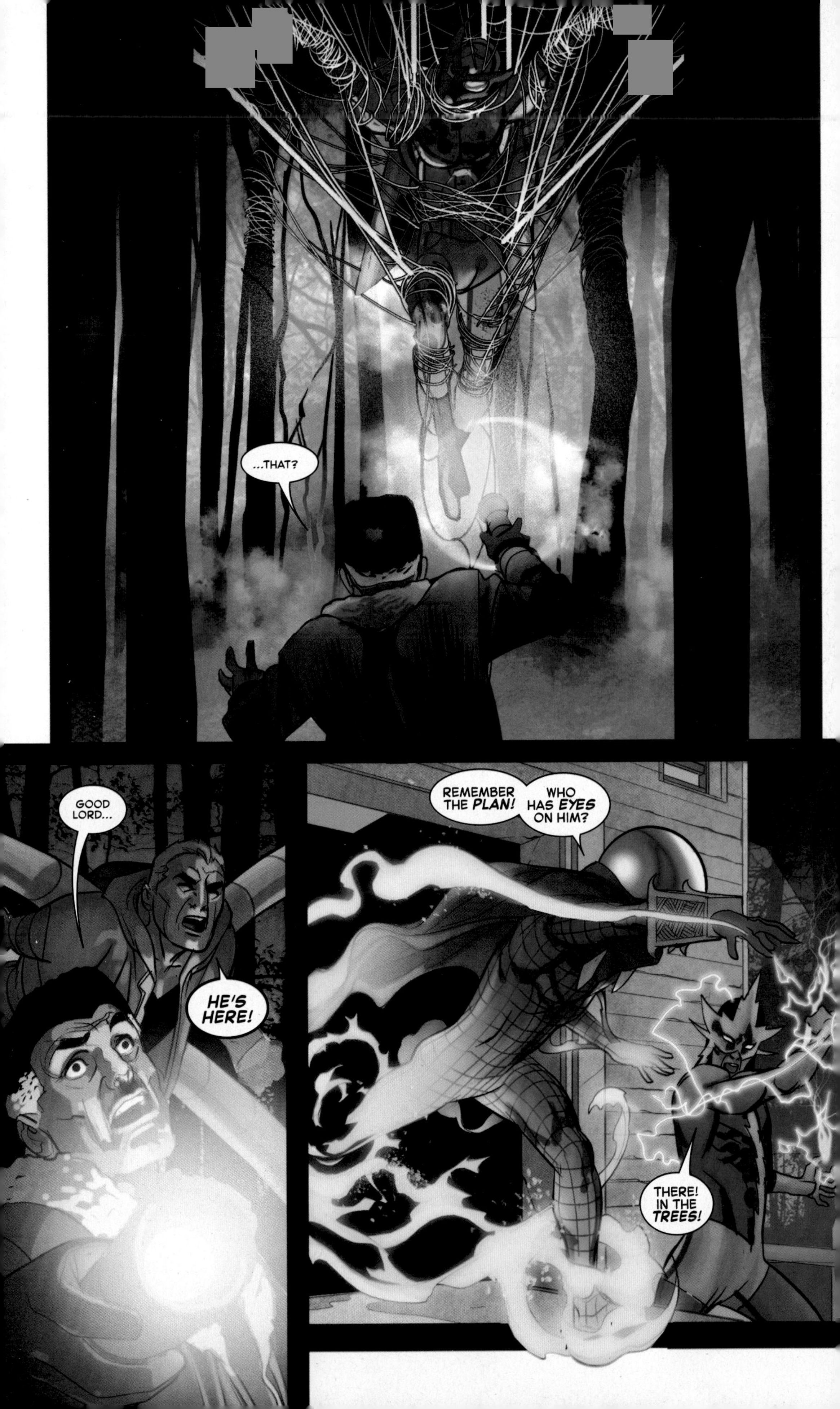
...THAT?
GOOD LORD...
HE'S HERE!
REMEMBER THE PLAN!
WHO HAS EYES ON HIM?
THERE! IN THE TREES!

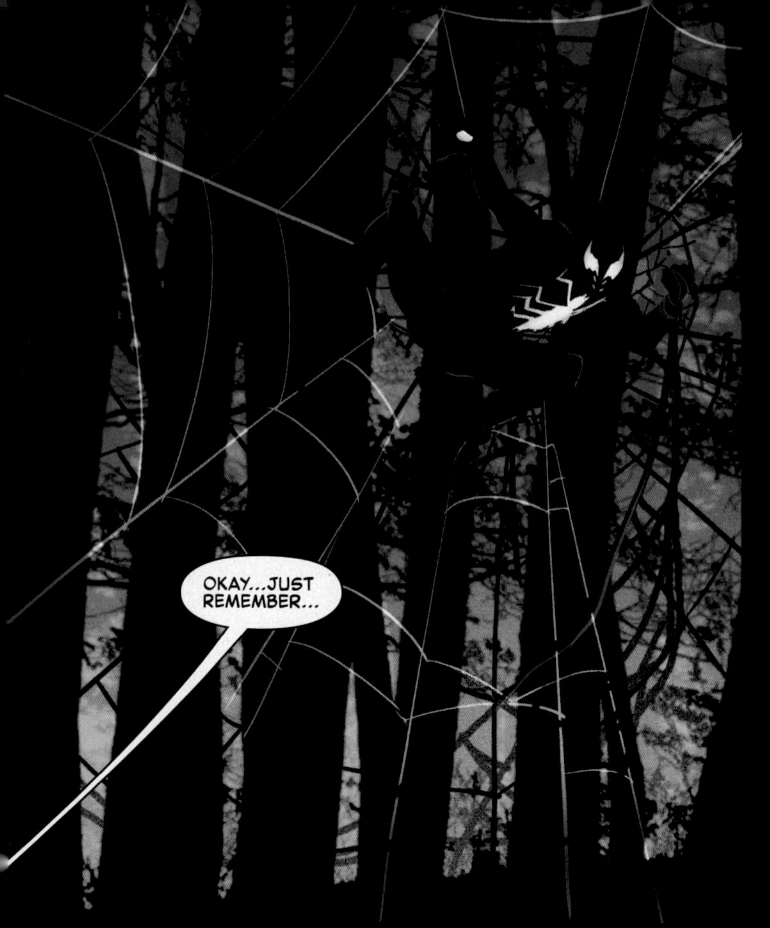
OKAY...JUST REMEMBER...

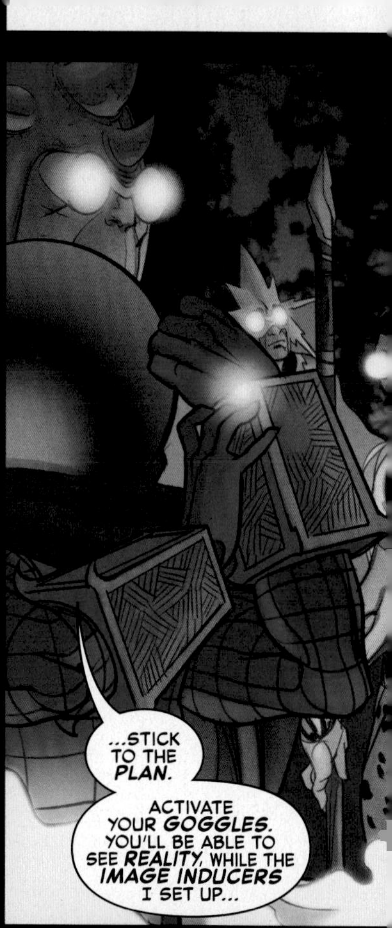
...STICK TO THE PLAN.
ACTIVATE YOUR GOGGLES. YOU'LL BE ABLE TO SEE REALITY, WHILE THE IMAGE INDUCERS I SET UP...

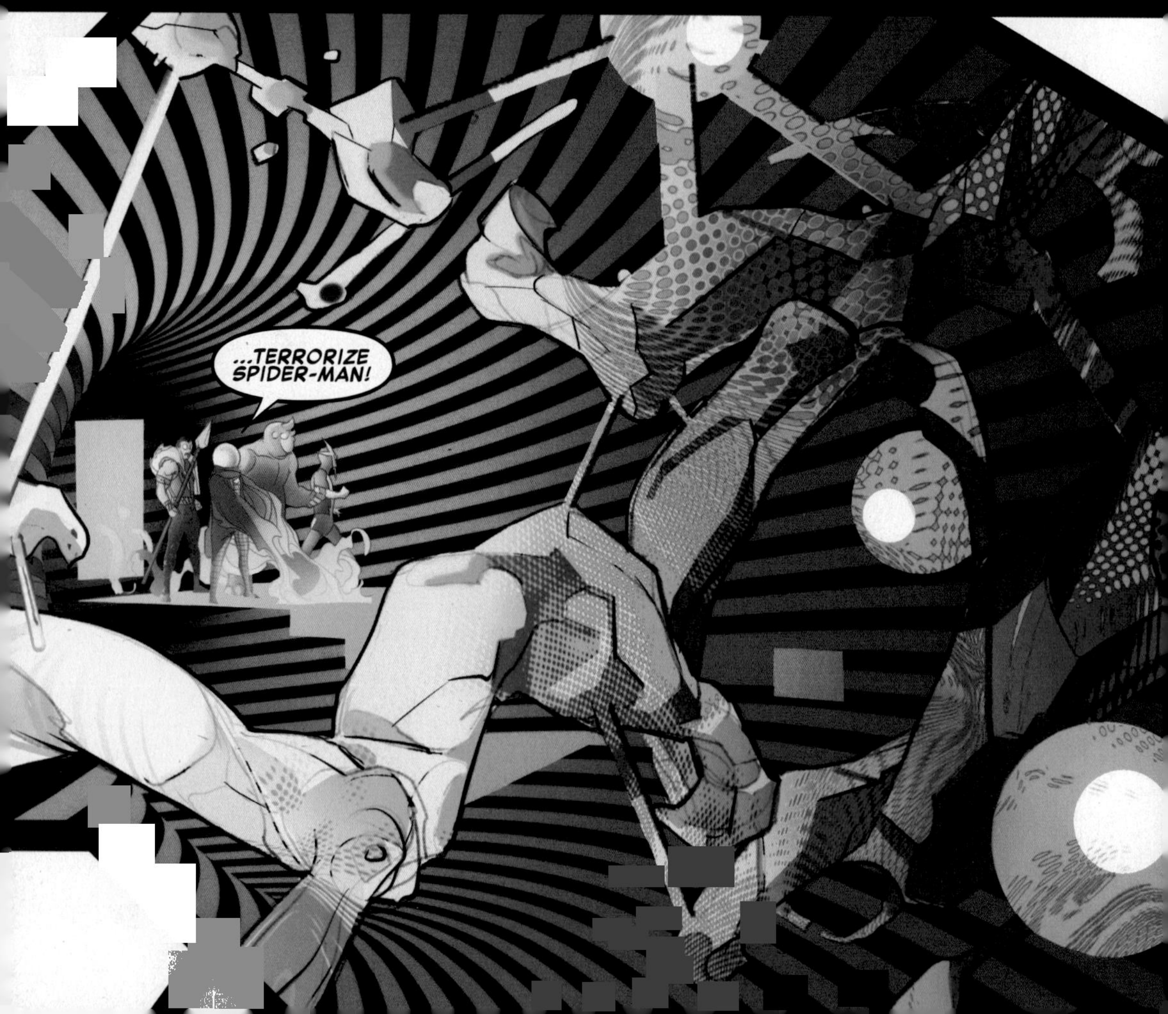
...TERRORIZE SPIDER-MAN!

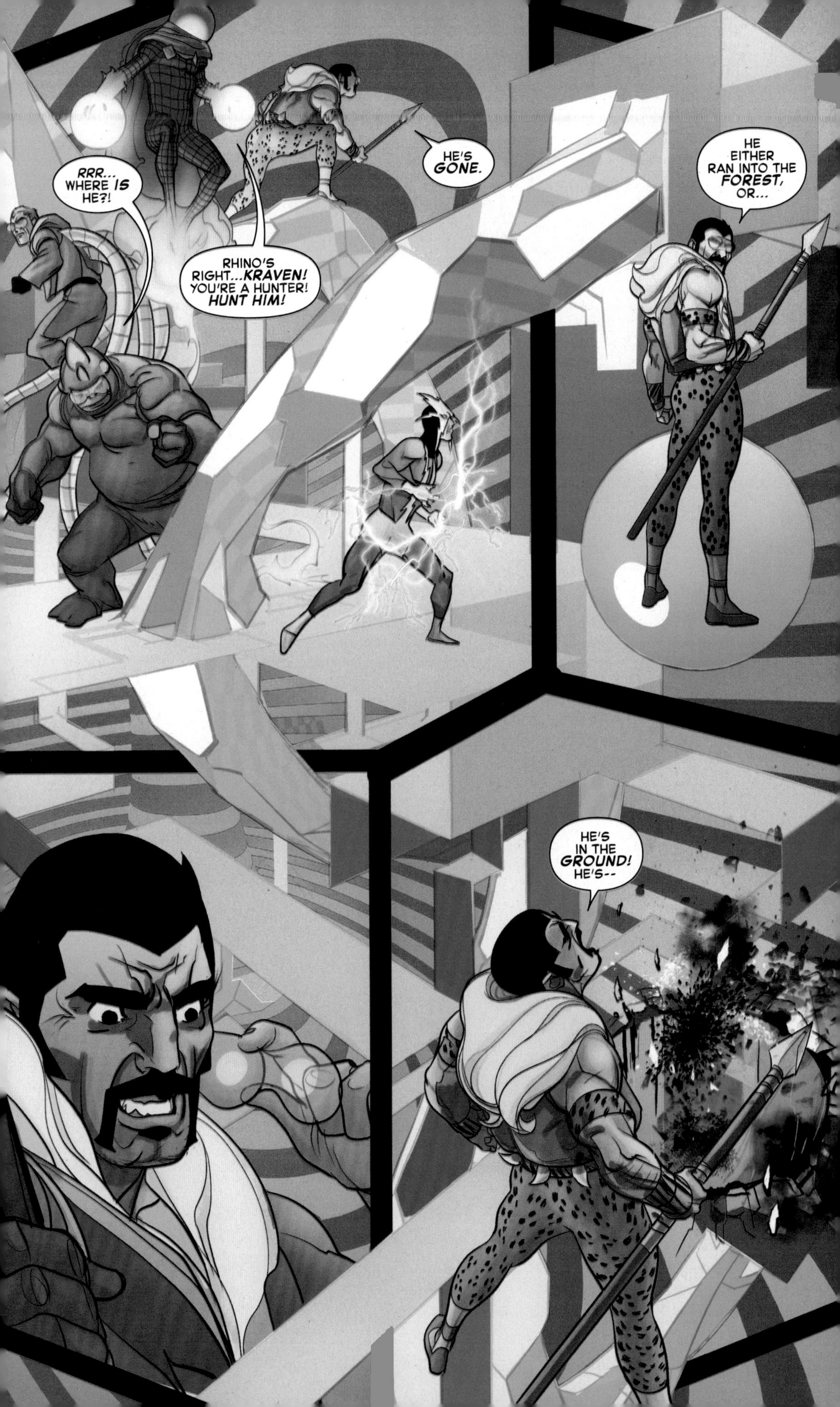

RRR... WHERE *IS* HE?!
RHINO'S RIGHT...*KRAVEN!* YOU'RE A HUNTER! *HUNT HIM!*
HE'S *GONE.*
HE EITHER RAN INTO THE *FOREST,* OR...
HE'S IN THE *GROUND!* HE'S--

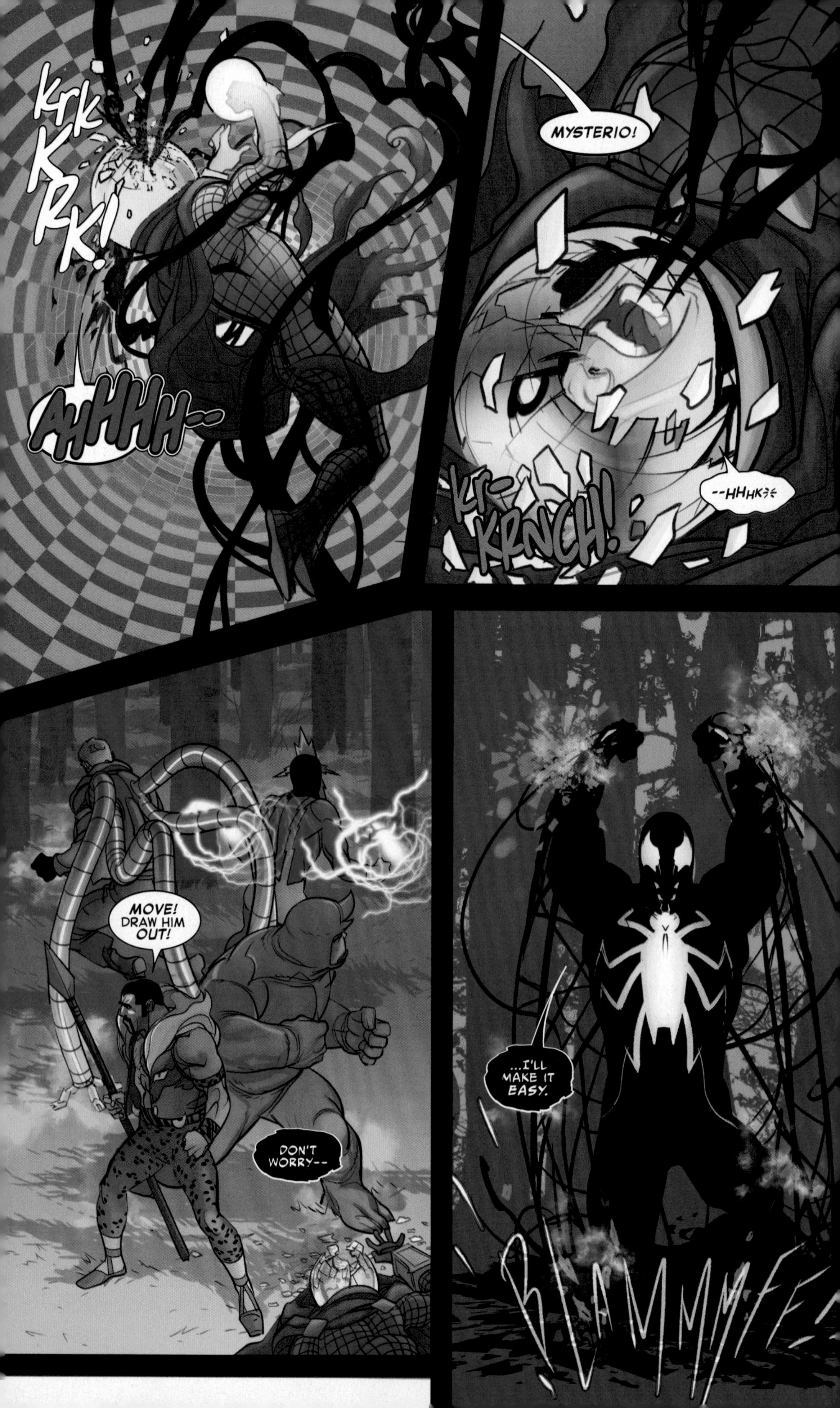
KRK KRK!
AHHHH--
MYSTERIO!
KR-KRNCH!
--HHHK
MOVE! DRAW HIM OUT!
DON'T WORRY--
...I'LL MAKE IT EASY.
BLAMMMF!

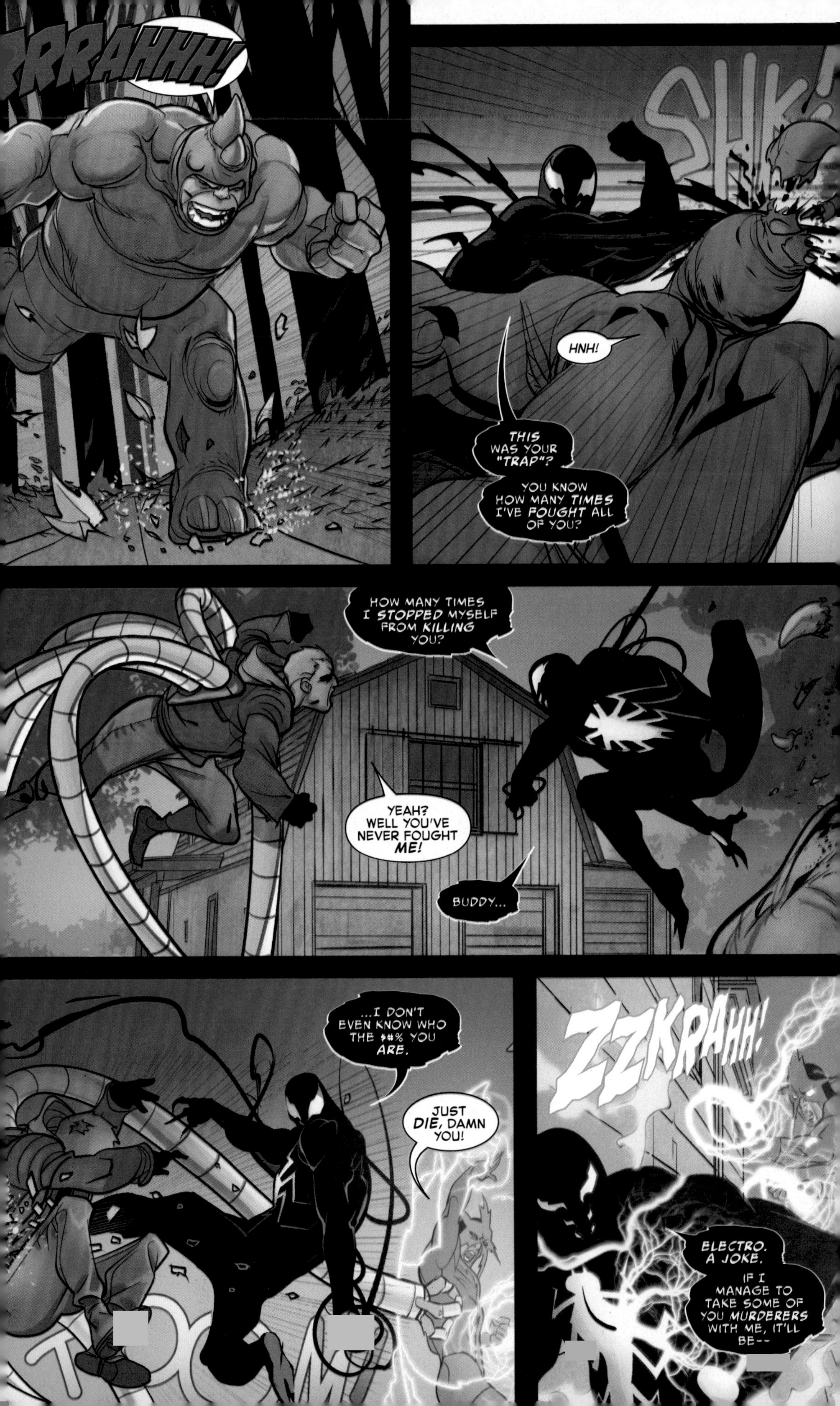
RRAHHH!
SHK!
HNH!
THIS WAS YOUR "TRAP"?
YOU KNOW HOW MANY TIMES I'VE FOUGHT ALL OF YOU?
HOW MANY TIMES I STOPPED MYSELF FROM KILLING YOU?
YEAH? WELL YOU'VE NEVER FOUGHT ME!
BUDDY...
...I DON'T EVEN KNOW WHO THE $#% YOU ARE.
JUST DIE, DAMN YOU!
TOOM
ZZKRAHH!
ELECTRO. A JOKE.
IF I MANAGE TO TAKE SOME OF YOU MURDERERS WITH ME, IT'LL BE--

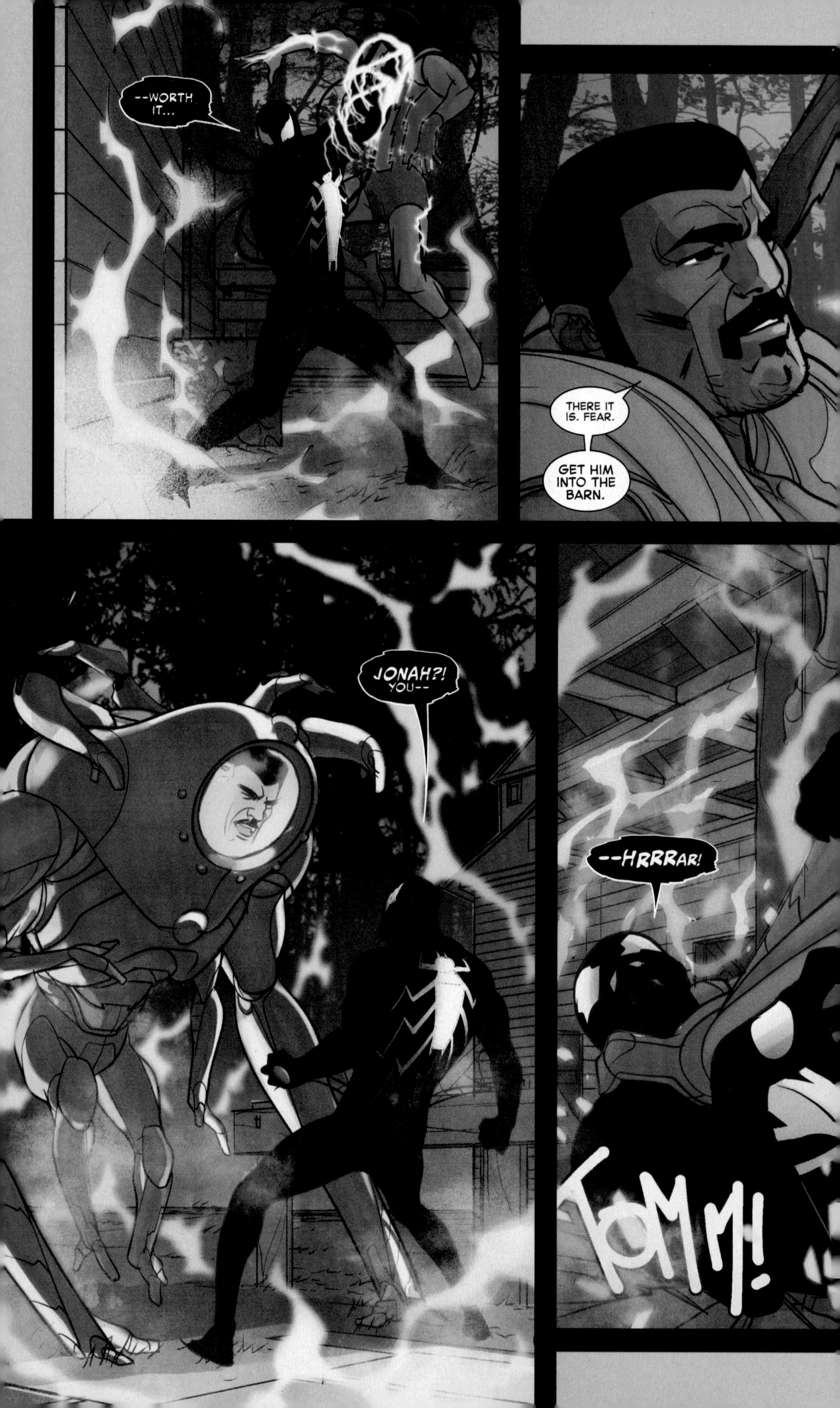
--WORTH IT...
THERE IT IS. FEAR.
GET HIM INTO THE BARN.
JONAH?! YOU--
--HRRRAR!
TOMM!

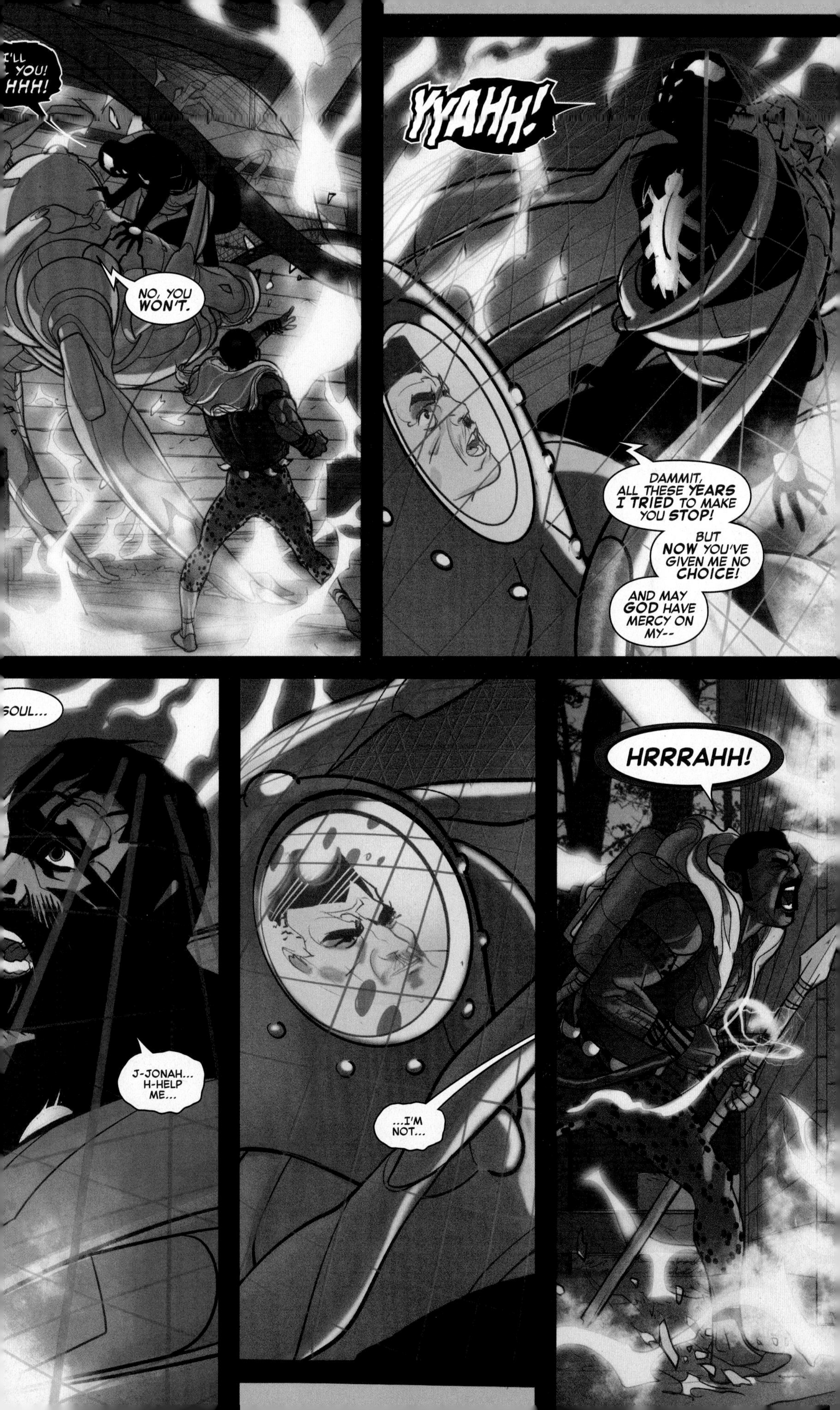
I'LL YOU! HHH!
NO, YOU WON'T.
YYAHH!
DAMMIT, ALL THESE YEARS I TRIED TO MAKE YOU STOP!
BUT NOW YOU'VE GIVEN ME NO CHOICE!
AND MAY GOD HAVE MERCY ON MY--
SOUL...
J-JONAH... H-HELP ME...
...I'M NOT...
HRRRAHH!

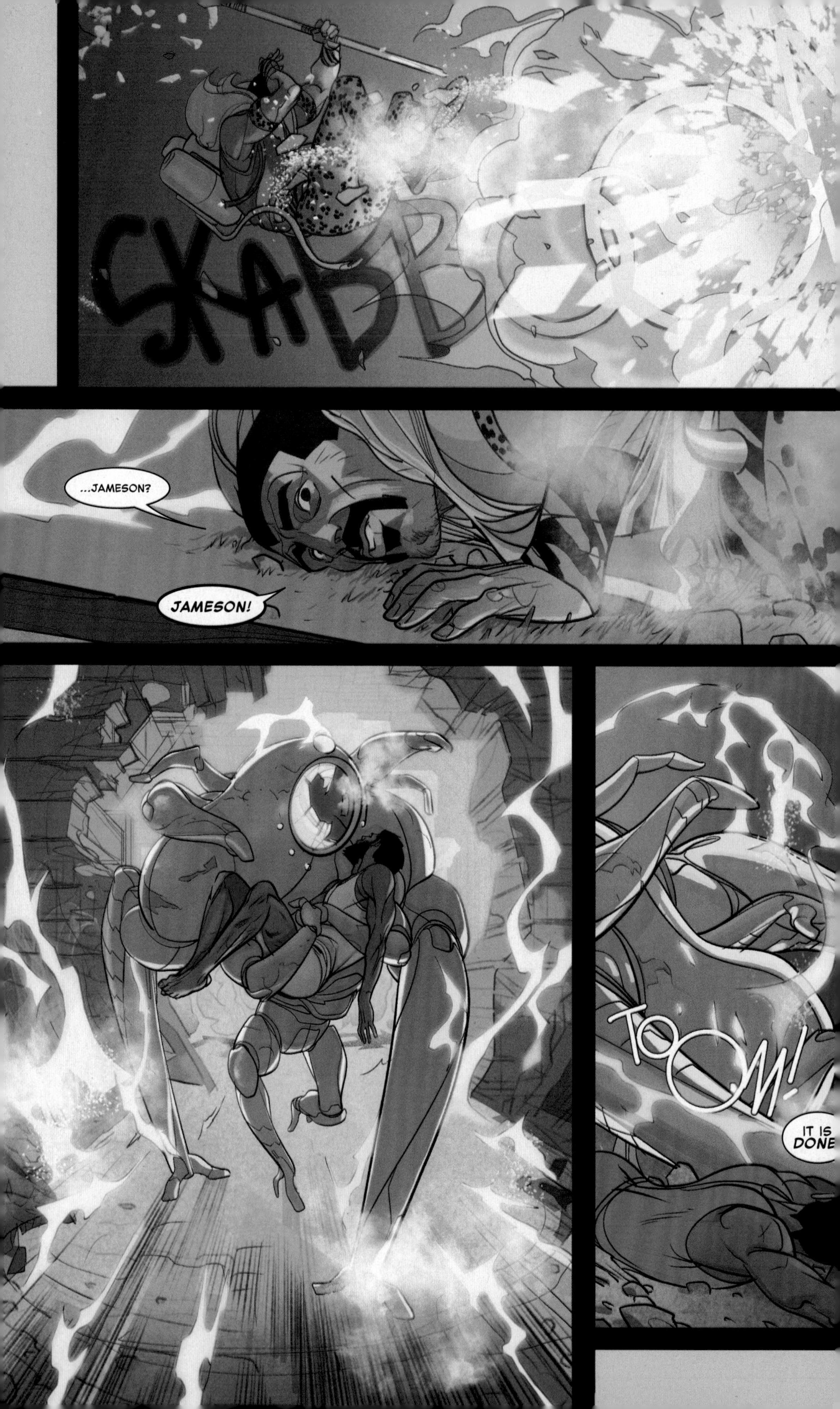
SKABB
...JAMESON?
JAMESON!
TOOM!
IT IS DONE

MANY WERE LOST...

...BUT THE HUNT IS CONCLUDED.

CHOK!

...DAMMIT.

DAMMIT, PARKER...

...WHY'D IT HAVE TO BE YOU?

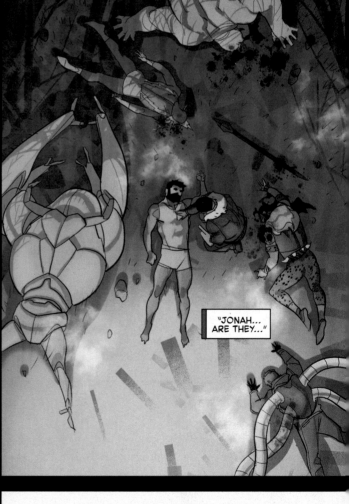

"JONAH... ARE THEY..."

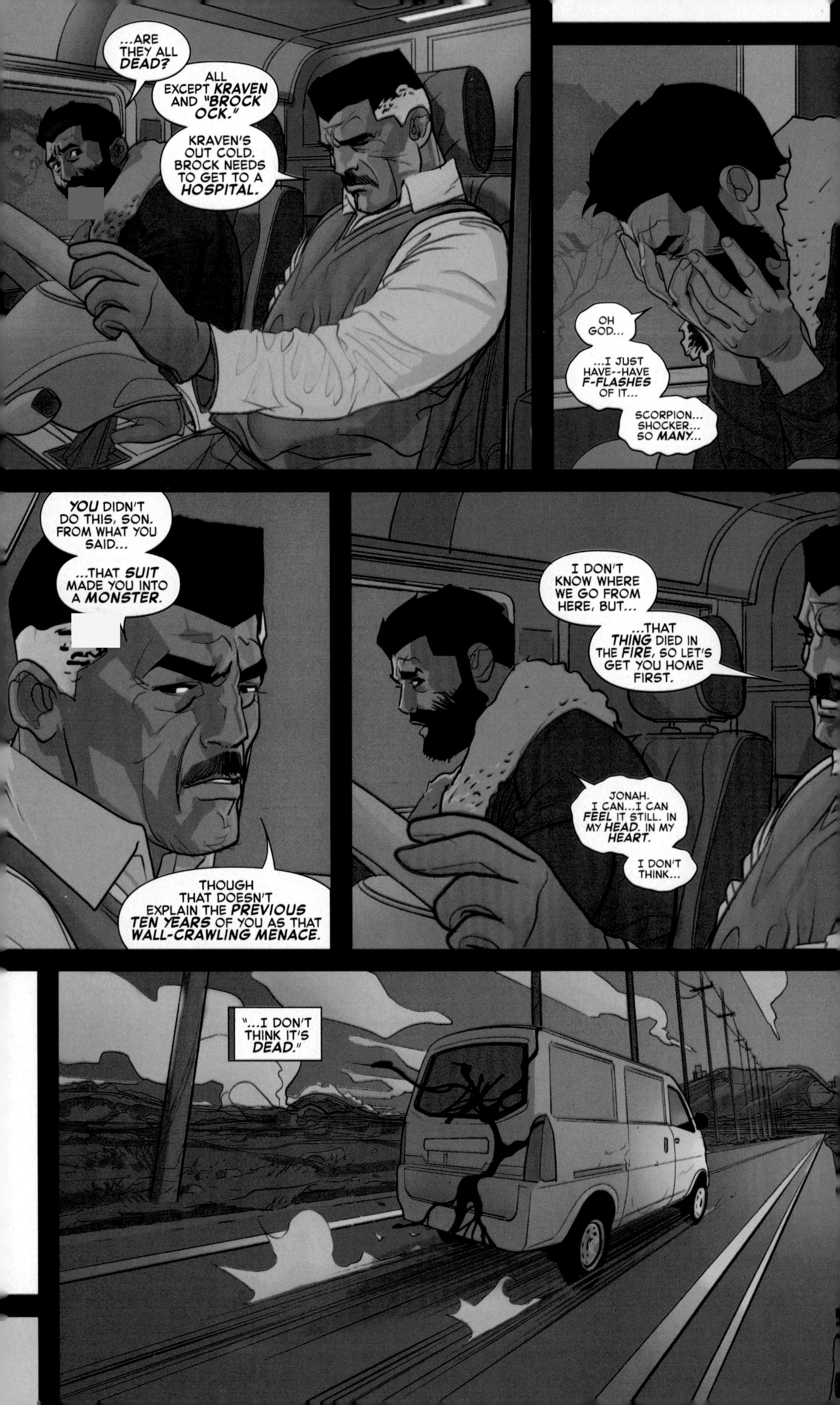
...ARE THEY ALL DEAD?
ALL EXCEPT KRAVEN AND "BROCK OCK."
KRAVEN'S OUT COLD. BROCK NEEDS TO GET TO A HOSPITAL.
OH GOD...
...I JUST HAVE--HAVE F-FLASHES OF IT...
SCORPION... SHOCKER... SO MANY...
YOU DIDN'T DO THIS, SON. FROM WHAT YOU SAID...
...THAT SUIT MADE YOU INTO A MONSTER.
THOUGH THAT DOESN'T EXPLAIN THE PREVIOUS TEN YEARS OF YOU AS THAT WALL-CRAWLING MENACE.
I DON'T KNOW WHERE WE GO FROM HERE, BUT...
...THAT THING DIED IN THE FIRE, SO LET'S GET YOU HOME FIRST.
JONAH. I CAN...I CAN FEEL IT STILL. IN MY HEAD. IN MY HEART.
I DON'T THINK...
"...I DON'T THINK IT'S DEAD."

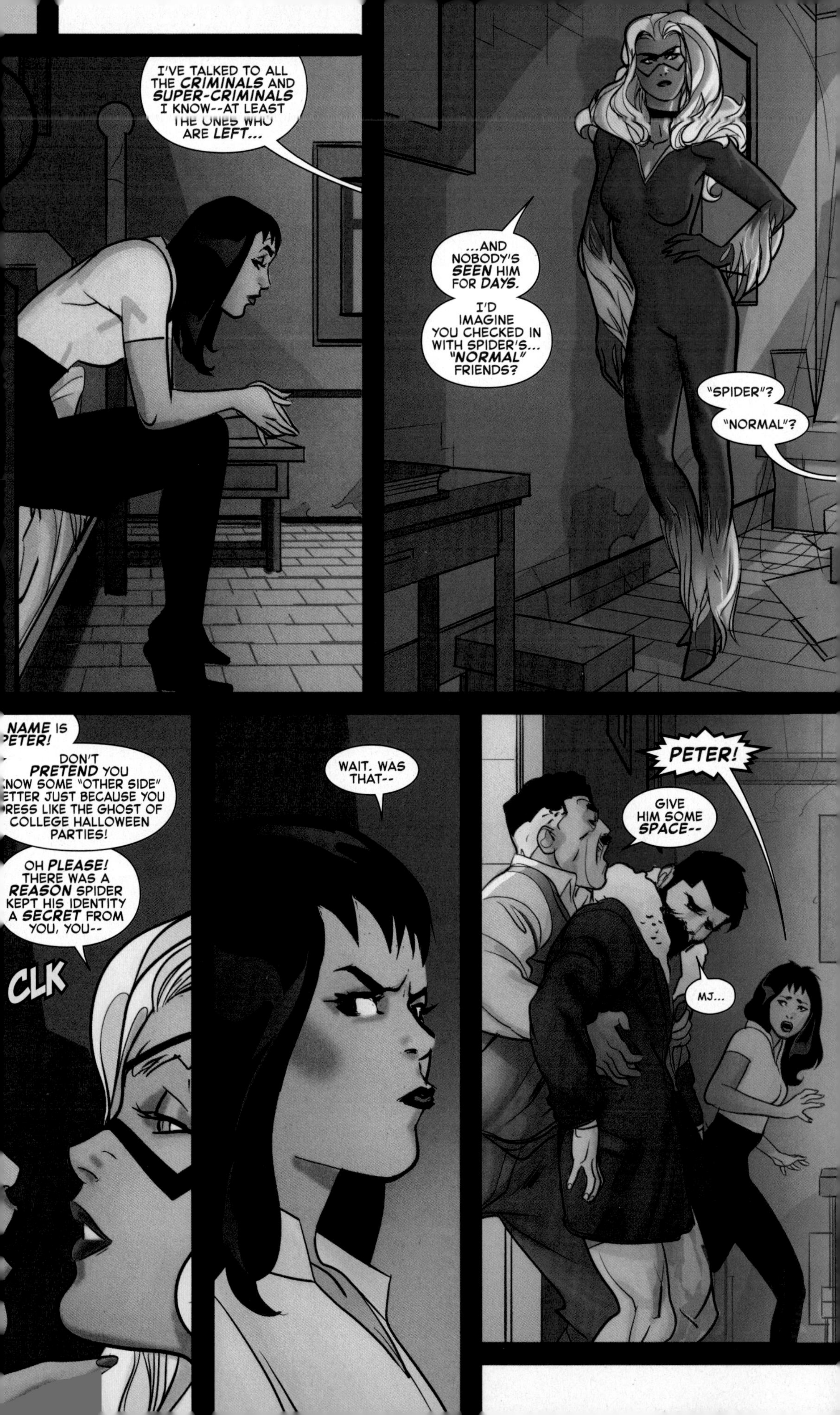
I'VE TALKED TO ALL THE CRIMINALS AND SUPER-CRIMINALS I KNOW--AT LEAST THE ONES WHO ARE LEFT...
...AND NOBODY'S SEEN HIM FOR DAYS.
I'D IMAGINE YOU CHECKED IN WITH SPIDER'S... "NORMAL" FRIENDS?
"SPIDER"?
"NORMAL"?
NAME IS PETER!
DON'T PRETEND YOU NOW SOME "OTHER SIDE" ETTER JUST BECAUSE YOU RESS LIKE THE GHOST OF COLLEGE HALLOWEEN PARTIES!
OH PLEASE! THERE WAS A REASON SPIDER KEPT HIS IDENTITY A SECRET FROM YOU, YOU--
CLK
WAIT. WAS THAT--
PETER!
GIVE HIM SOME SPACE--
MJ...

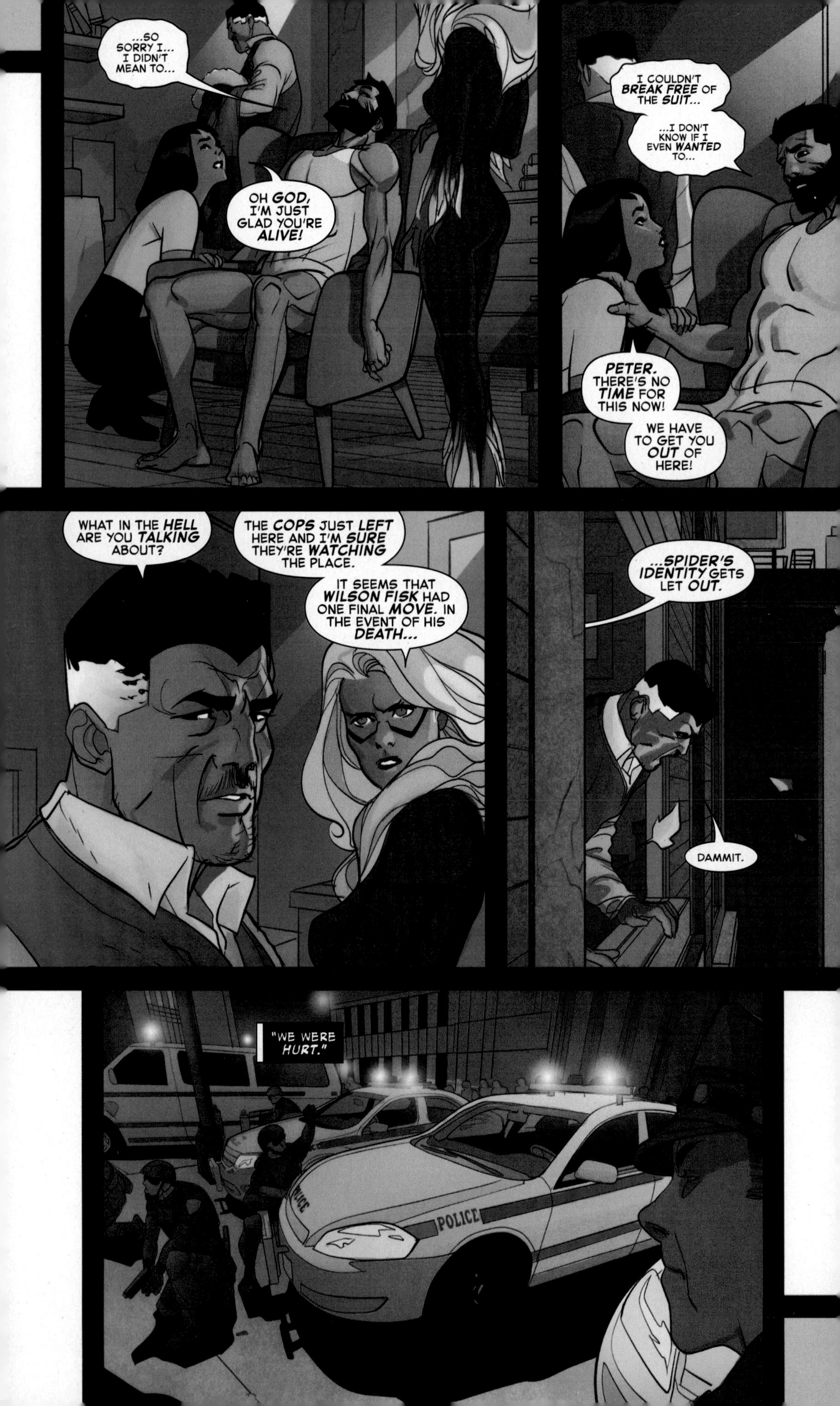
...SO SORRY I... I DIDN'T MEAN TO...
OH GOD, I'M JUST GLAD YOU'RE ALIVE!
I COULDN'T BREAK FREE OF THE SUIT...
...I DON'T KNOW IF I EVEN WANTED TO...
PETER. THERE'S NO TIME FOR THIS NOW!
WE HAVE TO GET YOU OUT OF HERE!
WHAT IN THE HELL ARE YOU TALKING ABOUT?
THE COPS JUST LEFT HERE AND I'M SURE THEY'RE WATCHING THE PLACE.
IT SEEMS THAT WILSON FISK HAD ONE FINAL MOVE. IN THE EVENT OF HIS DEATH...
...SPIDER'S IDENTITY GETS LET OUT.
DAMMIT.
"WE WERE HURT."
POLICE
POLICE

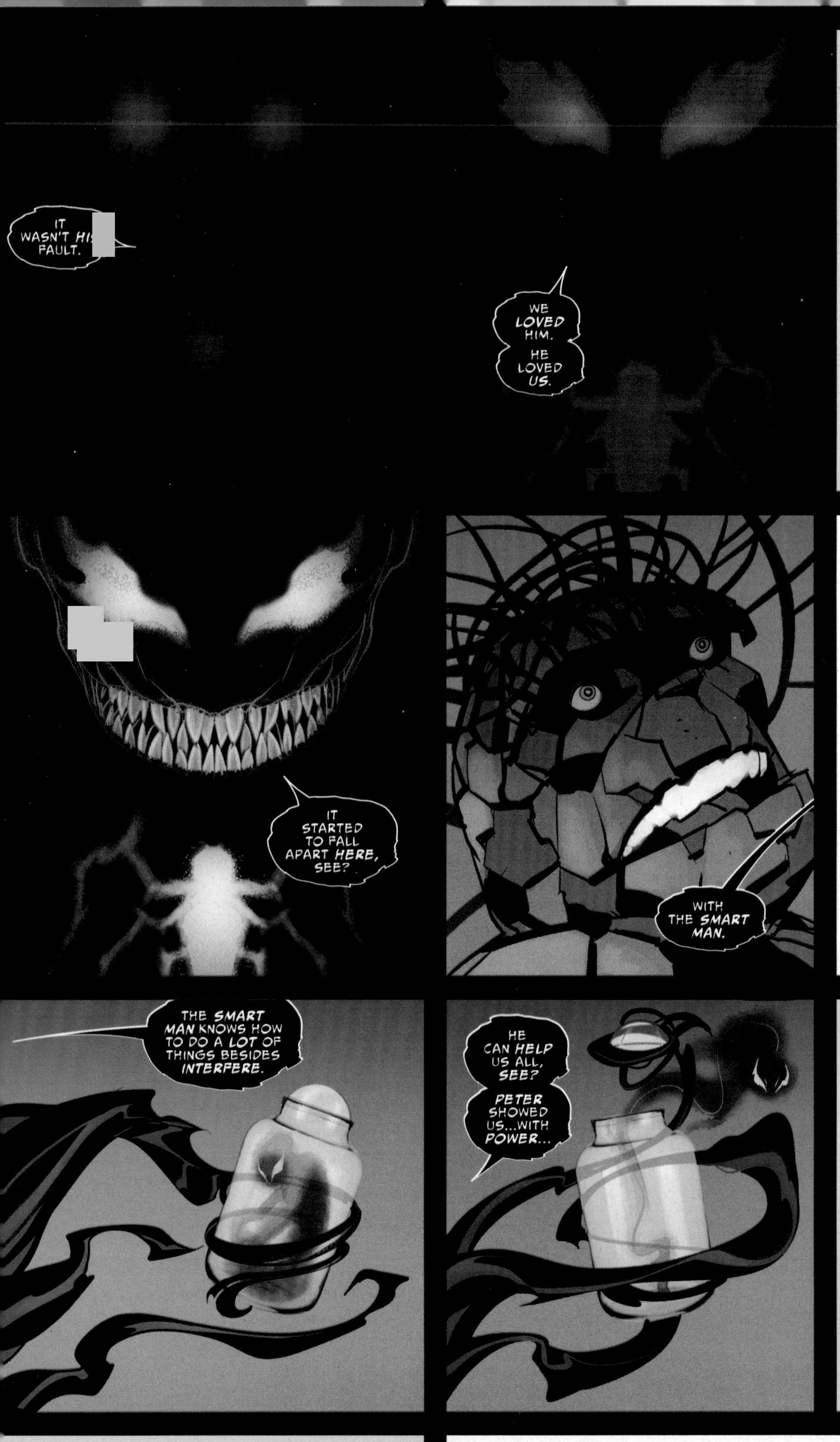
IT WASN'T HI FAULT.
WE LOVED HIM.
HE LOVED US.
IT STARTED TO FALL APART HERE, SEE?
WITH THE SMART MAN.
THE SMART MAN KNOWS HOW TO DO A LOT OF THINGS BESIDES INTERFERE.
HE CAN HELP US ALL, SEE?
PETER SHOWED US...WITH POWER...

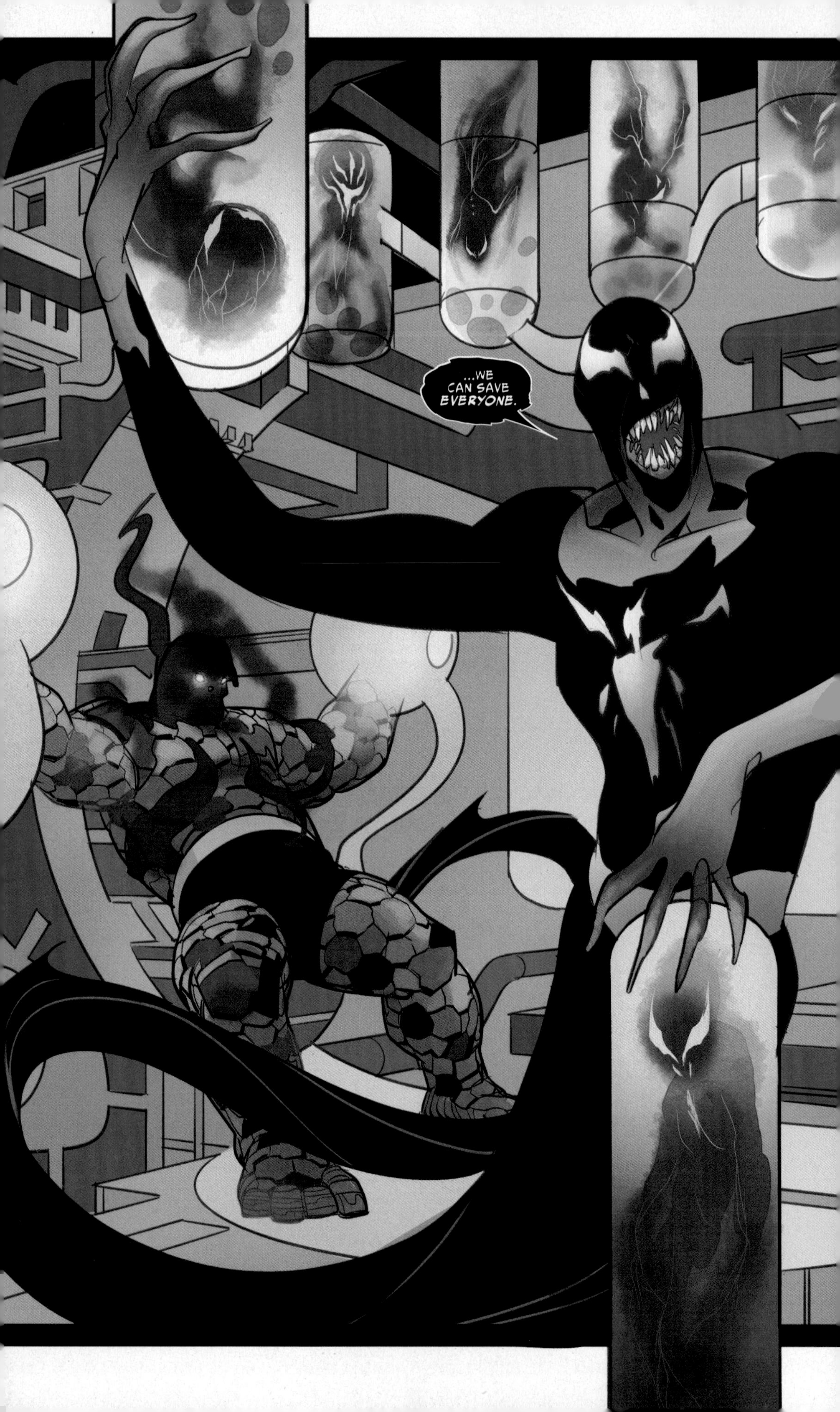
...WE CAN SAVE EVERYONE.

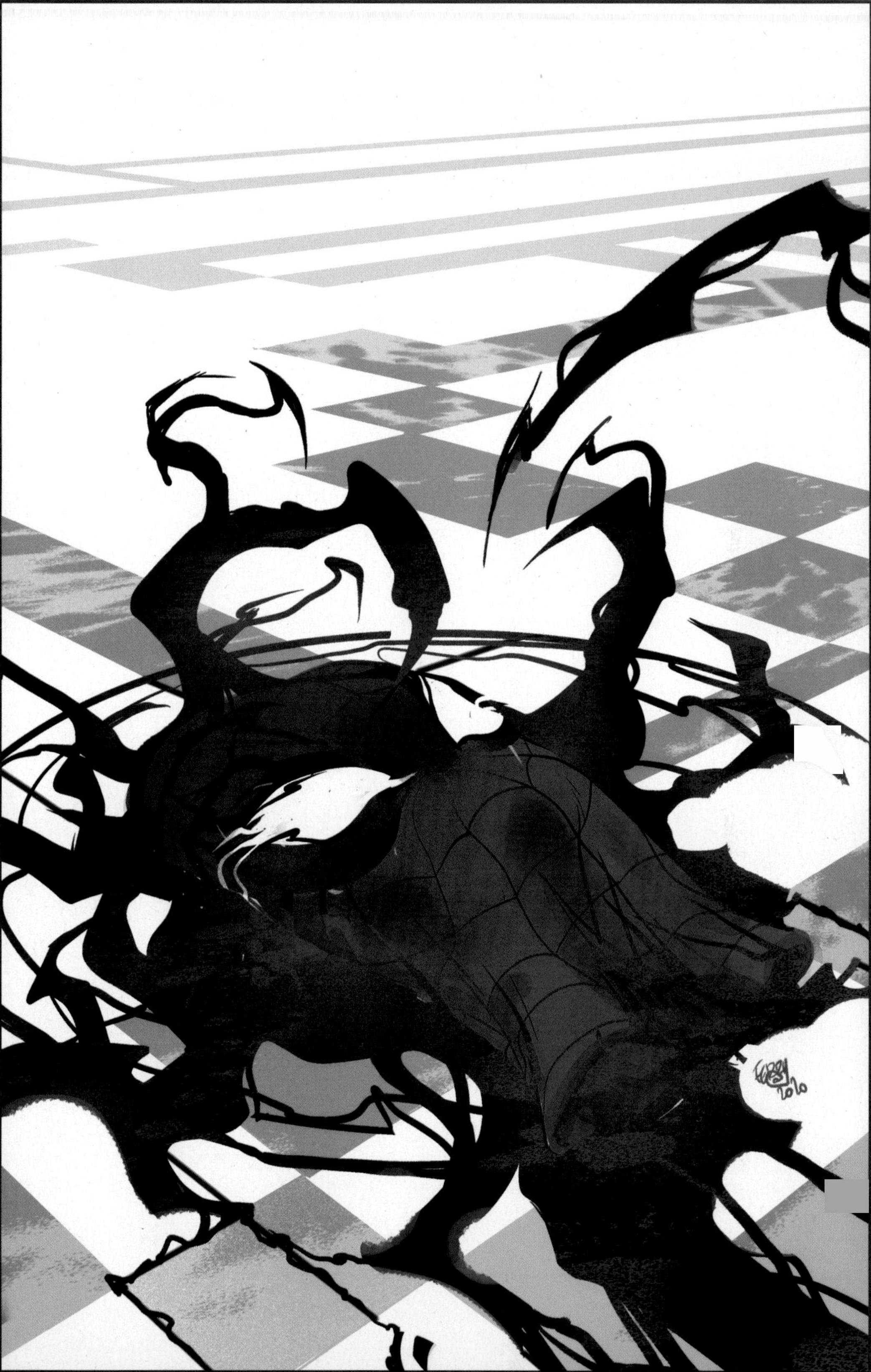
FERRY 2020

#1 VARIANT BY PASQUAL FERRY

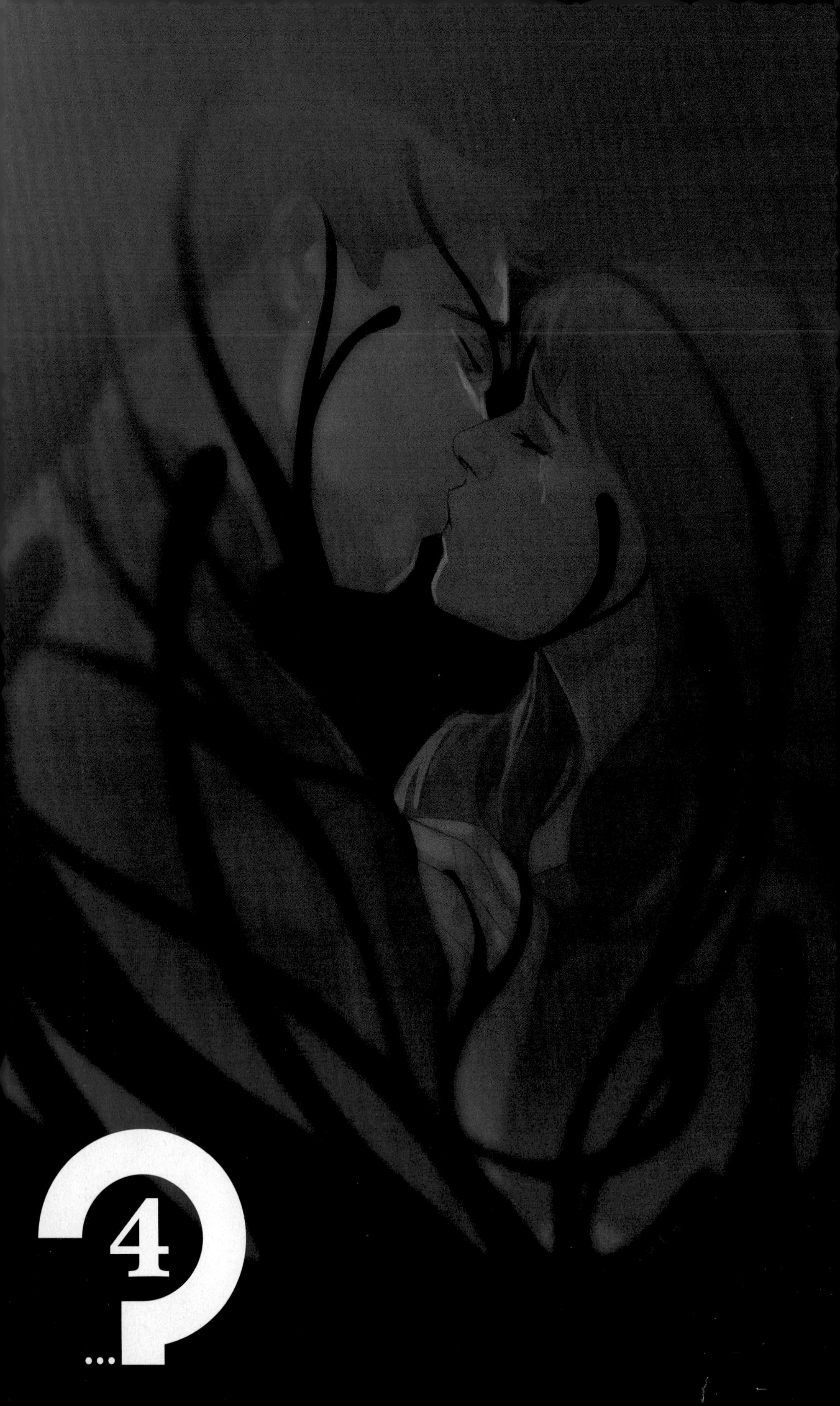
4
...

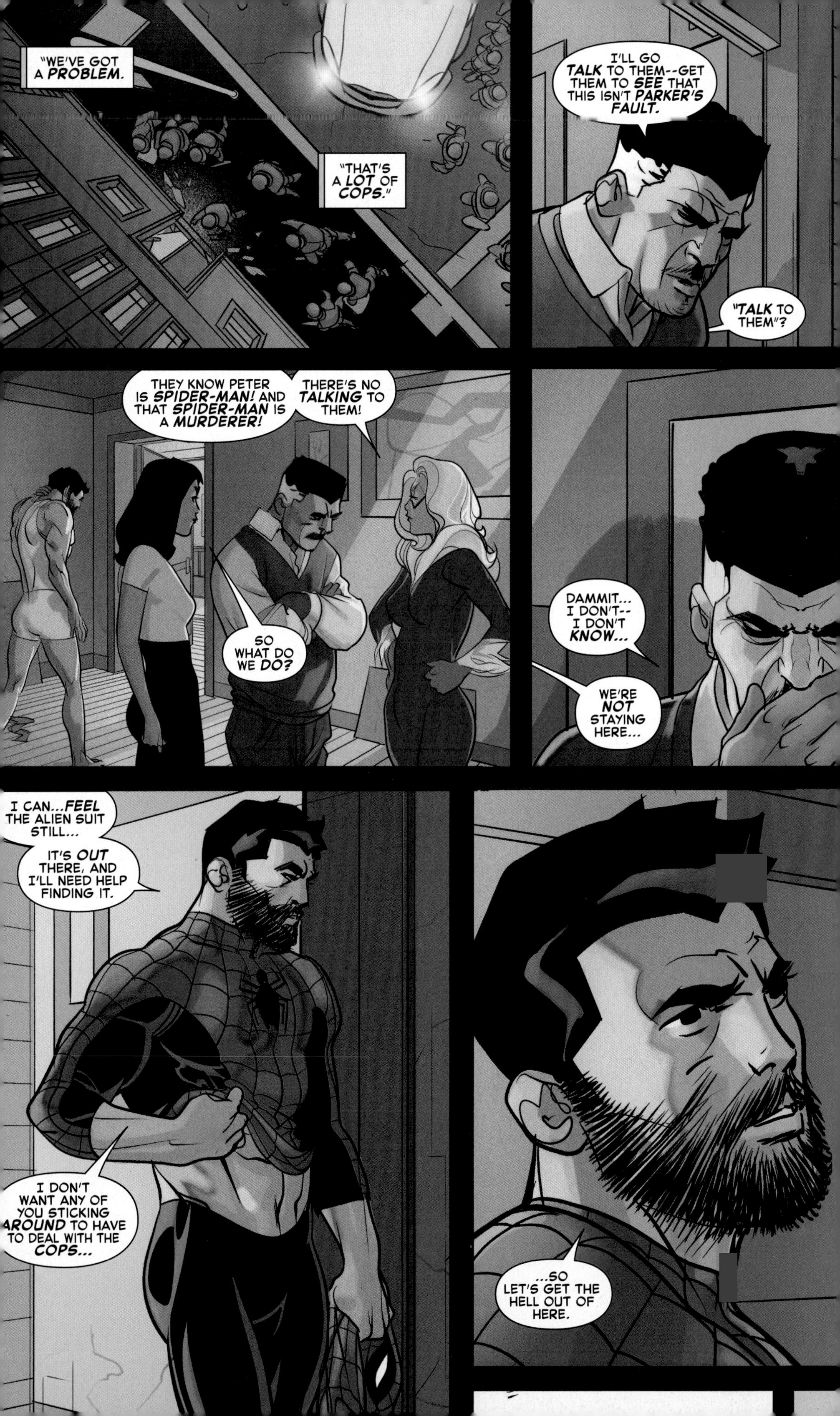
"WE'VE GOT A PROBLEM.
"THAT'S A LOT OF COPS."
I'LL GO TALK TO THEM--GET THEM TO SEE THAT THIS ISN'T PARKER'S FAULT.
"TALK TO THEM"?
THEY KNOW PETER IS SPIDER-MAN! AND THAT SPIDER-MAN IS A MURDERER!
THERE'S NO TALKING TO THEM!
SO WHAT DO WE DO?
DAMMIT... I DON'T-- I DON'T KNOW...
WE'RE NOT STAYING HERE...
I CAN...FEEL THE ALIEN SUIT STILL...
IT'S OUT THERE, AND I'LL NEED HELP FINDING IT.
I DON'T WANT ANY OF YOU STICKING AROUND TO HAVE TO DEAL WITH THE COPS...
...SO LET'S GET THE HELL OUT OF HERE.

ALL RIGHT, WHERE TO FIRST?

BLACK CAT, YOU TAKE JONAH HOME, AND I'LL...

...I'LL TAKE MJ HOME. ALL OF YOU NEED TO LIE LOW.

THEN I'LL GO SEE REED RICHARDS. HE STUDIED THE SUIT. HE'LL KNOW WHAT TO DO.

WHAT, YOU THINK YOU'RE CUTTING ME OUT OF THIS, PARKER

I'M J. JONAH JAMESON DAMMIT! I'LL--I'LL HEAD TO THE BUGLE AND TELL THIS STORY PROPERLY!

A CASH REWARD FO INFO ON YOU BLASTED EV PAJAMAS I'LL--

JONAH! FOR ONCE IN YOUR STUBBORN LIFE, LISTEN TO ME!

GO HOME AND WAIT! THIS THING COULD BE AFTER YOU NOW TOO!

I'LL LET YOU KNOW WHEN IT'S SAFE!

IF IT'S SAFE.

GOD, HOW DID I LET IT GET SO OUT OF CONTROL? I NEED TO--

OH NO...

PETER WHAT'

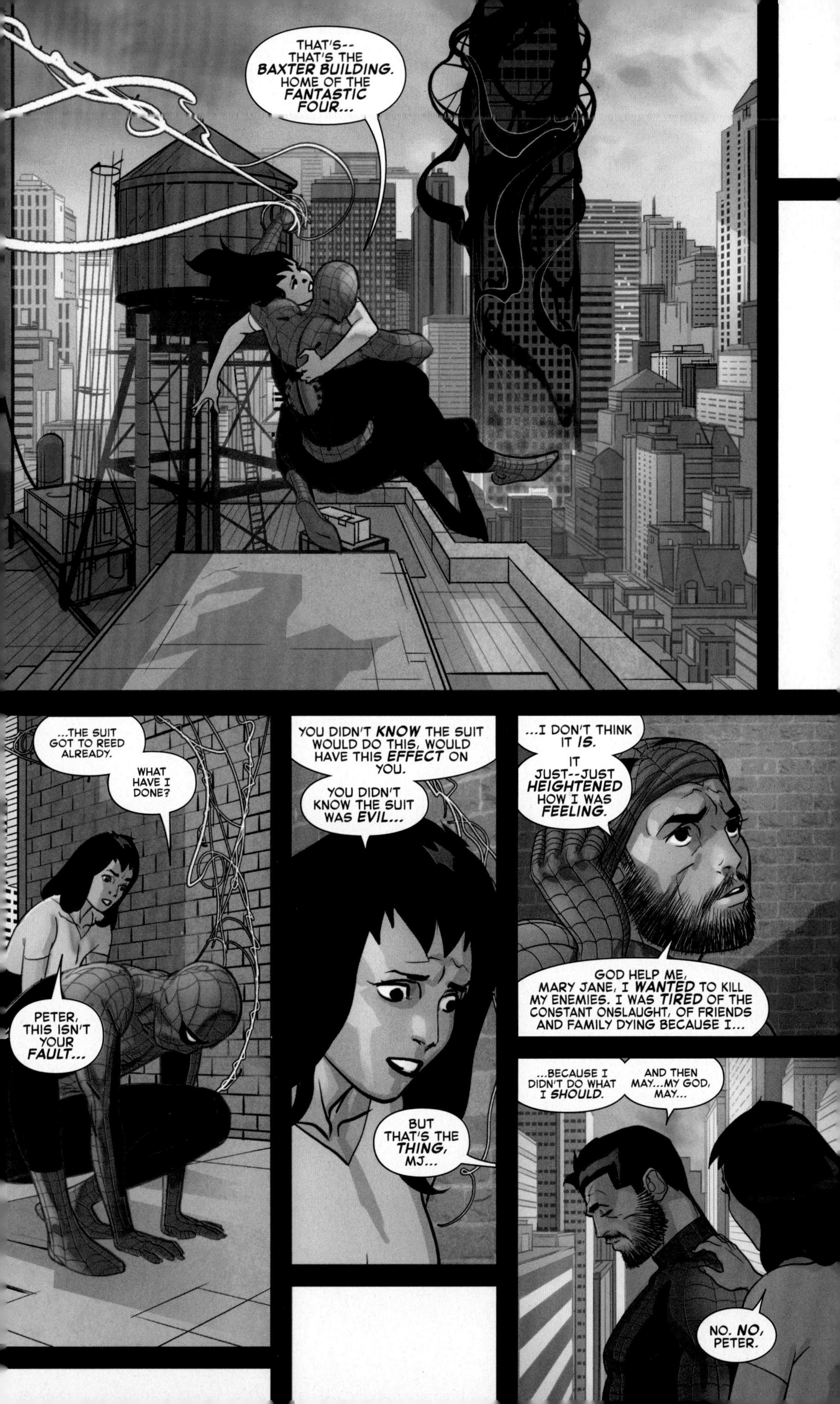
THAT'S--
THAT'S THE BAXTER BUILDING. HOME OF THE FANTASTIC FOUR...
...THE SUIT GOT TO REED ALREADY.
WHAT HAVE I DONE?
PETER, THIS ISN'T YOUR FAULT...
YOU DIDN'T KNOW THE SUIT WOULD DO THIS, WOULD HAVE THIS EFFECT ON YOU.
YOU DIDN'T KNOW THE SUIT WAS EVIL...
BUT THAT'S THE THING, MJ...
...I DON'T THINK IT IS.
IT JUST--JUST HEIGHTENED HOW I WAS FEELING.
GOD HELP ME, MARY JANE, I WANTED TO KILL MY ENEMIES. I WAS TIRED OF THE CONSTANT ONSLAUGHT, OF FRIENDS AND FAMILY DYING BECAUSE I...
...BECAUSE I DIDN'T DO WHAT I SHOULD.
AND THEN MAY...MY GOD, MAY...
NO. NO, PETER.

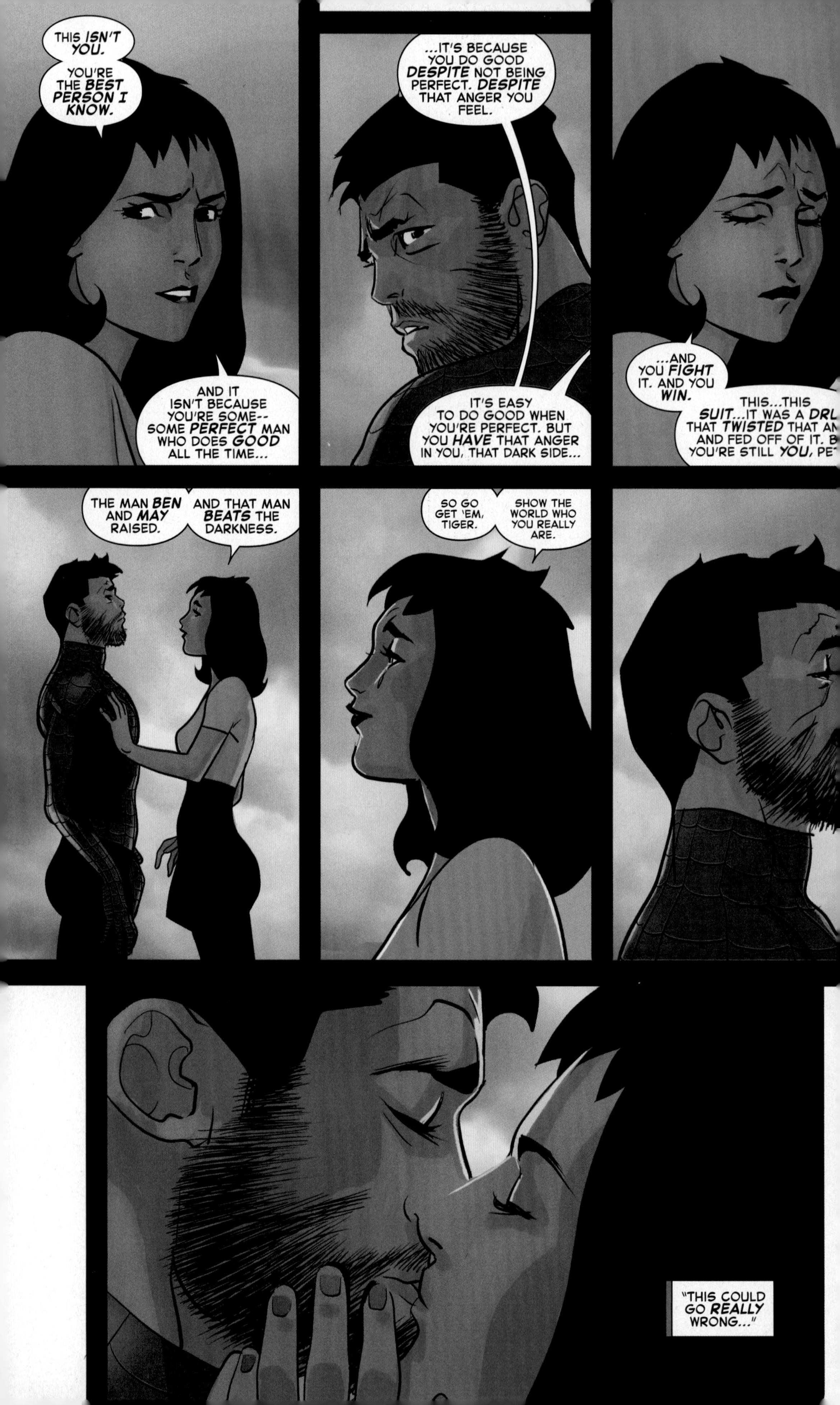
THIS ISN'T YOU.
YOU'RE THE BEST PERSON I KNOW.
AND IT ISN'T BECAUSE YOU'RE SOME-- SOME PERFECT MAN WHO DOES GOOD ALL THE TIME...
...IT'S BECAUSE YOU DO GOOD DESPITE NOT BEING PERFECT. DESPITE THAT ANGER YOU FEEL.
IT'S EASY TO DO GOOD WHEN YOU'RE PERFECT. BUT YOU HAVE THAT ANGER IN YOU, THAT DARK SIDE...
...AND YOU FIGHT IT. AND YOU WIN.
THIS...THIS SUIT...IT WAS A DRL THAT TWISTED THAT AN AND FED OFF OF IT. B YOU'RE STILL YOU, PE
THE MAN BEN AND MAY RAISED.
AND THAT MAN BEATS THE DARKNESS.
SO GO GET 'EM, TIGER.
SHOW THE WORLD WHO YOU REALLY ARE.
"THIS COULD GO REALLY WRONG..."

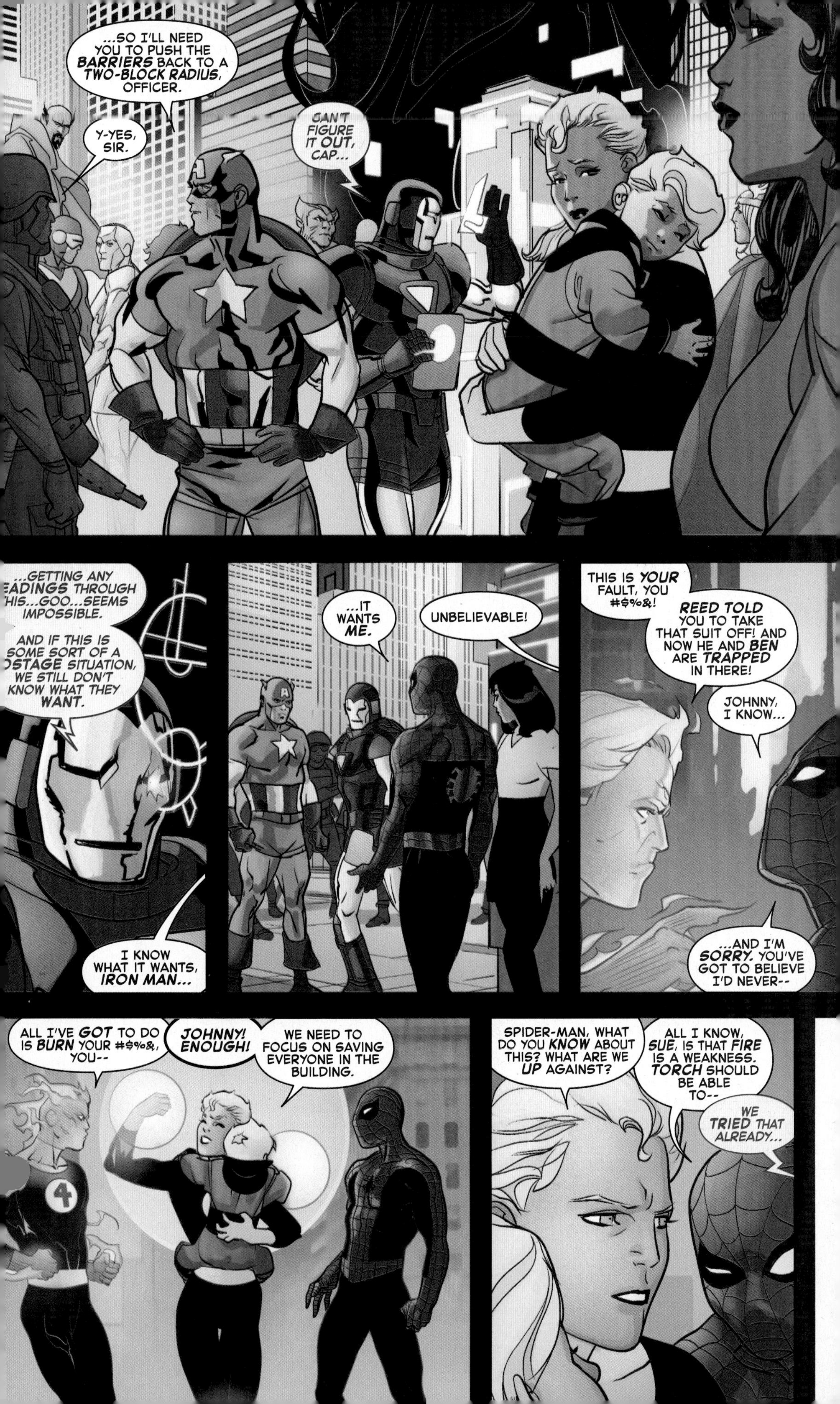
...SO I'LL NEED YOU TO PUSH THE BARRIERS BACK TO A TWO-BLOCK RADIUS, OFFICER.
Y-YES, SIR.
CAN'T FIGURE IT OUT, CAP...
...GETTING ANY EADINGS THROUGH THIS...GOO...SEEMS IMPOSSIBLE.
AND IF THIS IS SOME SORT OF A OSTAGE SITUATION, WE STILL DON'T KNOW WHAT THEY WANT.
I KNOW WHAT IT WANTS, IRON MAN...
...IT WANTS ME.
UNBELIEVABLE!
THIS IS YOUR FAULT, YOU #$%&!
REED TOLD YOU TO TAKE THAT SUIT OFF! AND NOW HE AND BEN ARE TRAPPED IN THERE!
JOHNNY, I KNOW...
...AND I'M SORRY. YOU'VE GOT TO BELIEVE I'D NEVER--
ALL I'VE GOT TO DO IS BURN YOUR #$%&, YOU--
JOHNNY! ENOUGH!
WE NEED TO FOCUS ON SAVING EVERYONE IN THE BUILDING.
SPIDER-MAN, WHAT DO YOU KNOW ABOUT THIS? WHAT ARE WE UP AGAINST?
ALL I KNOW, SUE, IS THAT FIRE IS A WEAKNESS. TORCH SHOULD BE ABLE TO--
WE TRIED THAT ALREADY...

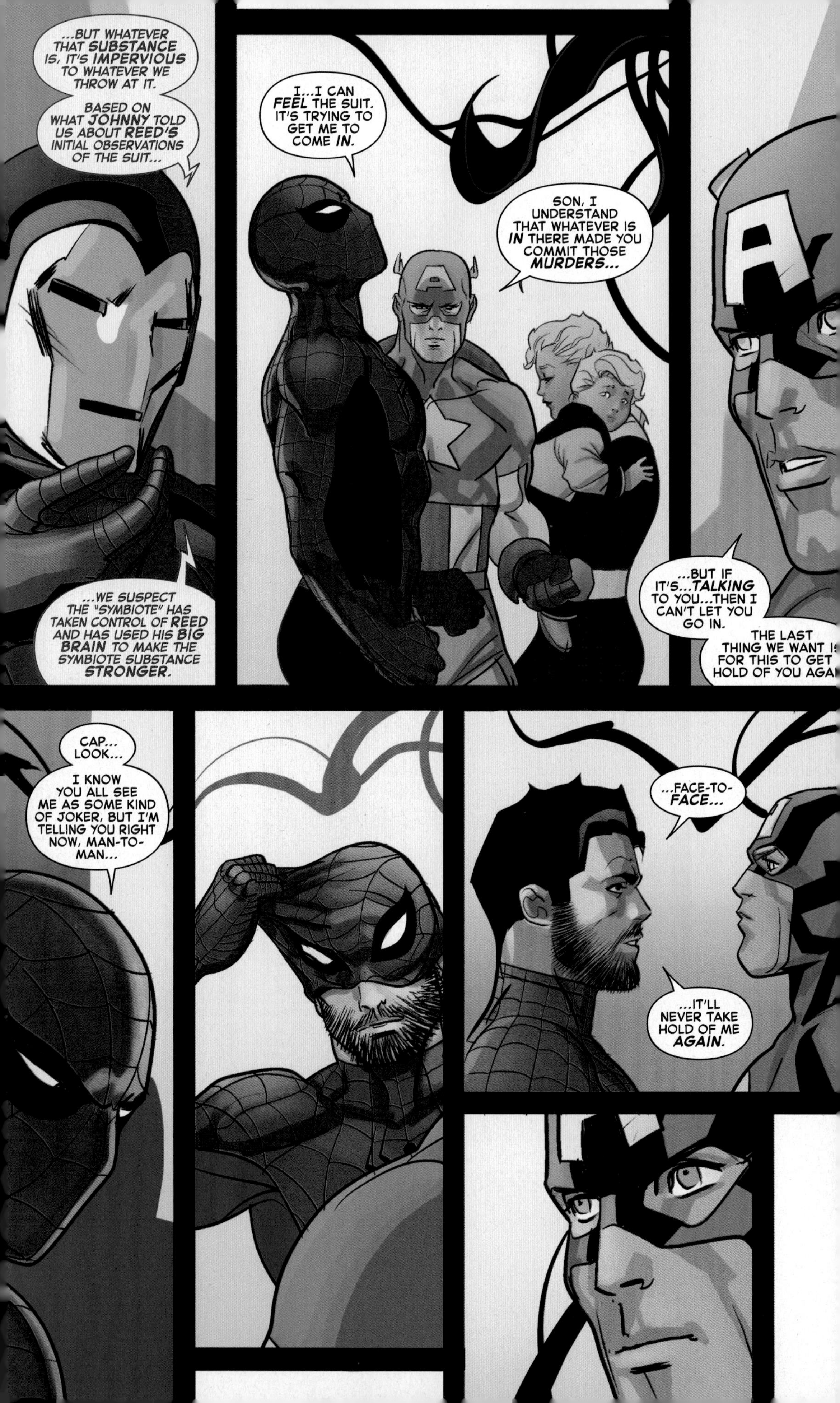
...BUT WHATEVER THAT SUBSTANCE IS, IT'S IMPERVIOUS TO WHATEVER WE THROW AT IT.
BASED ON WHAT JOHNNY TOLD US ABOUT REED'S INITIAL OBSERVATIONS OF THE SUIT...
...WE SUSPECT THE "SYMBIOTE" HAS TAKEN CONTROL OF REED AND HAS USED HIS BIG BRAIN TO MAKE THE SYMBIOTE SUBSTANCE STRONGER.
I...I CAN FEEL THE SUIT. IT'S TRYING TO GET ME TO COME IN.
SON, I UNDERSTAND THAT WHATEVER IS IN THERE MADE YOU COMMIT THOSE MURDERS...
...BUT IF IT'S...TALKING TO YOU...THEN I CAN'T LET YOU GO IN.
THE LAST THING WE WANT IS FOR THIS TO GET HOLD OF YOU AGA
CAP... LOOK...
I KNOW YOU ALL SEE ME AS SOME KIND OF JOKER, BUT I'M TELLING YOU RIGHT NOW, MAN-TO-MAN...
...FACE-TO-FACE...
...IT'LL NEVER TAKE HOLD OF ME AGAIN.

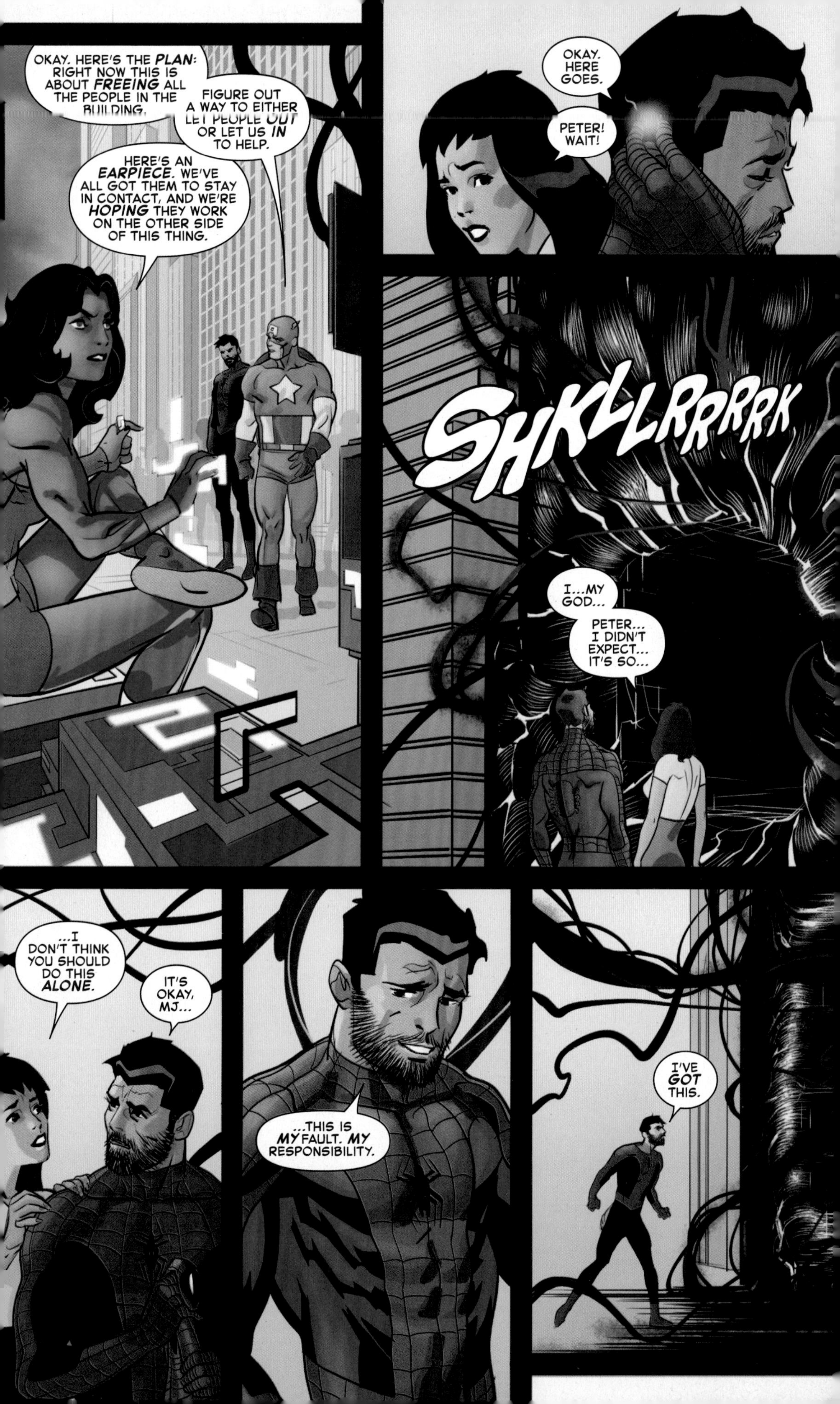
OKAY. HERE'S THE PLAN: RIGHT NOW THIS IS ABOUT FREEING ALL THE PEOPLE IN THE BUILDING.
FIGURE OUT A WAY TO EITHER LET PEOPLE OUT OR LET US IN TO HELP.
HERE'S AN EARPIECE. WE'VE ALL GOT THEM TO STAY IN CONTACT, AND WE'RE HOPING THEY WORK ON THE OTHER SIDE OF THIS THING.
OKAY. HERE GOES.
PETER! WAIT!
SHKLLRRRRK
I...MY GOD...
PETER... I DIDN'T EXPECT... IT'S SO...
...I DON'T THINK YOU SHOULD DO THIS ALONE.
IT'S OKAY, MJ...
...THIS IS MY FAULT. MY RESPONSIBILITY.
I'VE GOT THIS.

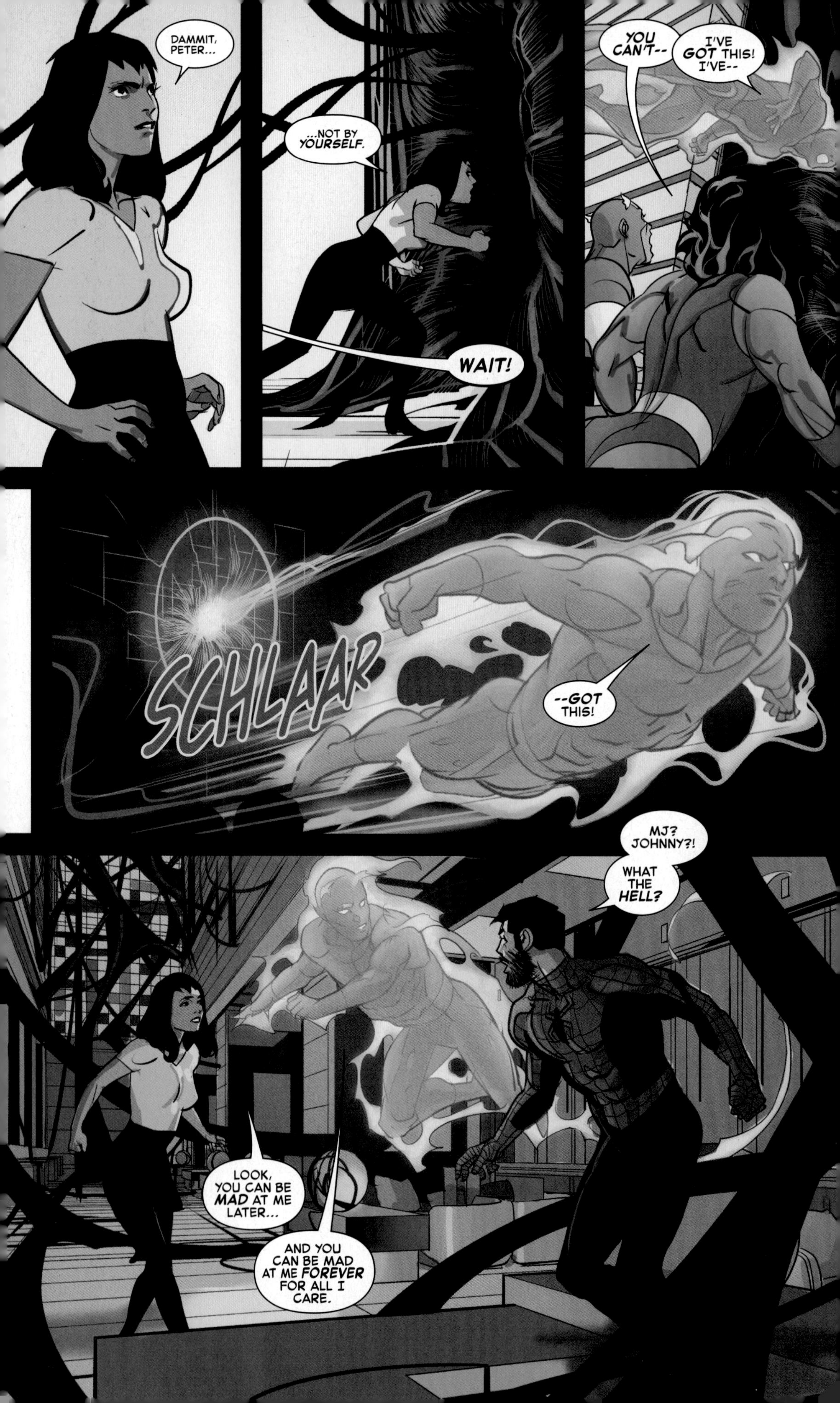
DAMMIT, PETER...
...NOT BY YOURSELF.
WAIT!
YOU CAN'T--
I'VE GOT THIS! I'VE--
SCHLAAR
--GOT THIS!
MJ? JOHNNY?!
WHAT THE HELL?
LOOK, YOU CAN BE MAD AT ME LATER...
AND YOU CAN BE MAD AT ME FOREVER FOR ALL I CARE.

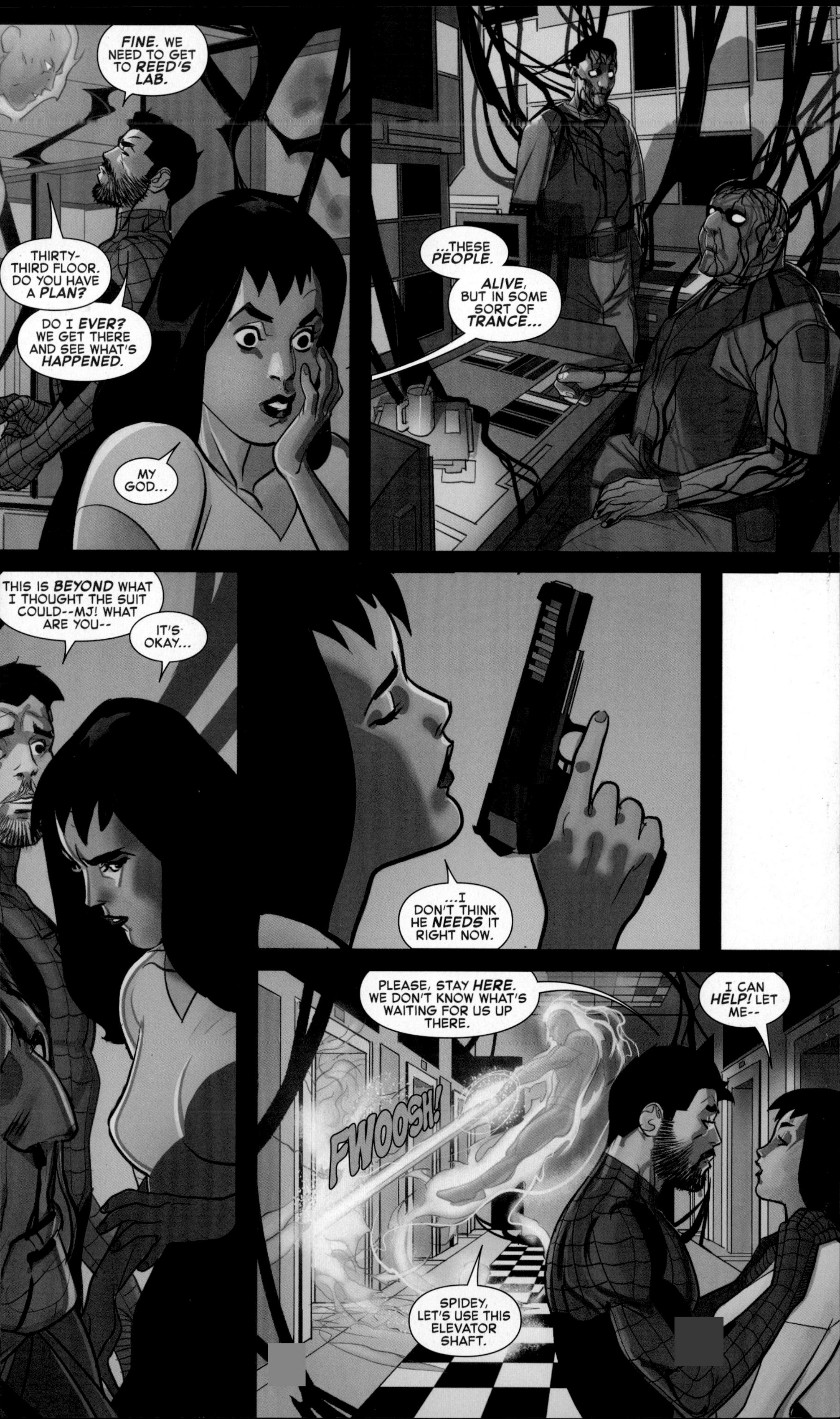

FINE. WE NEED TO GET TO REED'S LAB.
THIRTY-THIRD FLOOR. DO YOU HAVE A PLAN?
DO I EVER? WE GET THERE AND SEE WHAT'S HAPPENED.
MY GOD...
...THESE PEOPLE.
ALIVE, BUT IN SOME SORT OF TRANCE...
THIS IS BEYOND WHAT I THOUGHT THE SUIT COULD--MJ! WHAT ARE YOU--
IT'S OKAY...
...I DON'T THINK HE NEEDS IT RIGHT NOW.
PLEASE, STAY HERE. WE DON'T KNOW WHAT'S WAITING FOR US UP THERE.
I CAN HELP! LET ME--
FWOOSH!
SPIDEY, LET'S USE THIS ELEVATOR SHAFT.

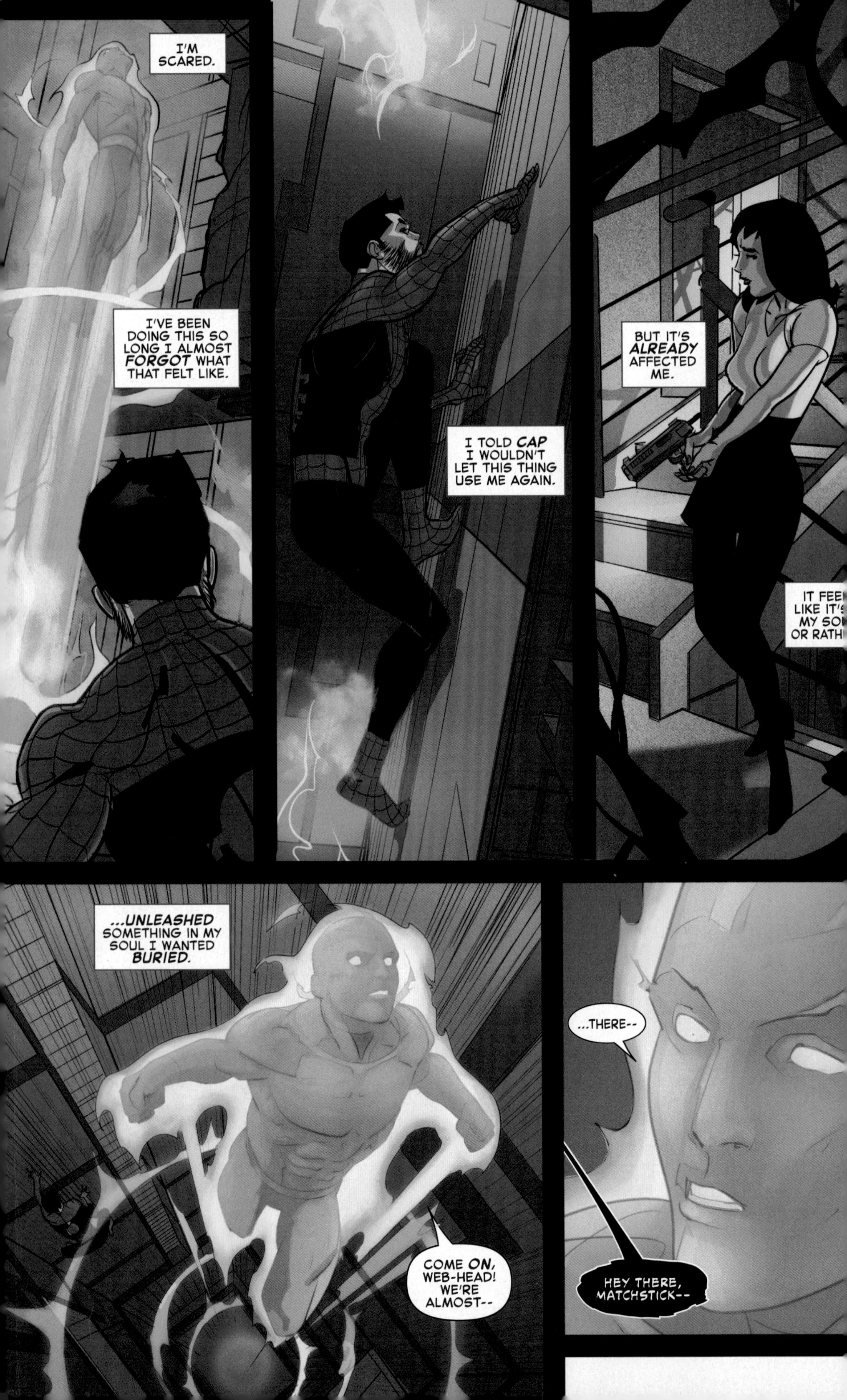
I'M SCARED.
I'VE BEEN DOING THIS SO LONG I ALMOST FORGOT WHAT THAT FELT LIKE.
I TOLD CAP I WOULDN'T LET THIS THING USE ME AGAIN.
BUT IT'S ALREADY AFFECTED ME.
IT FEE LIKE IT'S MY SO OR RATH
...UNLEASHED SOMETHING IN MY SOUL I WANTED BURIED.
COME ON, WEB-HEAD! WE'RE ALMOST--
...THERE--
HEY THERE, MATCHSTICK--

--MIND IF I *STRIKE* YA?

DAMMIT! BEN'S BEEN--BEEN *INFECTED!*

TORCH BLASTED INTO ANOTHER *FLOOR!*

BUT THERE'S NOWHERE *I* CAN GO TO GET OUT OF--

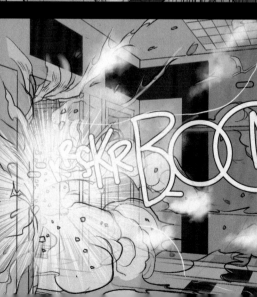

FSKR**BOOM**

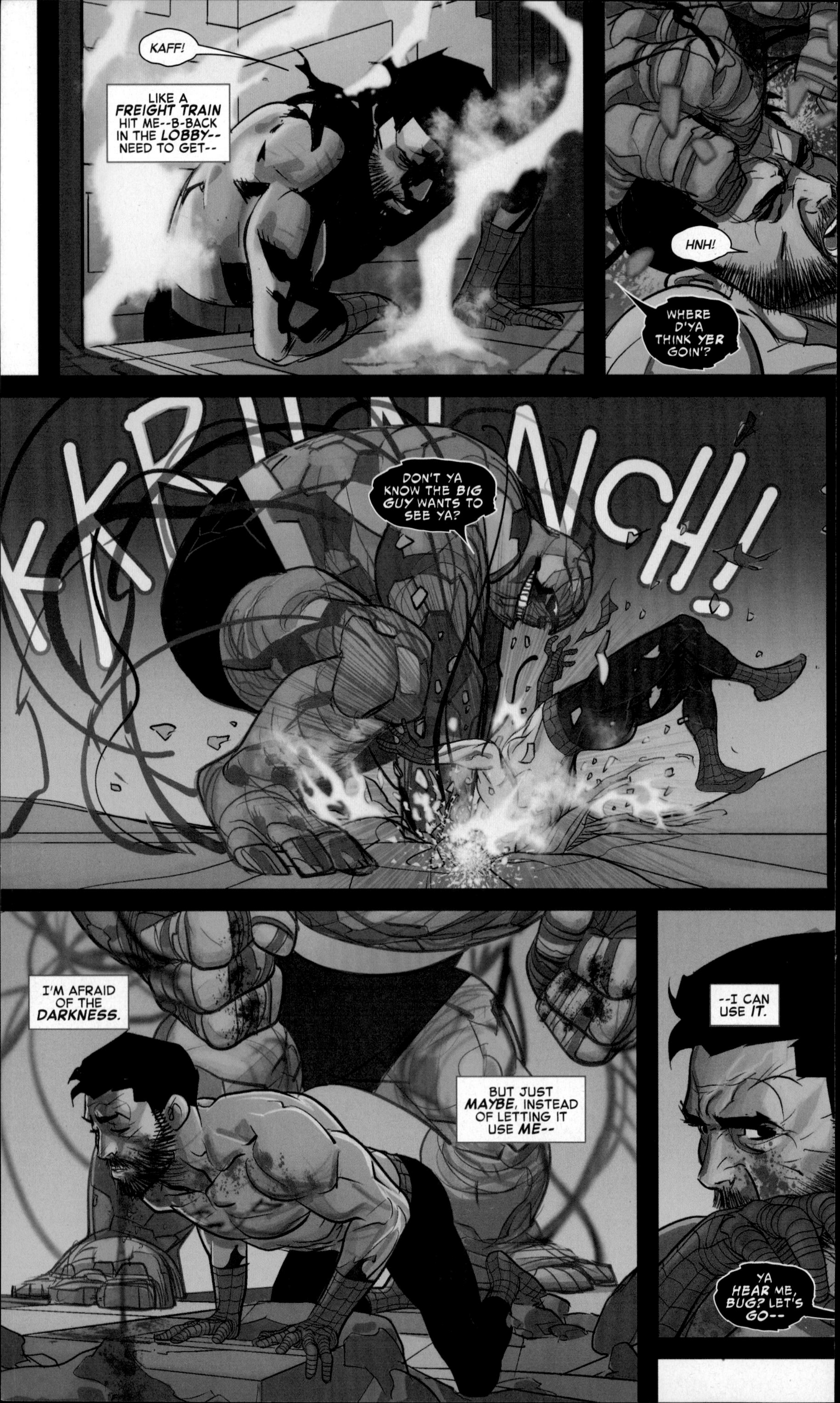
KAFF!
LIKE A FREIGHT TRAIN HIT ME--B-BACK IN THE LOBBY--NEED TO GET--
HNH!
WHERE D'YA THINK YER GOIN'?
KRUNCH!
DON'T YA KNOW THE BIG GUY WANTS TO SEE YA?
I'M AFRAID OF THE DARKNESS.
BUT JUST MAYBE, INSTEAD OF LETTING IT USE ME--
--I CAN USE IT.
YA HEAR ME, BUG? LET'S GO--

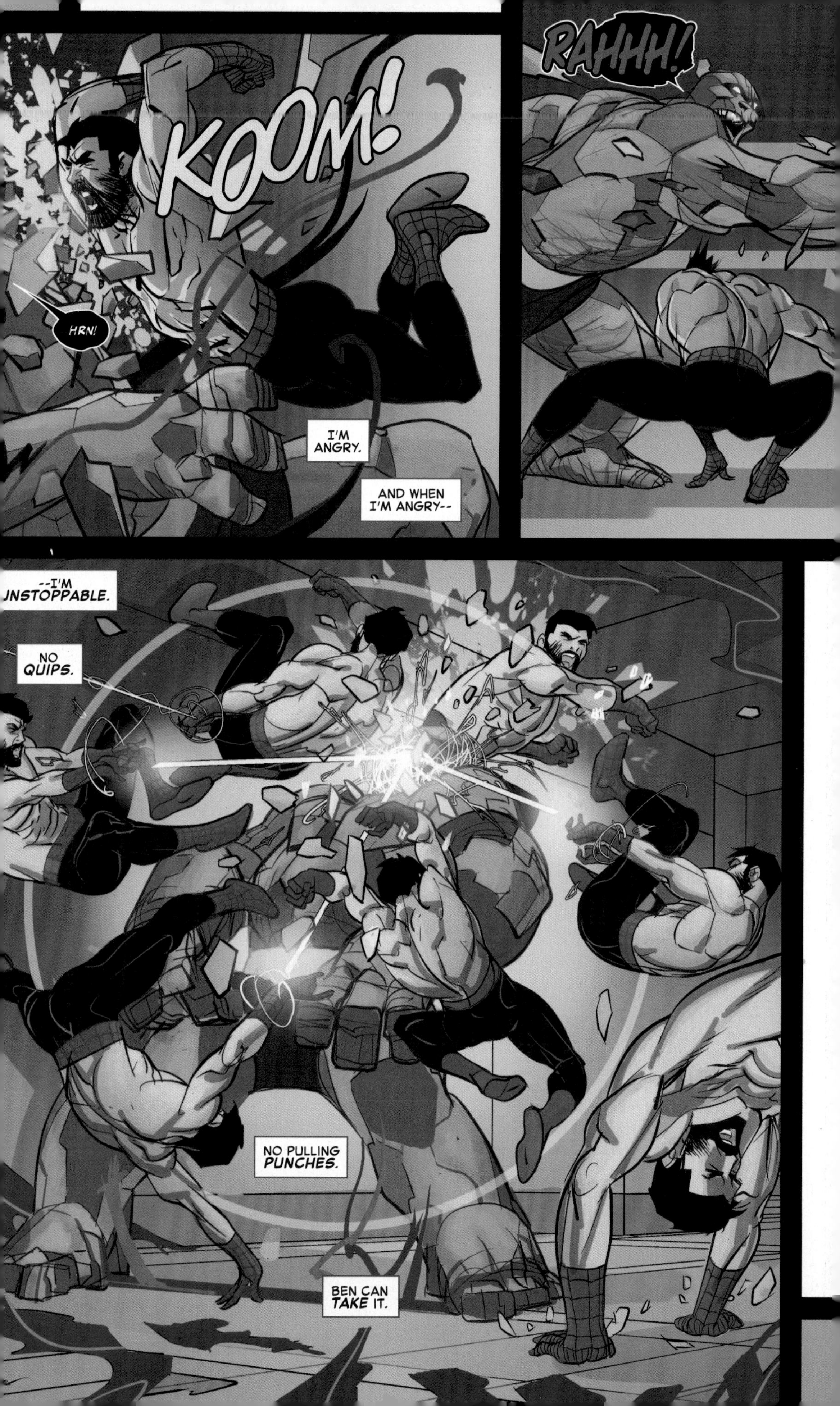
KOOM!
HRN!
I'M ANGRY.
AND WHEN I'M ANGRY--
RAHHH!
--I'M UNSTOPPABLE.
NO QUIPS.
NO PULLING PUNCHES.
BEN CAN TAKE IT.

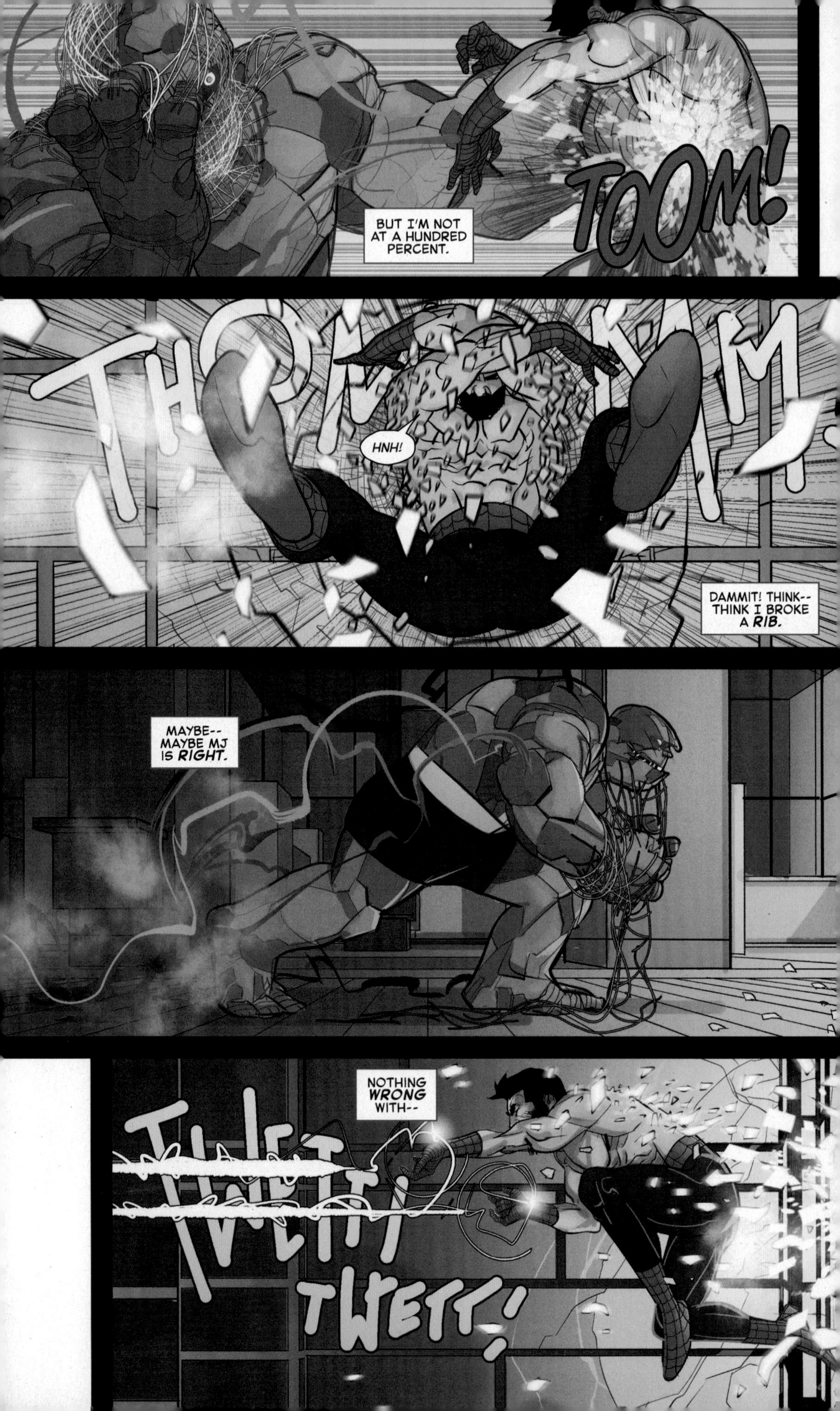
BUT I'M NOT AT A HUNDRED PERCENT.
TOOM!
THOOOM!
HNH!
DAMMIT! THINK-- THINK I BROKE A RIB.
MAYBE-- MAYBE MJ IS RIGHT.
NOTHING WRONG WITH--
TWETT!
TWETT!

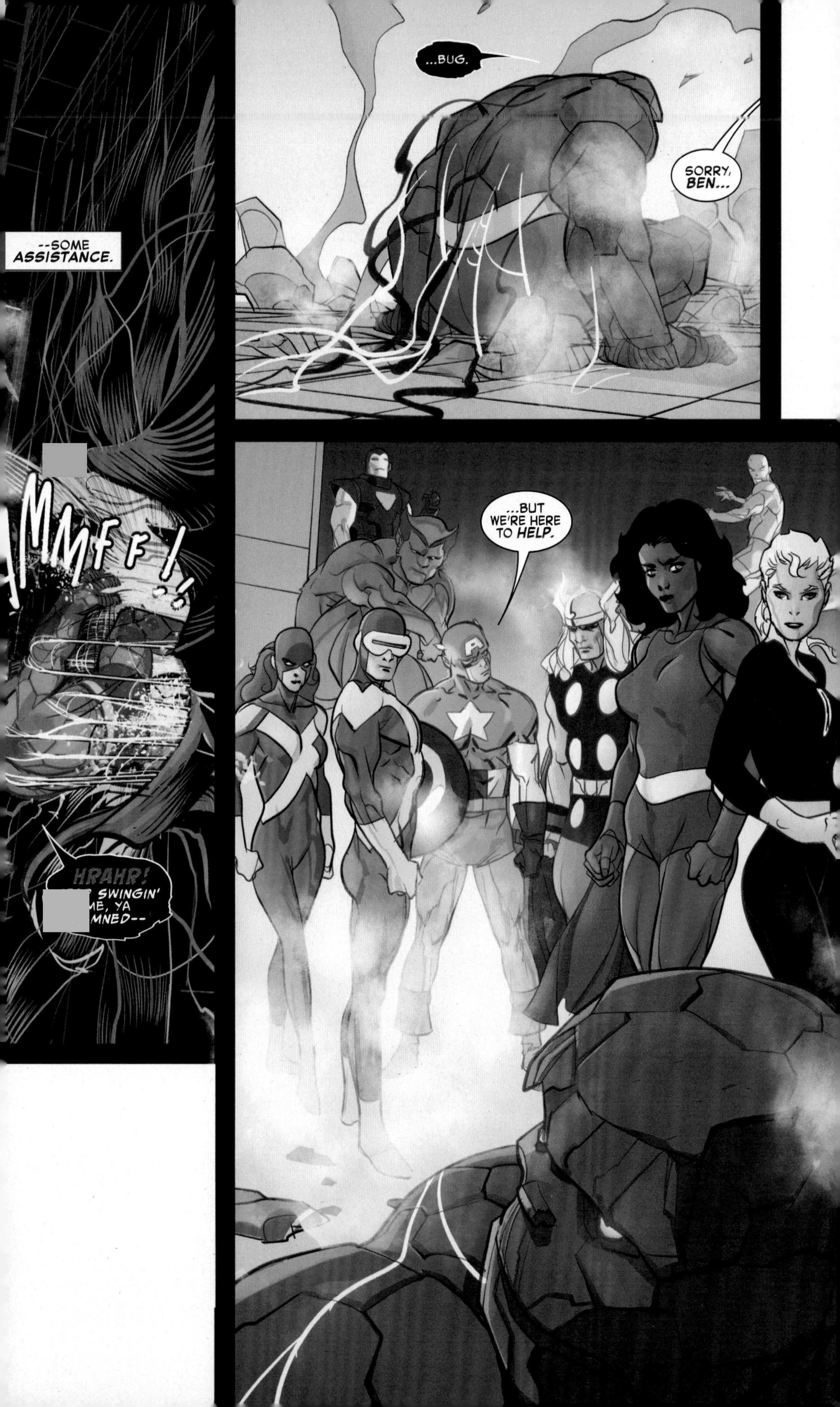
--SOME ASSISTANCE.
MMFF!!
HRAHR!
SWINGIN'
ME, YA
MNED--
...BUG.
SORRY, BEN...
...BUT WE'RE HERE TO HELP.

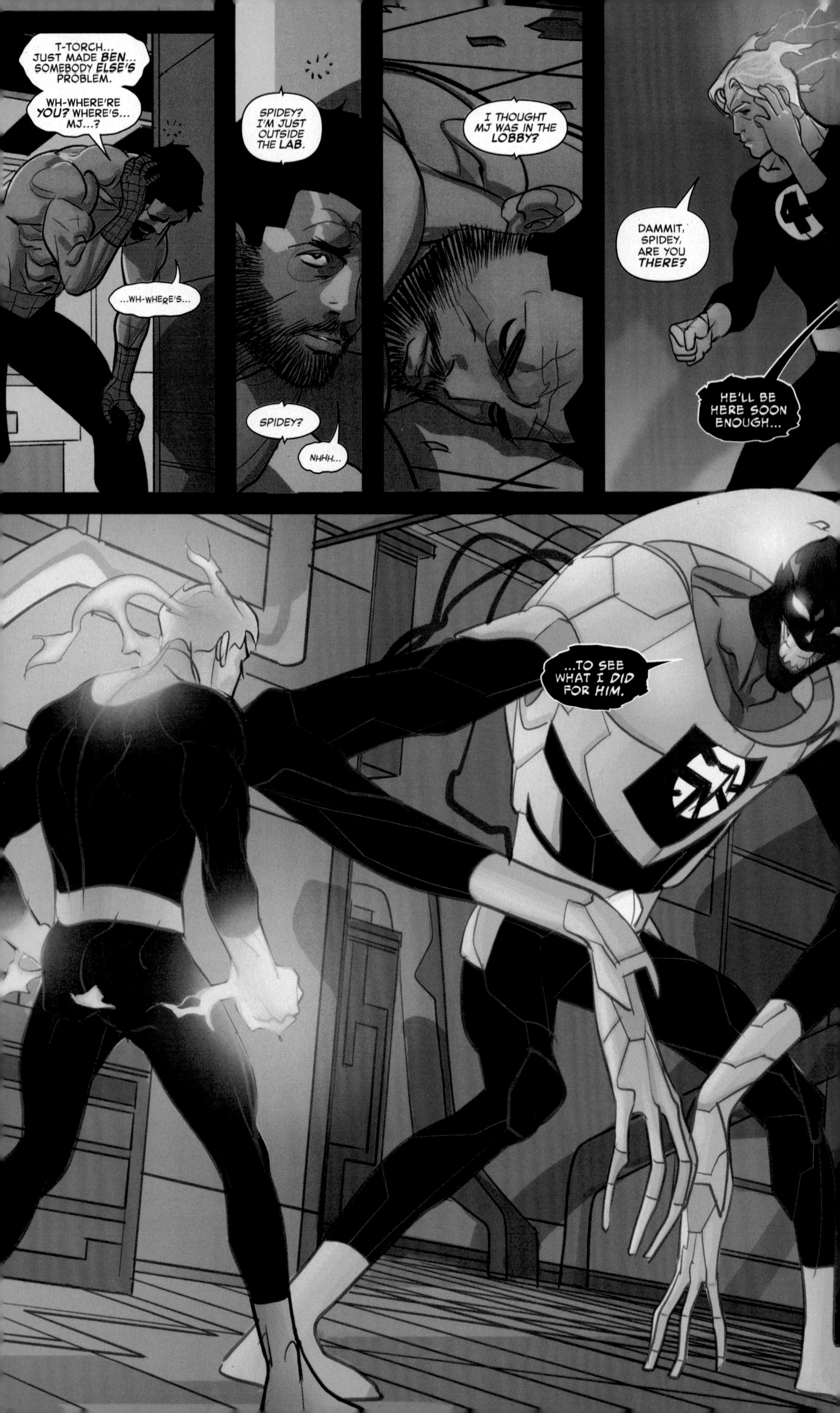
T-TORCH... JUST MADE BEN... SOMEBODY ELSE'S PROBLEM.
WH-WHERE'RE YOU? WHERE'S... MJ...?
...WH-WHERE'S...
SPIDEY? I'M JUST OUTSIDE THE LAB.
SPIDEY?
NHHH...
I THOUGHT MJ WAS IN THE LOBBY?
DAMMIT, SPIDEY, ARE YOU THERE?
HE'LL BE HERE SOON ENOUGH...
...TO SEE WHAT I DID FOR HIM.

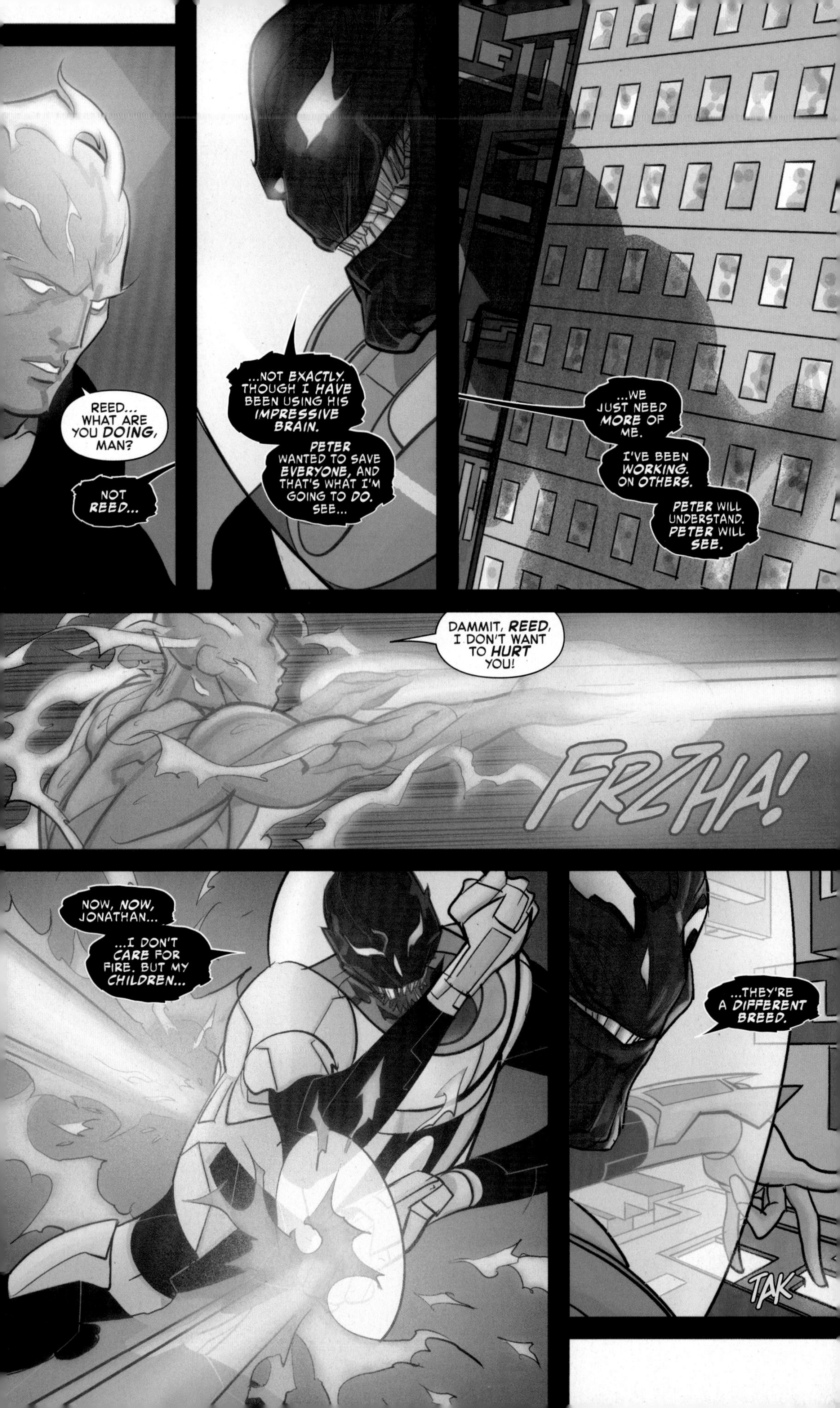

REED... WHAT ARE YOU DOING, MAN?
NOT REED...
...NOT EXACTLY. THOUGH I HAVE BEEN USING HIS IMPRESSIVE BRAIN.
PETER WANTED TO SAVE EVERYONE, AND THAT'S WHAT I'M GOING TO DO. SEE...
...WE JUST NEED MORE OF ME.
I'VE BEEN WORKING. ON OTHERS.
PETER WILL UNDERSTAND. PETER WILL SEE.
DAMMIT, REED, I DON'T WANT TO HURT YOU!
FRZHA!
NOW, NOW, JONATHAN...
...I DON'T CARE FOR FIRE. BUT MY CHILDREN...
...THEY'RE A DIFFERENT BREED.
TAK

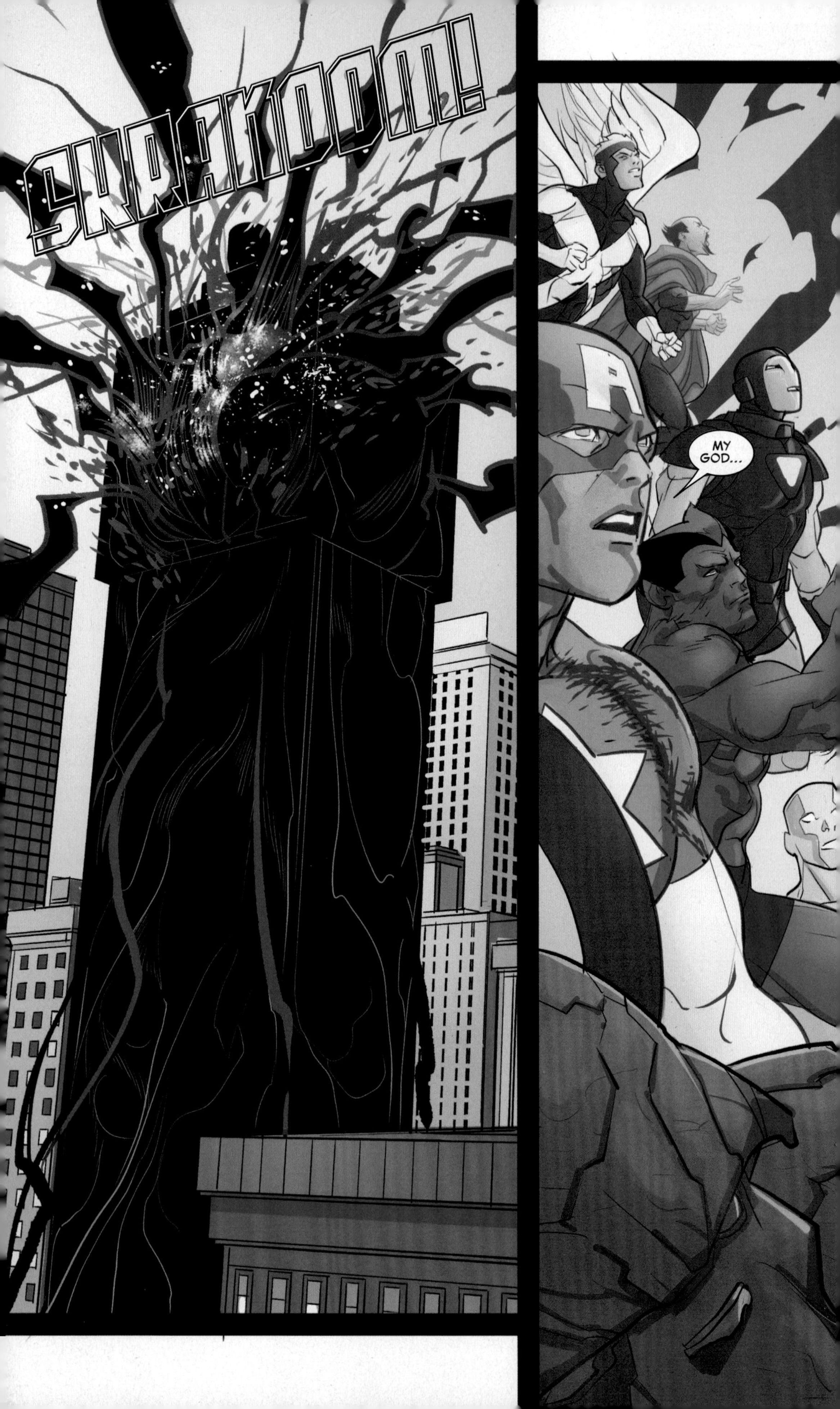
SKRAKOOOM!
MY GOD...

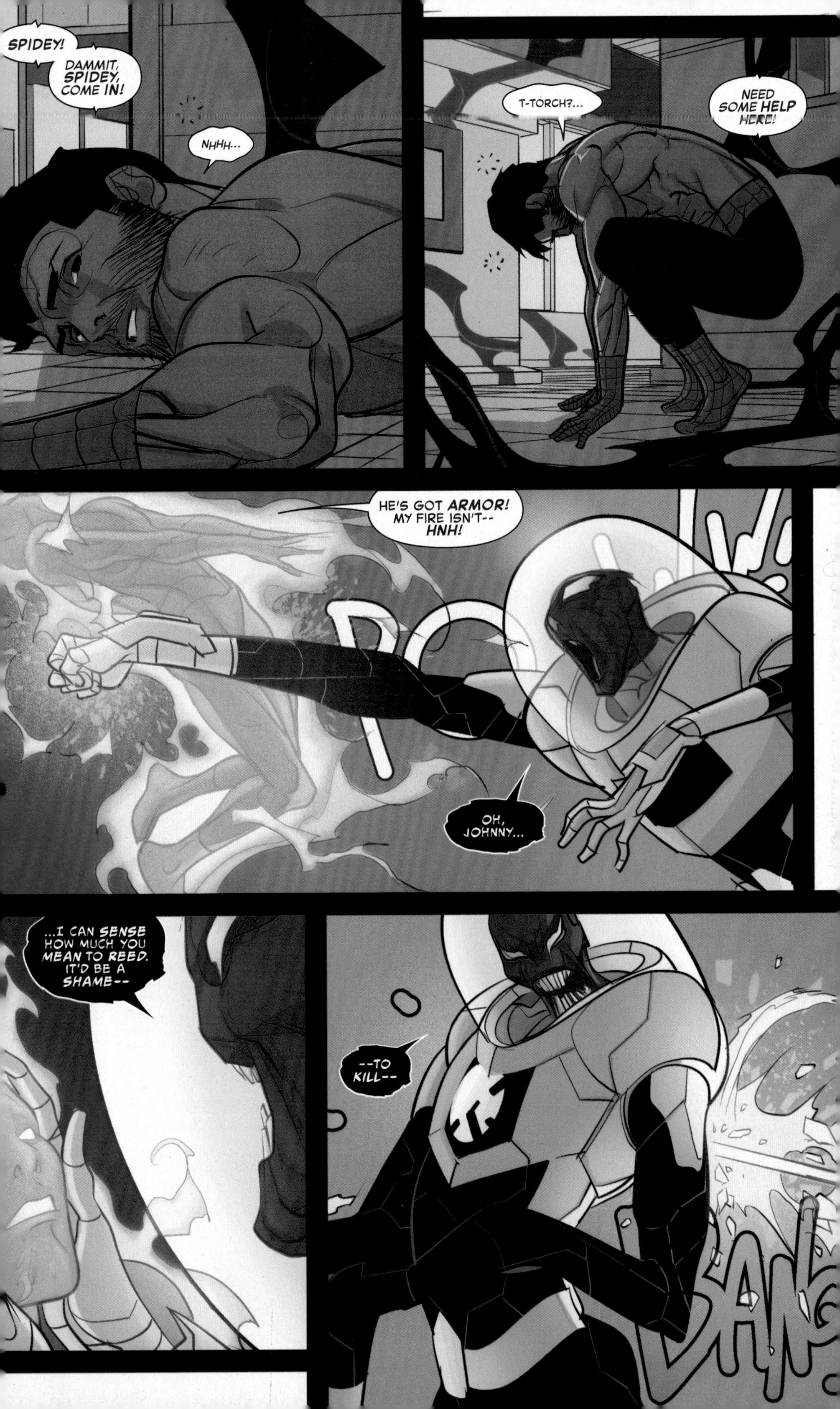
SPIDEY!
DAMMIT, SPIDEY, COME IN!
NHHH...
T-TORCH?...
NEED SOME HELP HERE!
HE'S GOT ARMOR! MY FIRE ISN'T-- HNH!
OH, JOHNNY...
...I CAN SENSE HOW MUCH YOU MEAN TO REED. IT'D BE A SHAME--
--TO KILL--

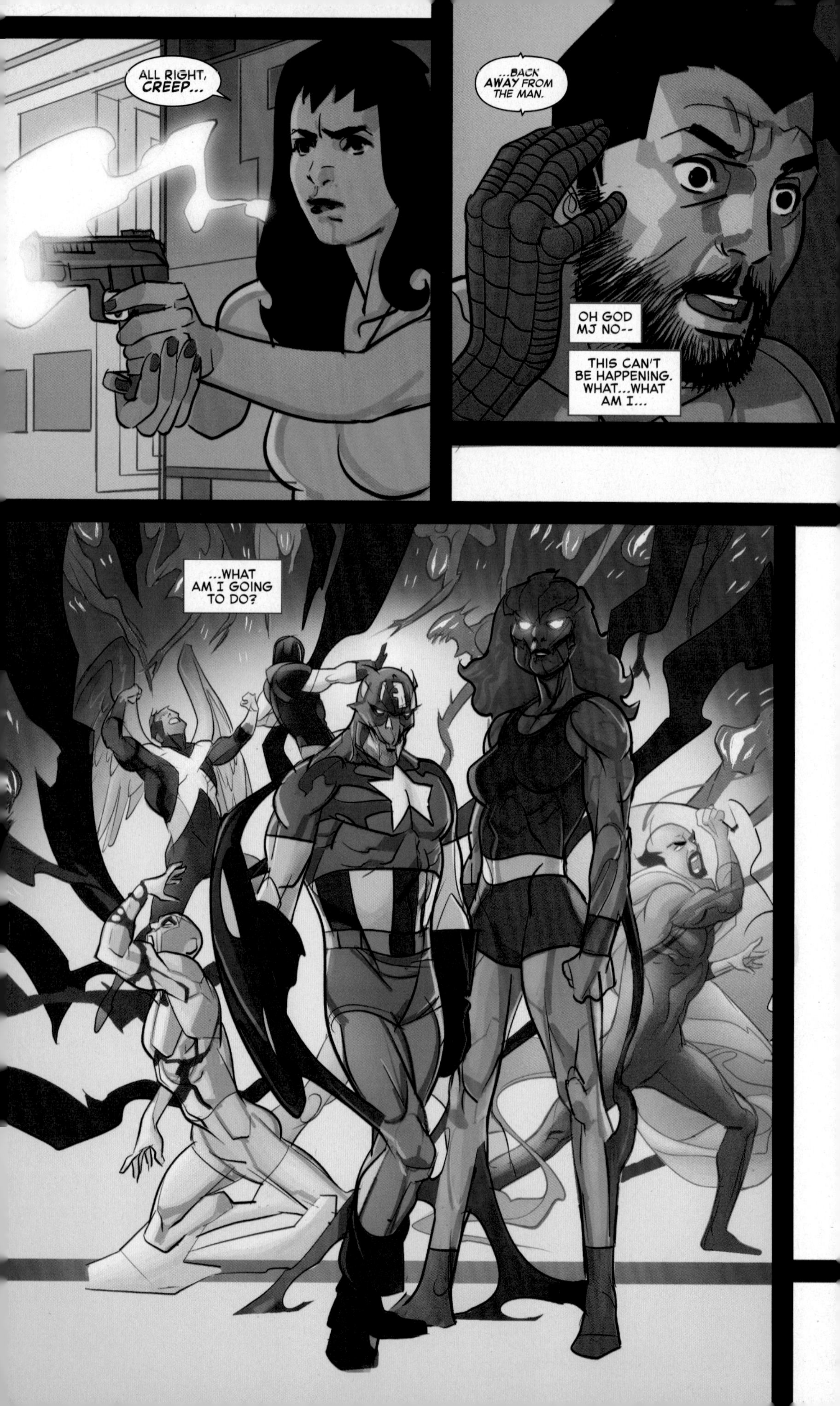
ALL RIGHT, CREEP...
...BACK AWAY FROM THE MAN.
OH GOD MJ NO--
THIS CAN'T BE HAPPENING. WHAT...WHAT AM I...
...WHAT AM I GOING TO DO?

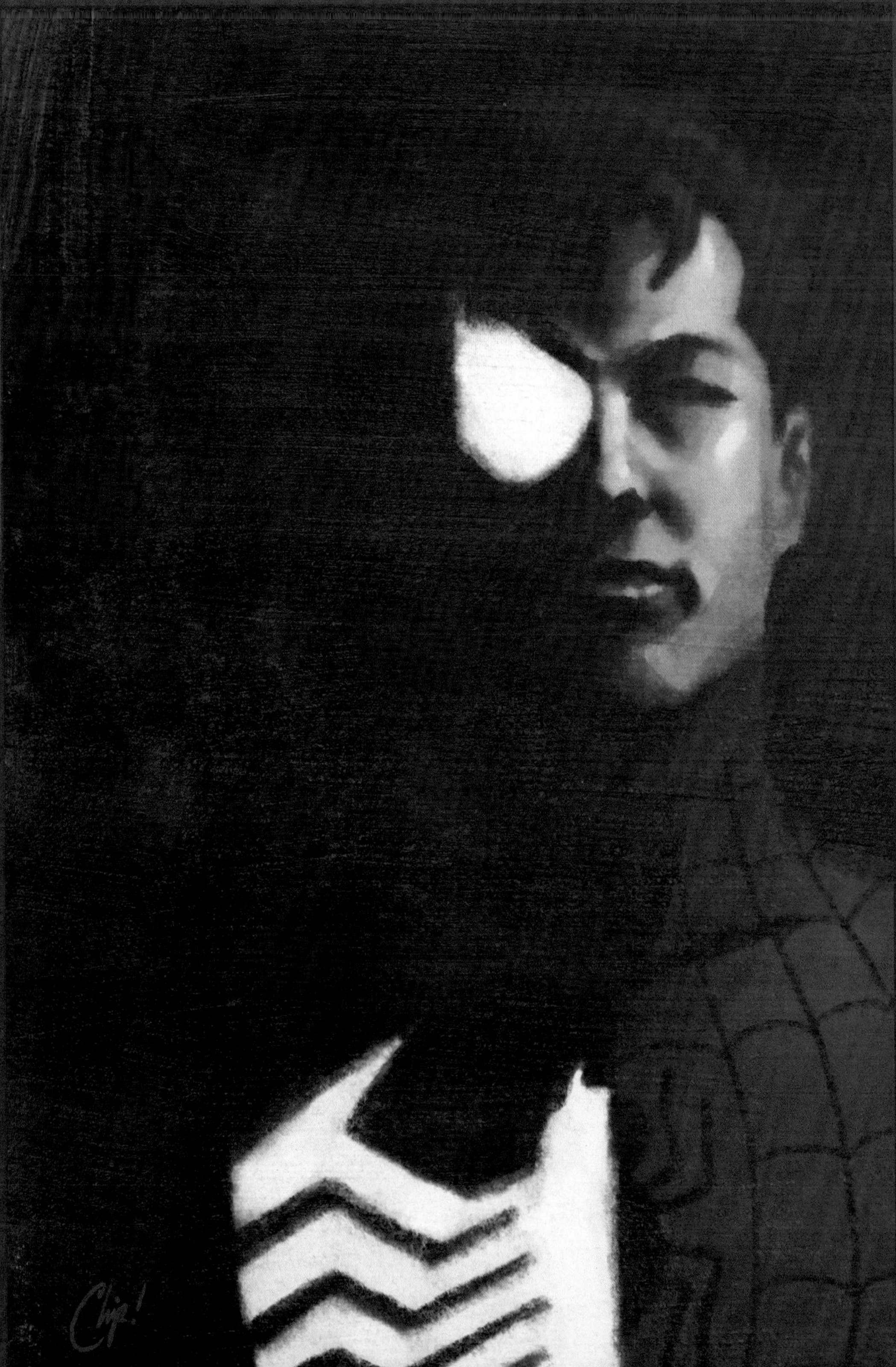
Chip!

#1 VARIANT BY CHIP ZDARSKY

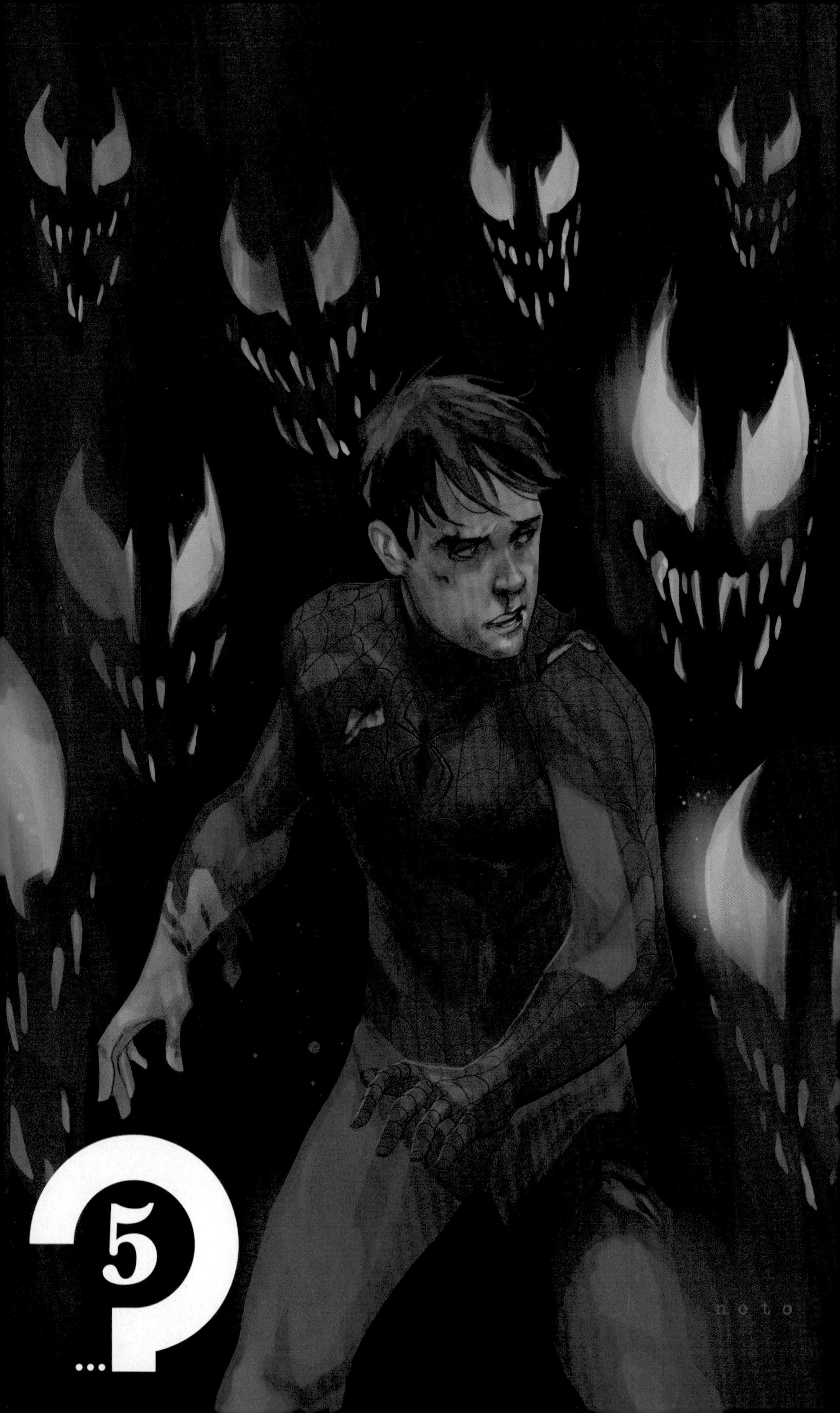
5

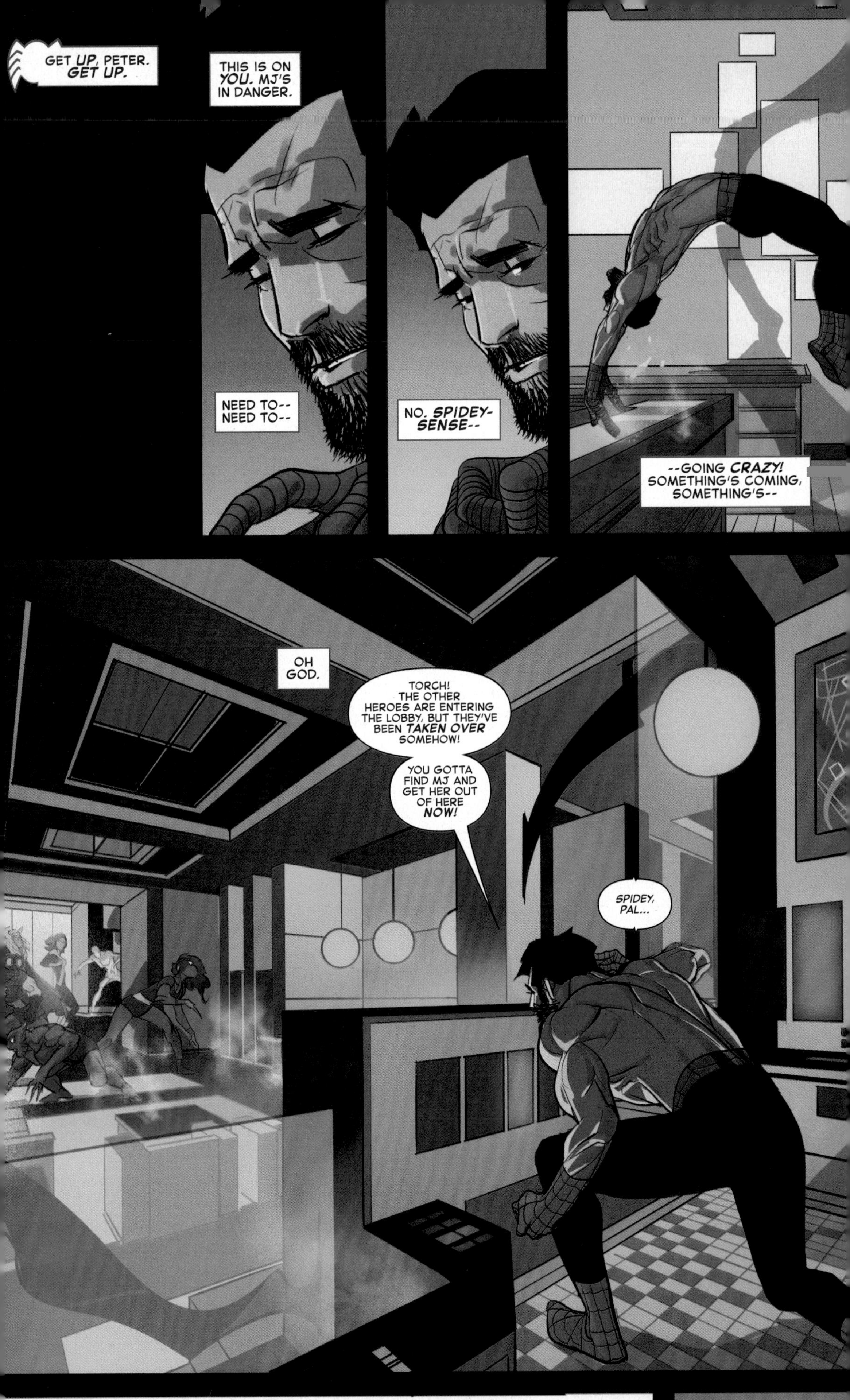
GET UP, PETER. GET UP.
THIS IS ON YOU. MJ'S IN DANGER.
NEED TO-- NEED TO--
NO. SPIDEY-SENSE--
--GOING CRAZY! SOMETHING'S COMING, SOMETHING'S--
OH GOD.
TORCH! THE OTHER HEROES ARE ENTERING THE LOBBY, BUT THEY'VE BEEN TAKEN OVER SOMEHOW!
YOU GOTTA FIND MJ AND GET HER OUT OF HERE NOW!
SPIDEY, PAL...

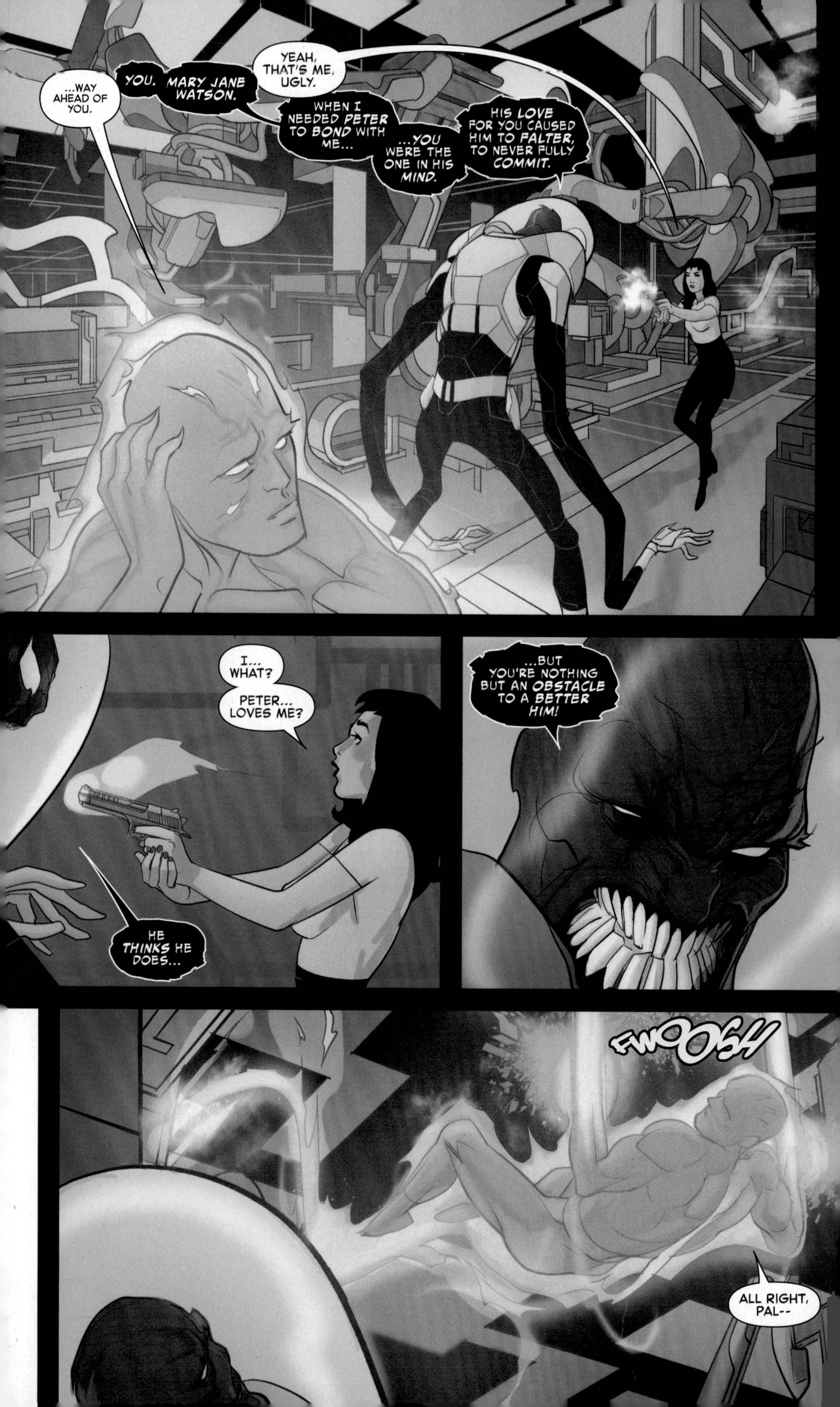

YOU. MARY JANE WATSON.
...WAY AHEAD OF YOU.
YEAH, THAT'S ME, UGLY.
WHEN I NEEDED PETER TO BOND WITH ME...
...YOU WERE THE ONE IN HIS MIND.
HIS LOVE FOR YOU CAUSED HIM TO FALTER, TO NEVER FULLY COMMIT.
I... WHAT?
PETER... LOVES ME?
HE THINKS HE DOES...
...BUT YOU'RE NOTHING BUT AN OBSTACLE TO A BETTER HIM!
FWOOSH
ALL RIGHT, PAL--

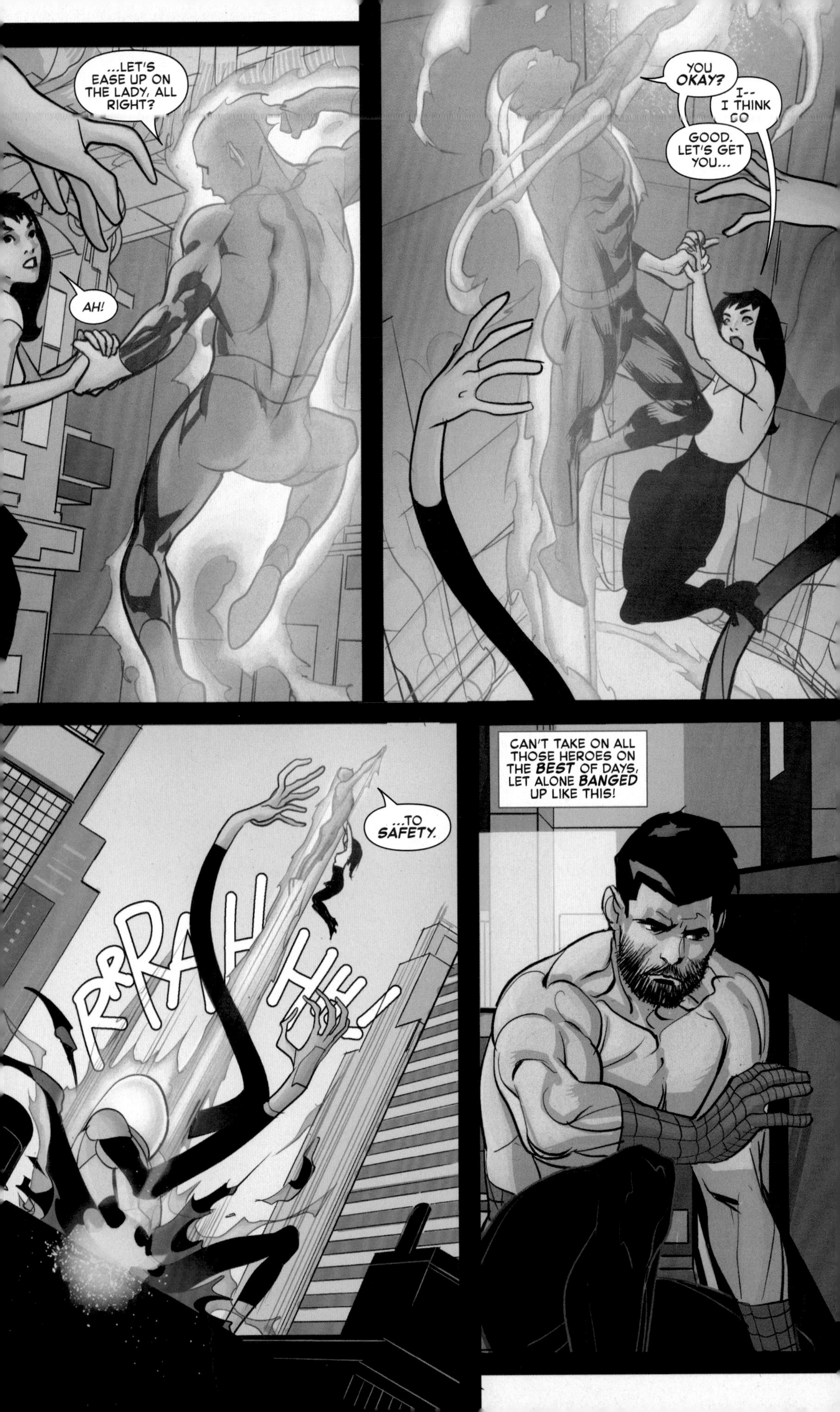
...LET'S EASE UP ON THE LADY, ALL RIGHT?
AH!
YOU OKAY?
I-- I THINK SO
GOOD. LET'S GET YOU...
...TO SAFETY.
RRRAHHH!
CAN'T TAKE ON ALL THOSE HEROES ON THE BEST OF DAYS, LET ALONE BANGED UP LIKE THIS!

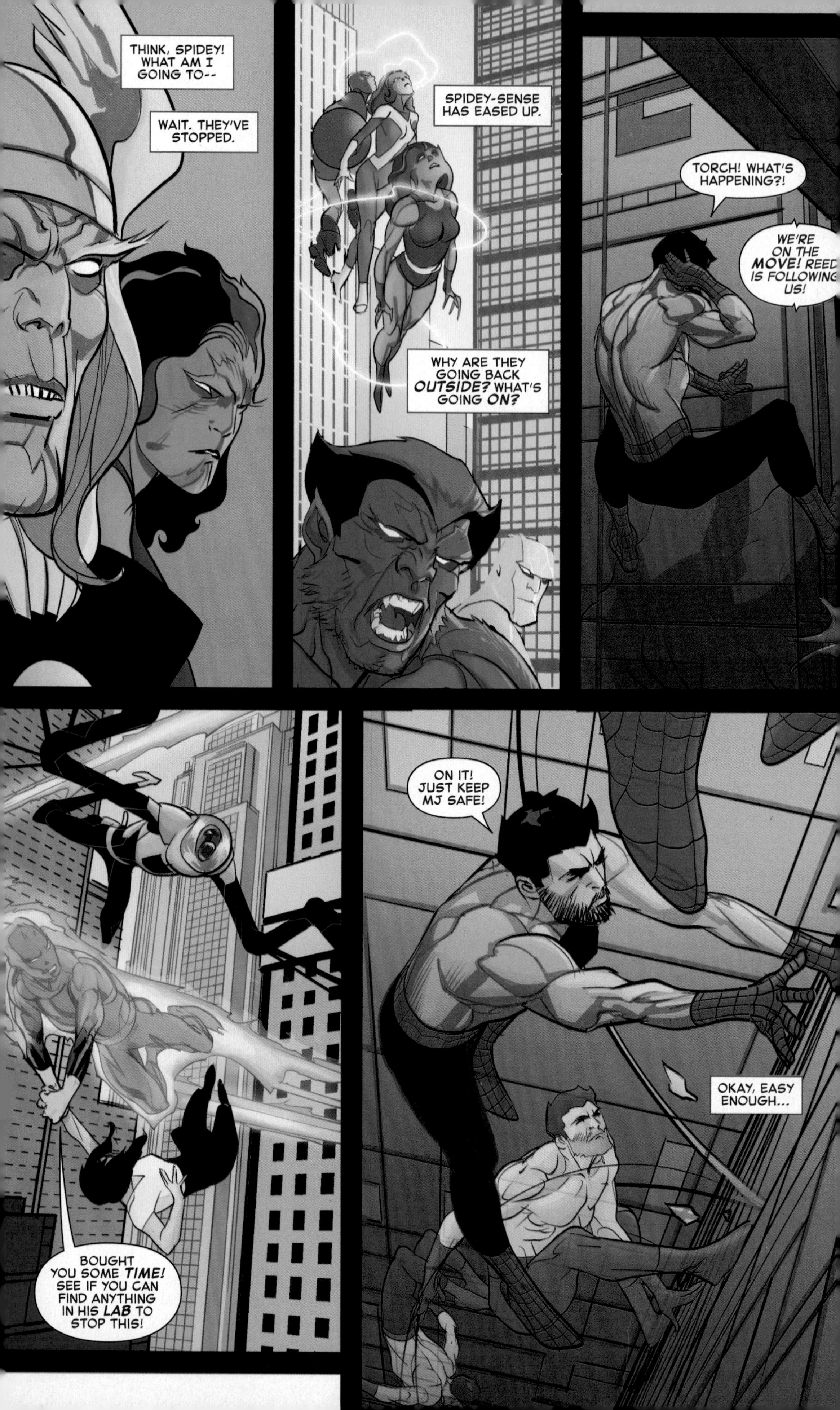
THINK, SPIDEY! WHAT AM I GOING TO--
WAIT. THEY'VE STOPPED.
SPIDEY-SENSE HAS EASED UP.
WHY ARE THEY GOING BACK OUTSIDE? WHAT'S GOING ON?
TORCH! WHAT'S HAPPENING?!
WE'RE ON THE MOVE! REED IS FOLLOWING US!
BOUGHT YOU SOME TIME! SEE IF YOU CAN FIND ANYTHING IN HIS LAB TO STOP THIS!
ON IT! JUST KEEP MJ SAFE!
OKAY, EASY ENOUGH...

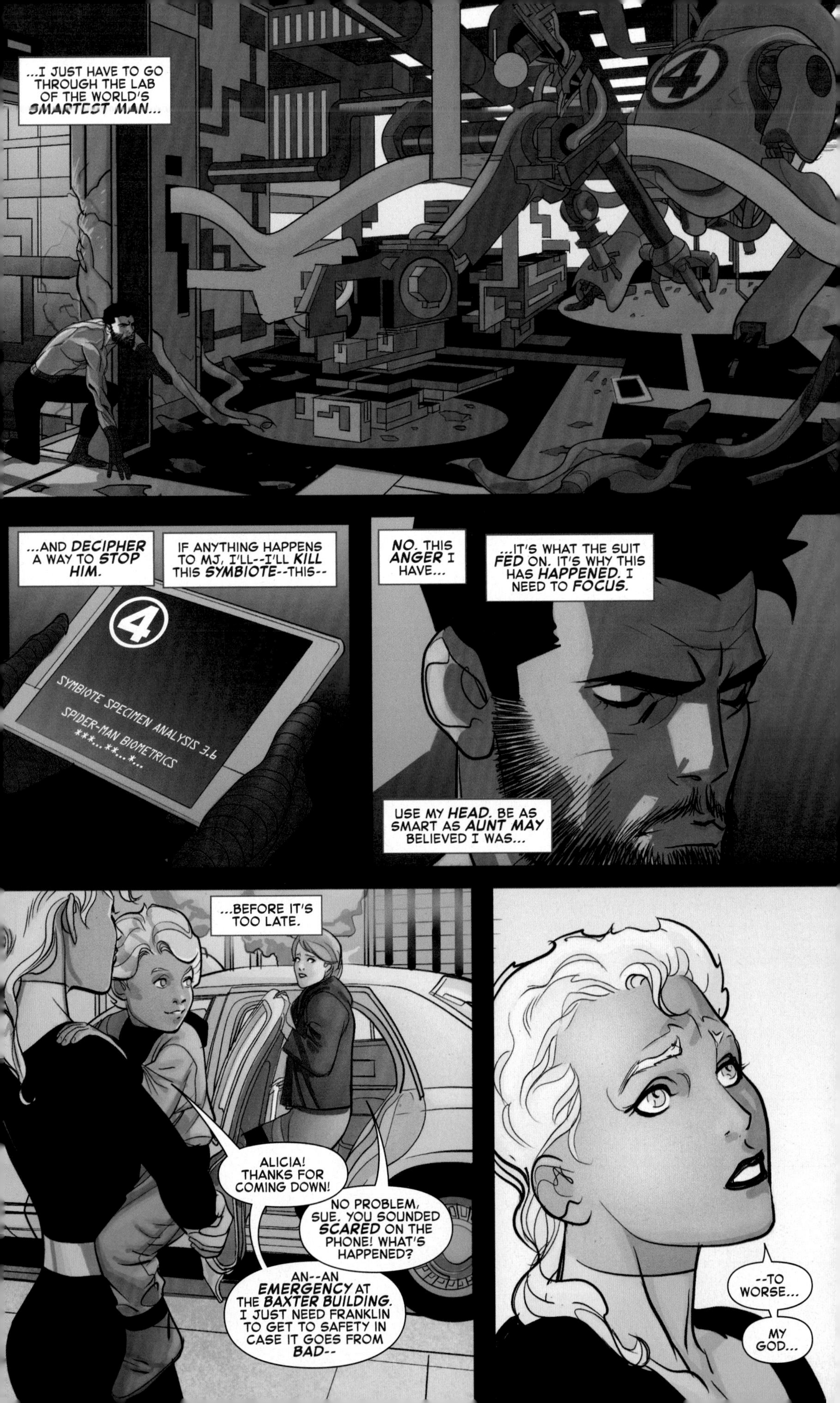

...I JUST HAVE TO GO THROUGH THE LAB OF THE WORLD'S SMARTEST MAN...
...AND DECIPHER A WAY TO STOP HIM.
IF ANYTHING HAPPENS TO MJ, I'LL--I'LL KILL THIS SYMBIOTE--THIS--
SYMBIOTE SPECIMEN ANALYSIS 3.6
SPIDER-MAN BIOMETRICS
***...**...*...
NO. THIS ANGER I HAVE...
...IT'S WHAT THE SUIT FED ON. IT'S WHY THIS HAS HAPPENED. I NEED TO FOCUS.
USE MY HEAD. BE AS SMART AS AUNT MAY BELIEVED I WAS...
...BEFORE IT'S TOO LATE.
ALICIA! THANKS FOR COMING DOWN!
NO PROBLEM, SUE. YOU SOUNDED SCARED ON THE PHONE! WHAT'S HAPPENED?
AN--AN EMERGENCY AT THE BAXTER BUILDING. I JUST NEED FRANKLIN TO GET TO SAFETY IN CASE IT GOES FROM BAD--
--TO WORSE...
MY GOD...

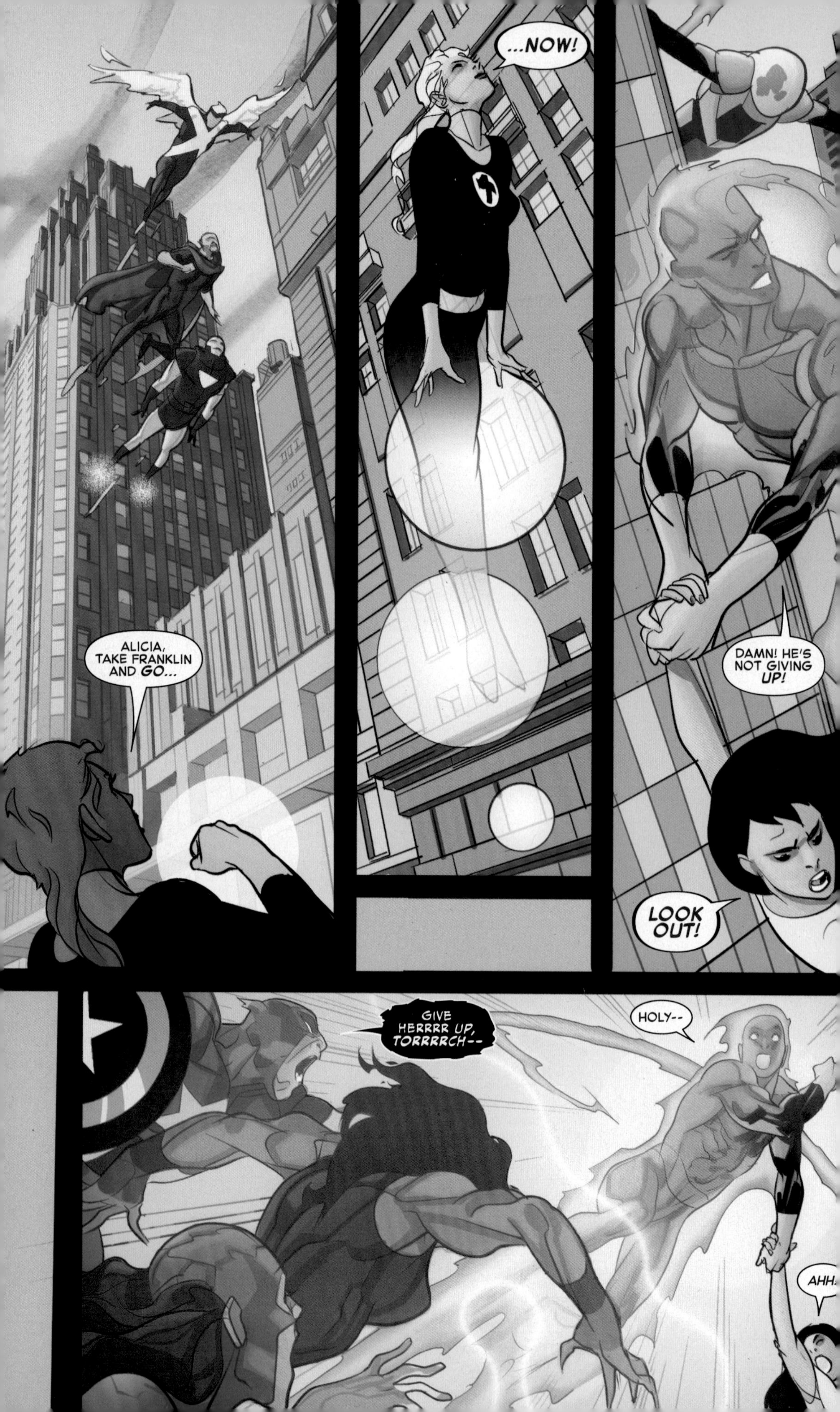
...NOW!
ALICIA, TAKE FRANKLIN AND GO...
DAMN! HE'S NOT GIVING UP!
LOOK OUT!
GIVE HERRRR UP, TORRRRCH--
HOLY--
AHH.

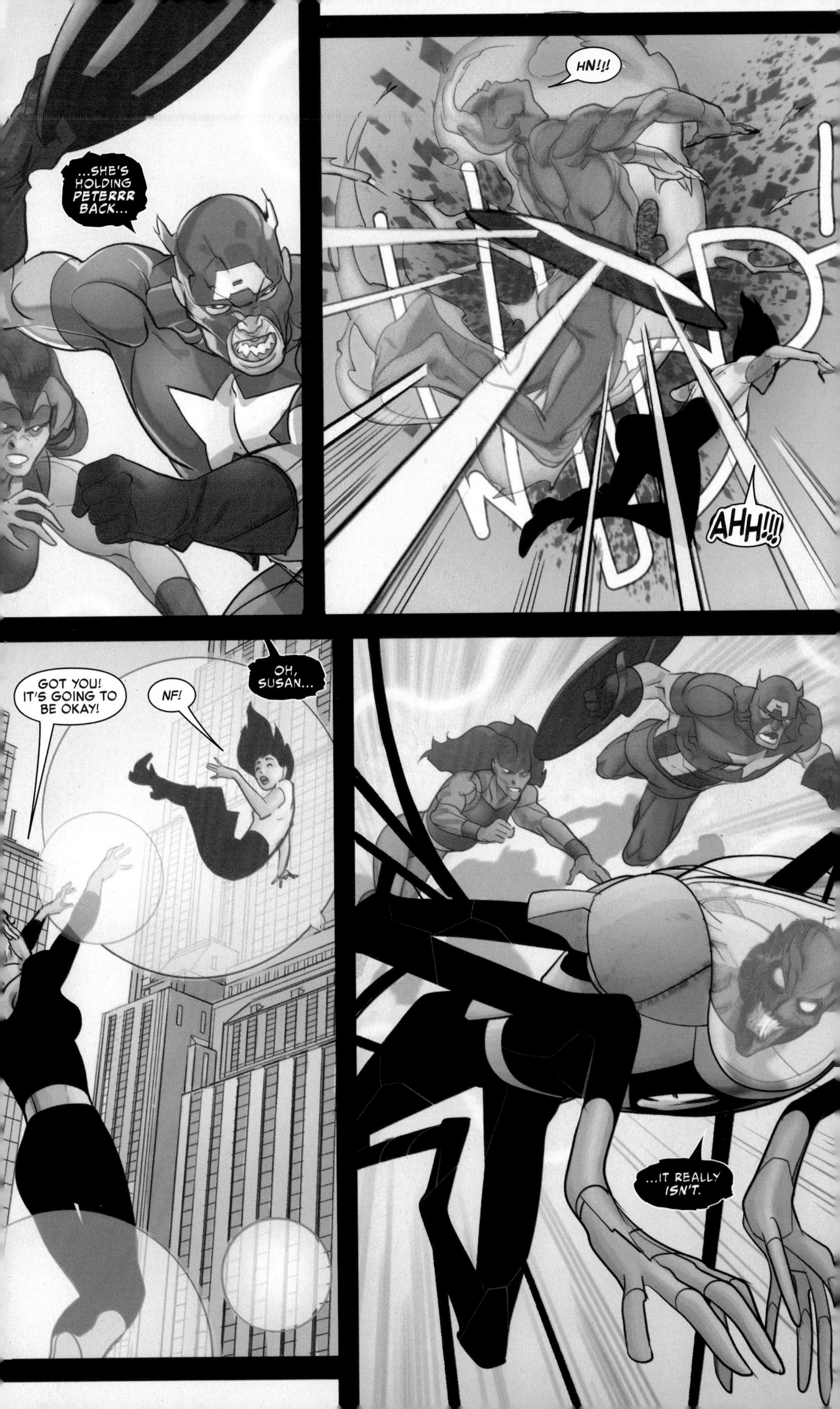

...SHE'S HOLDING PETERRR BACK...
HN!!!
AHH!!!
GOT YOU! IT'S GOING TO BE OKAY!
NF!
OH, SUSAN...
...IT REALLY ISN'T.

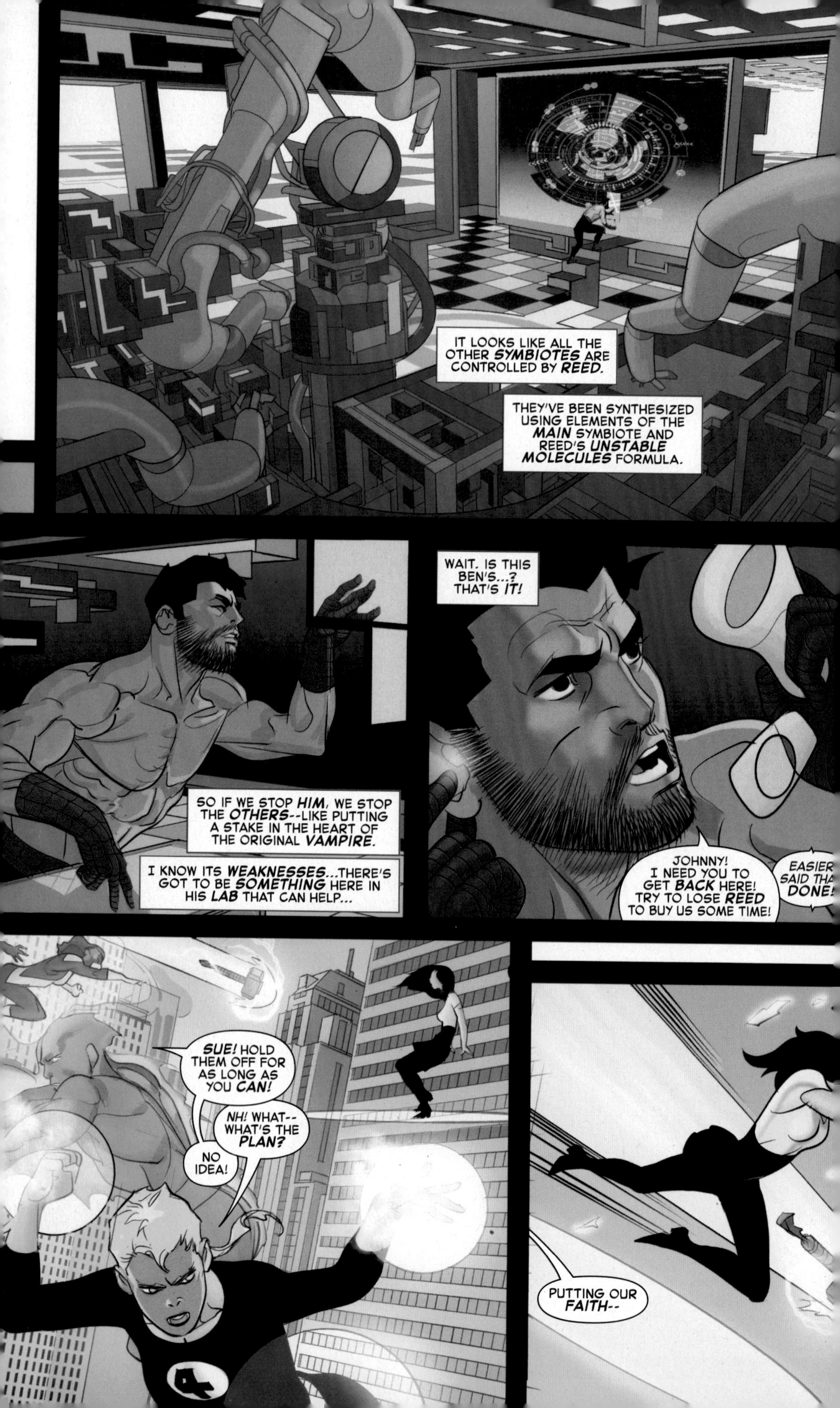

IT LOOKS LIKE ALL THE OTHER SYMBIOTES ARE CONTROLLED BY REED.
THEY'VE BEEN SYNTHESIZED USING ELEMENTS OF THE MAIN SYMBIOTE AND REED'S UNSTABLE MOLECULES FORMULA.
SO IF WE STOP HIM, WE STOP THE OTHERS--LIKE PUTTING A STAKE IN THE HEART OF THE ORIGINAL VAMPIRE.
I KNOW ITS WEAKNESSES...THERE'S GOT TO BE SOMETHING HERE IN HIS LAB THAT CAN HELP...
WAIT. IS THIS BEN'S...? THAT'S IT!
JOHNNY! I NEED YOU TO GET BACK HERE! TRY TO LOSE REED TO BUY US SOME TIME!
EASIER SAID THA DONE!
SUE! HOLD THEM OFF FOR AS LONG AS YOU CAN!
NH! WHAT-- WHAT'S THE PLAN?
NO IDEA!
PUTTING OUR FAITH--

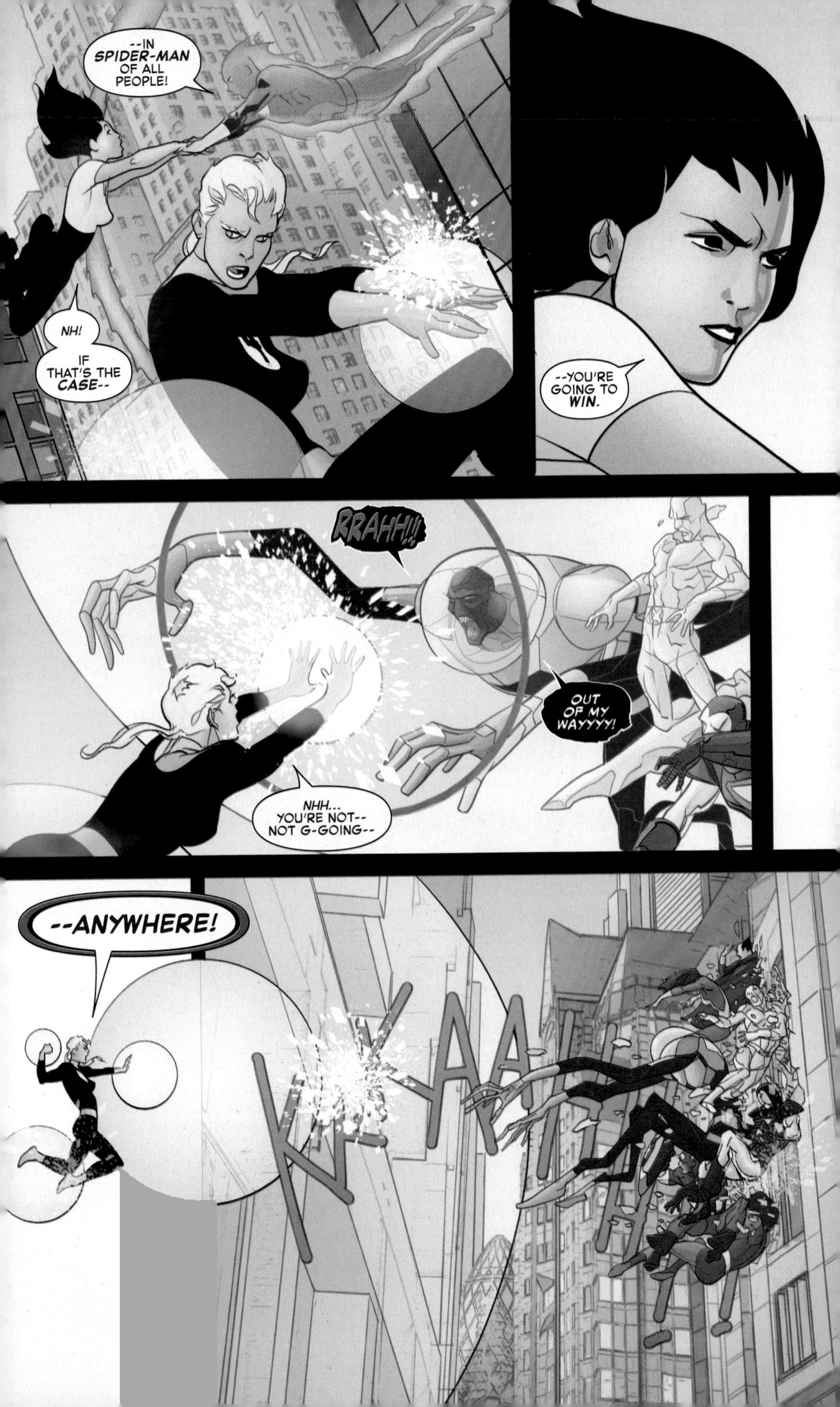
--IN SPIDER-MAN OF ALL PEOPLE!
NH!
IF THAT'S THE CASE--
--YOU'RE GOING TO WIN.
KRAHH!!!
OUT OF MY WAYYYY!
NHH... YOU'RE NOT-- NOT G-GOING--
--ANYWHERE!

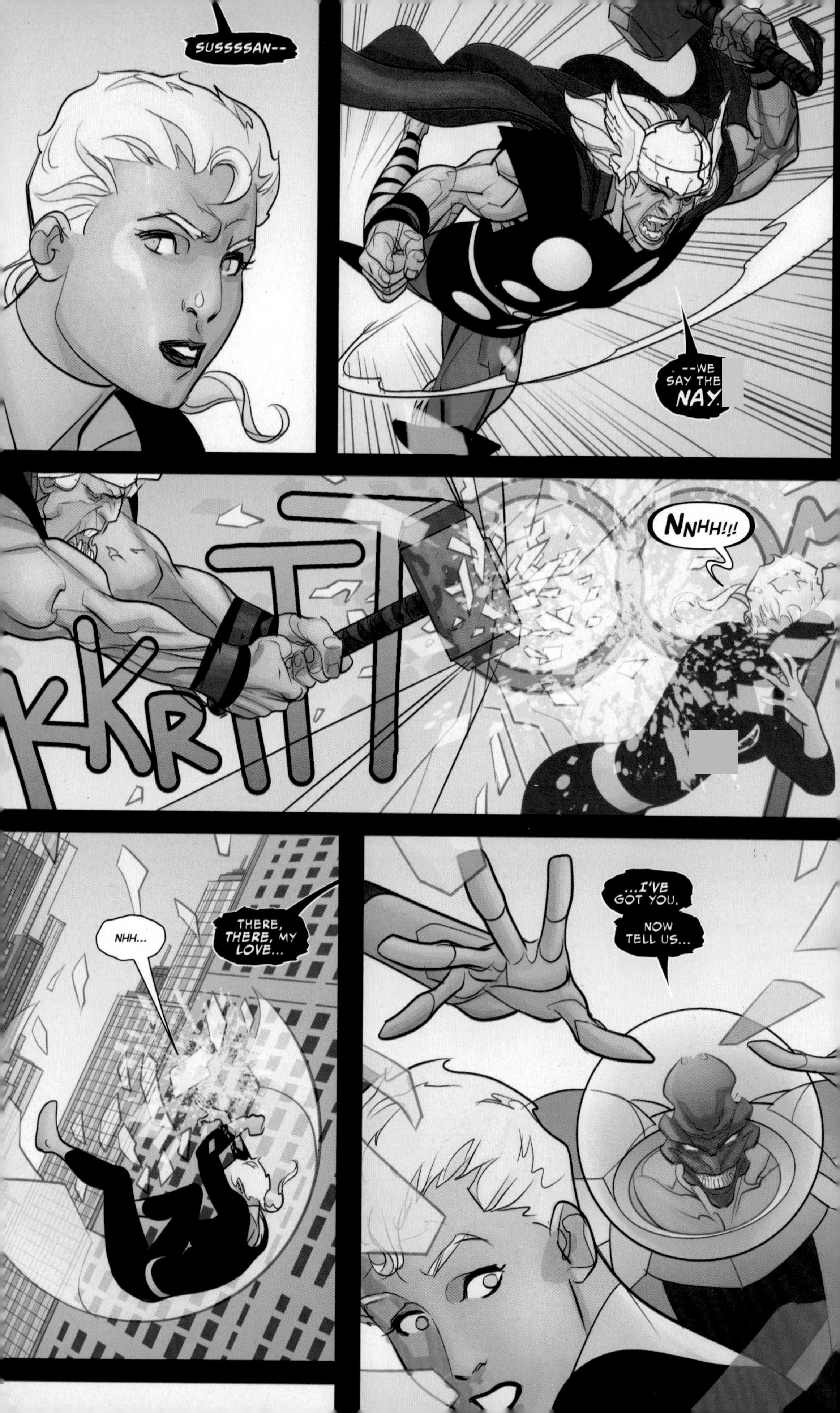

SUSSSSAN--
--WE SAY THE NAY.
KKRTT
NNHH!!!
NHH...
THERE, THERE, MY LOVE...
...I'VE GOT YOU.
NOW TELL US...

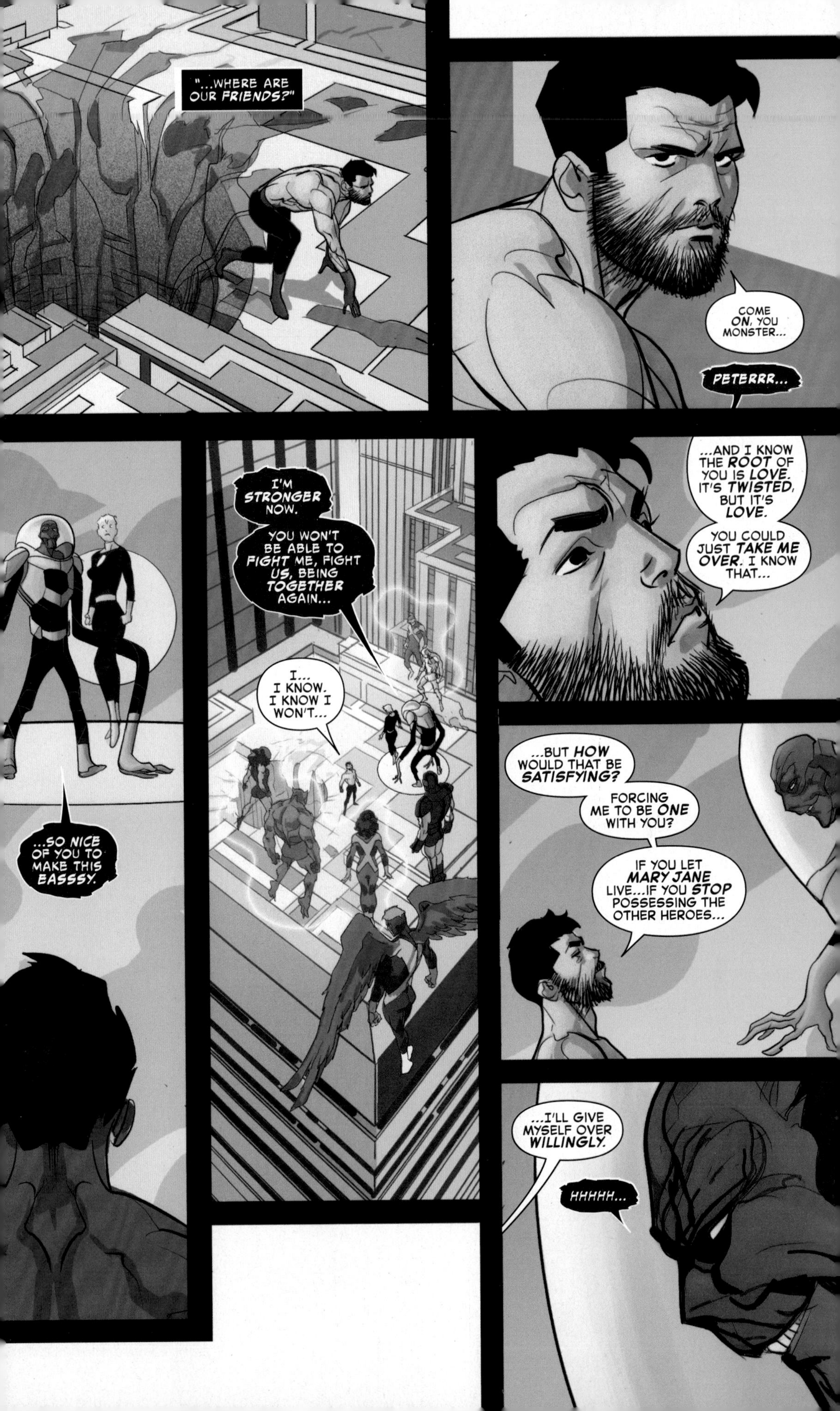

"...WHERE ARE OUR FRIENDS?"
COME ON, YOU MONSTER...
PETERRR...
...SO NICE OF YOU TO MAKE THIS EASSSY.
I'M STRONGER NOW.
YOU WON'T BE ABLE TO FIGHT ME, FIGHT US, BEING TOGETHER AGAIN...
I... I KNOW. I KNOW I WON'T...
...AND I KNOW THE ROOT OF YOU IS LOVE. IT'S TWISTED, BUT IT'S LOVE.
YOU COULD JUST TAKE ME OVER. I KNOW THAT...
...BUT HOW WOULD THAT BE SATISFYING?
FORCING ME TO BE ONE WITH YOU?
IF YOU LET MARY JANE LIVE...IF YOU STOP POSSESSING THE OTHER HEROES...
...I'LL GIVE MYSELF OVER WILLINGLY.
HHHHH...

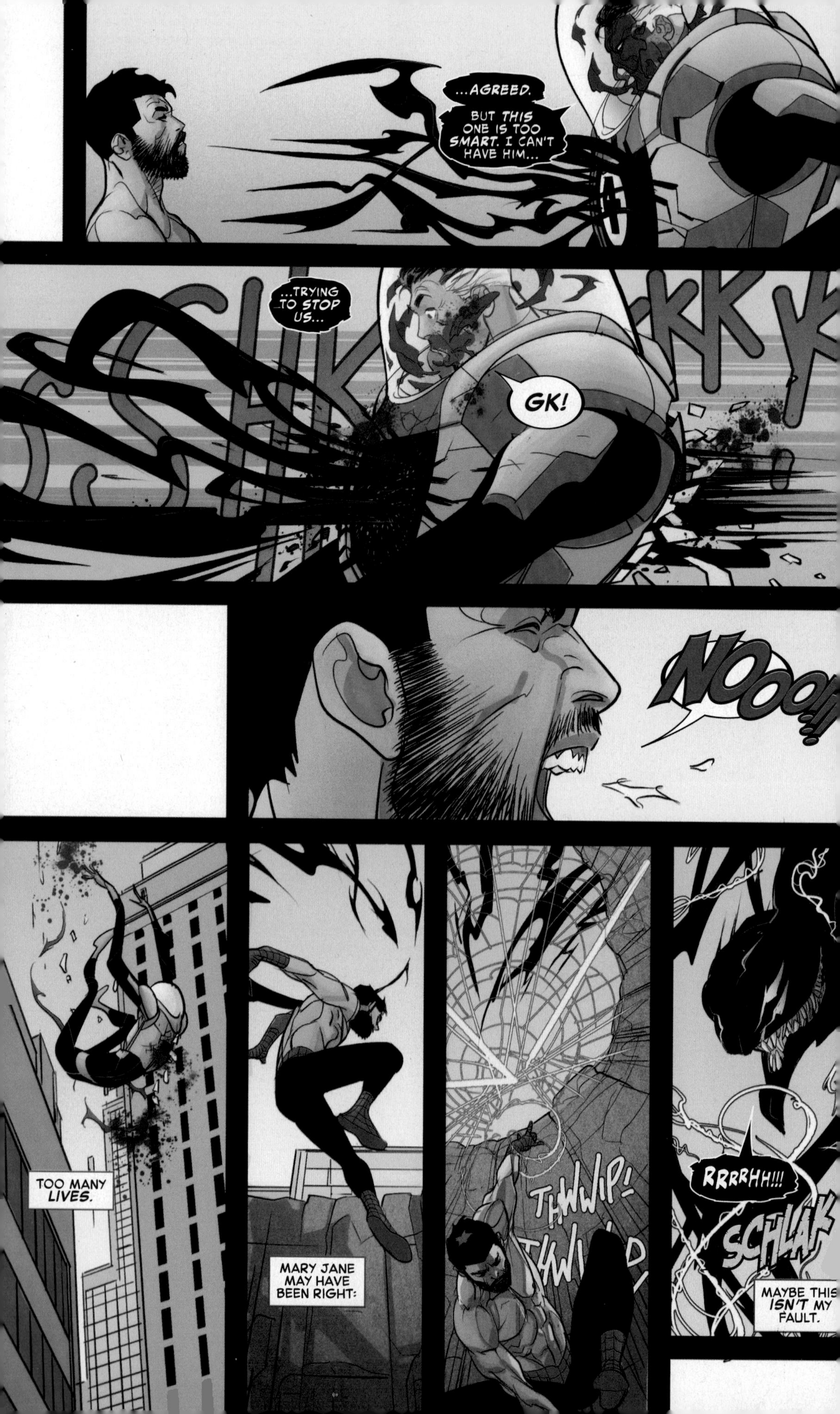
...AGREED.
BUT THIS ONE IS TOO SMART. I CAN'T HAVE HIM...
...TRYING TO STOP US...
GK!
NOOO!!!
TOO MANY LIVES.
MARY JANE MAY HAVE BEEN RIGHT:
THWWIP!
RRRRHH!!!
SCHLAK
MAYBE THIS ISN'T MY FAULT.

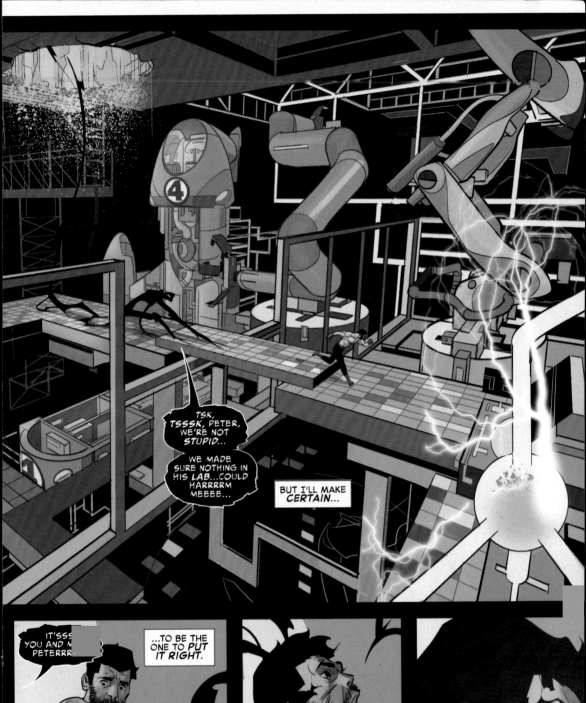

TSK, TSSSK, PETER, WE'RE NOT STUPID...

WE MADE SURE NOTHING IN HIS LAB...COULD HARRRRM MEEEE...

BUT I'LL MAKE CERTAIN...

IT'SSS YOU AND M... PETERRR...

...TO BE THE ONE TO PUT IT RIGHT.

REED ALWAYS FELT GUILTY FOR TURNING BEN INTO THE THING...

...SO HE TRIED TO FIX HIS MISTAKES. MAKING IT SO BEN COULD WALK AROUND AND LOOK HUMAN...

...WAIT... ...HAT ISSSS THISSSS...?

...WITH AN IMAGE INDUCER.

FLAME ON.

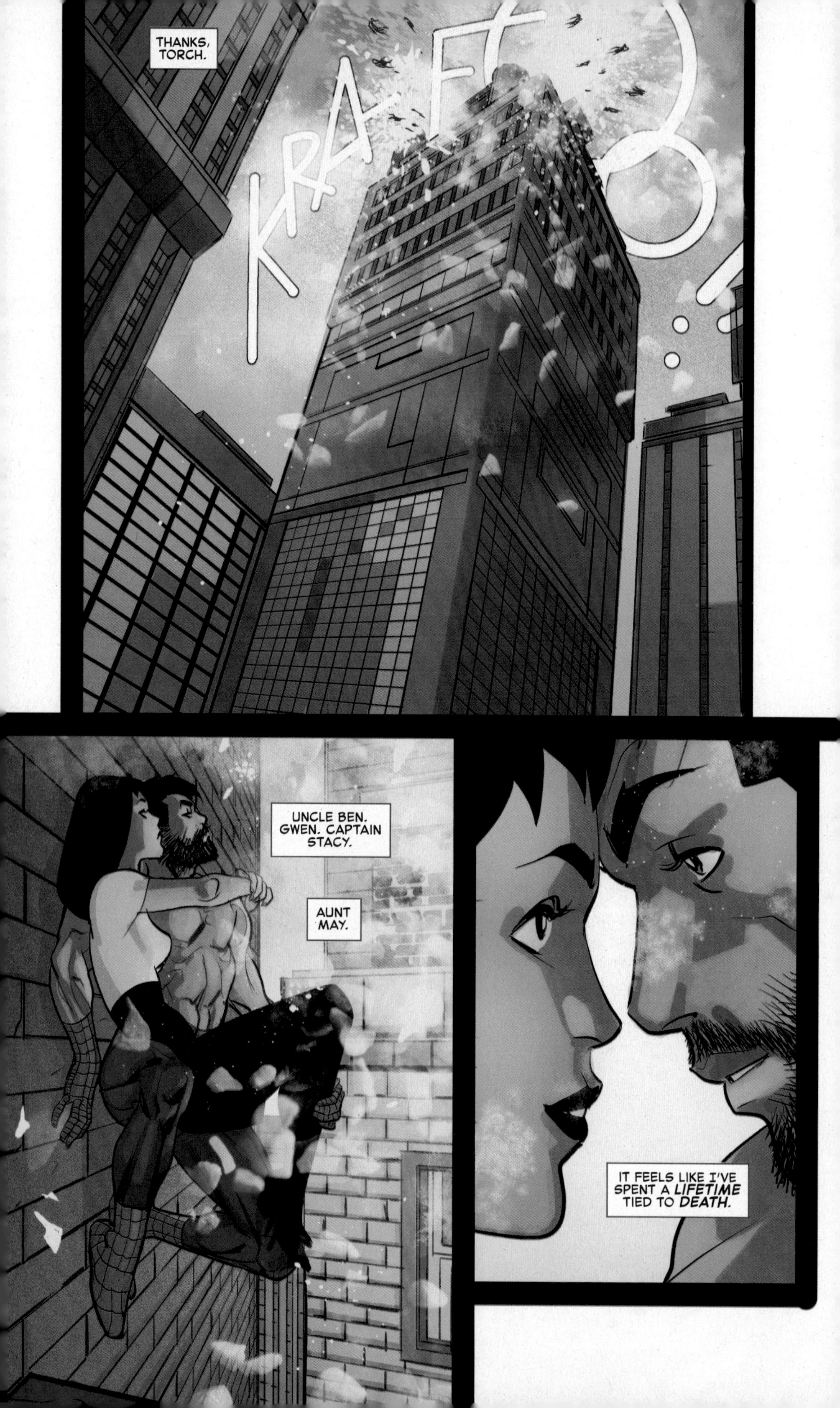
THANKS, TORCH.
KRAFTOOM
UNCLE BEN. GWEN. CAPTAIN STACY.
AUNT MAY.
IT FEELS LIKE I'VE SPENT A *LIFETIME* TIED TO *DEATH*.

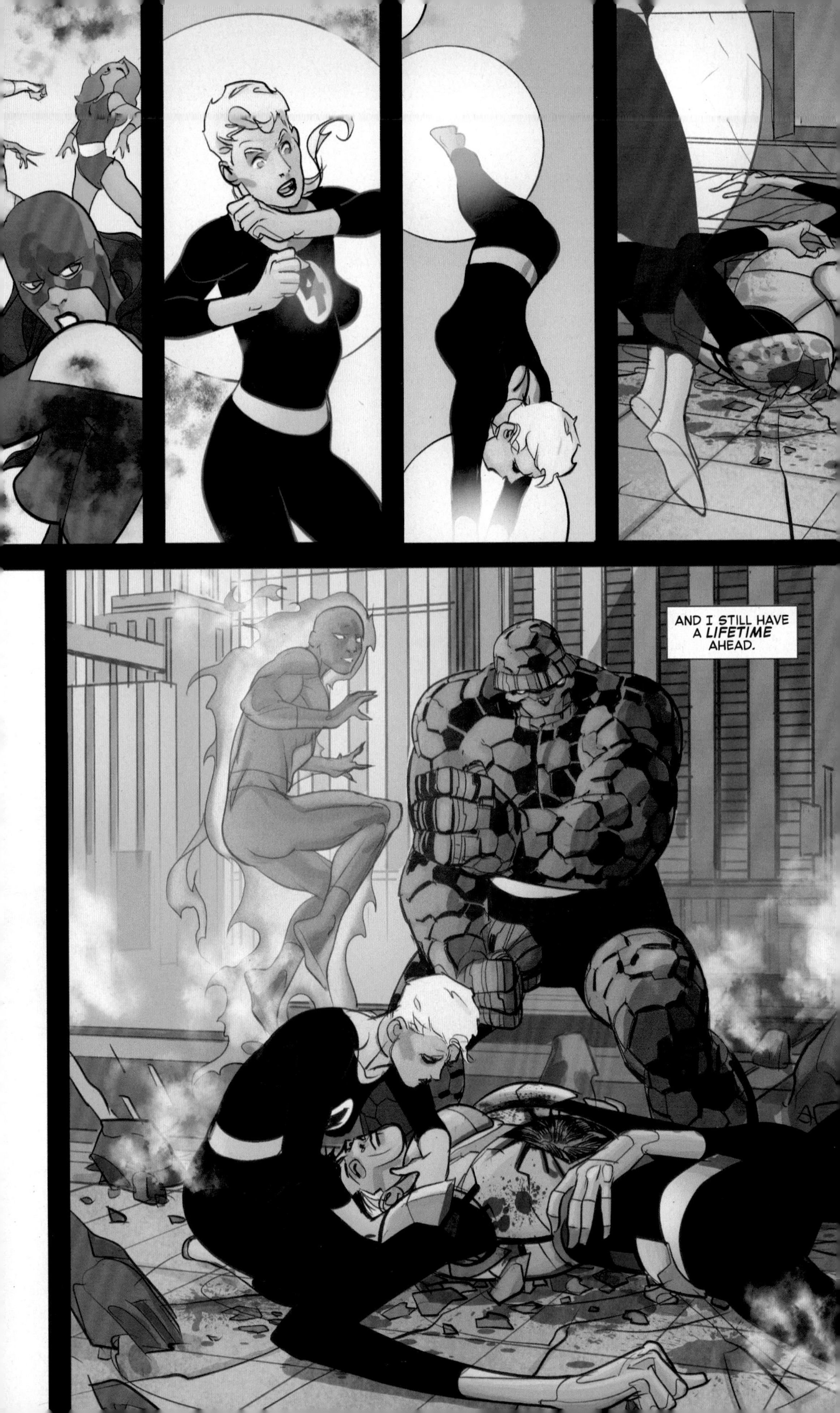
AND I STILL HAVE A *LIFETIME* AHEAD.

"YOU'VE GOT
TO LET *GO*."

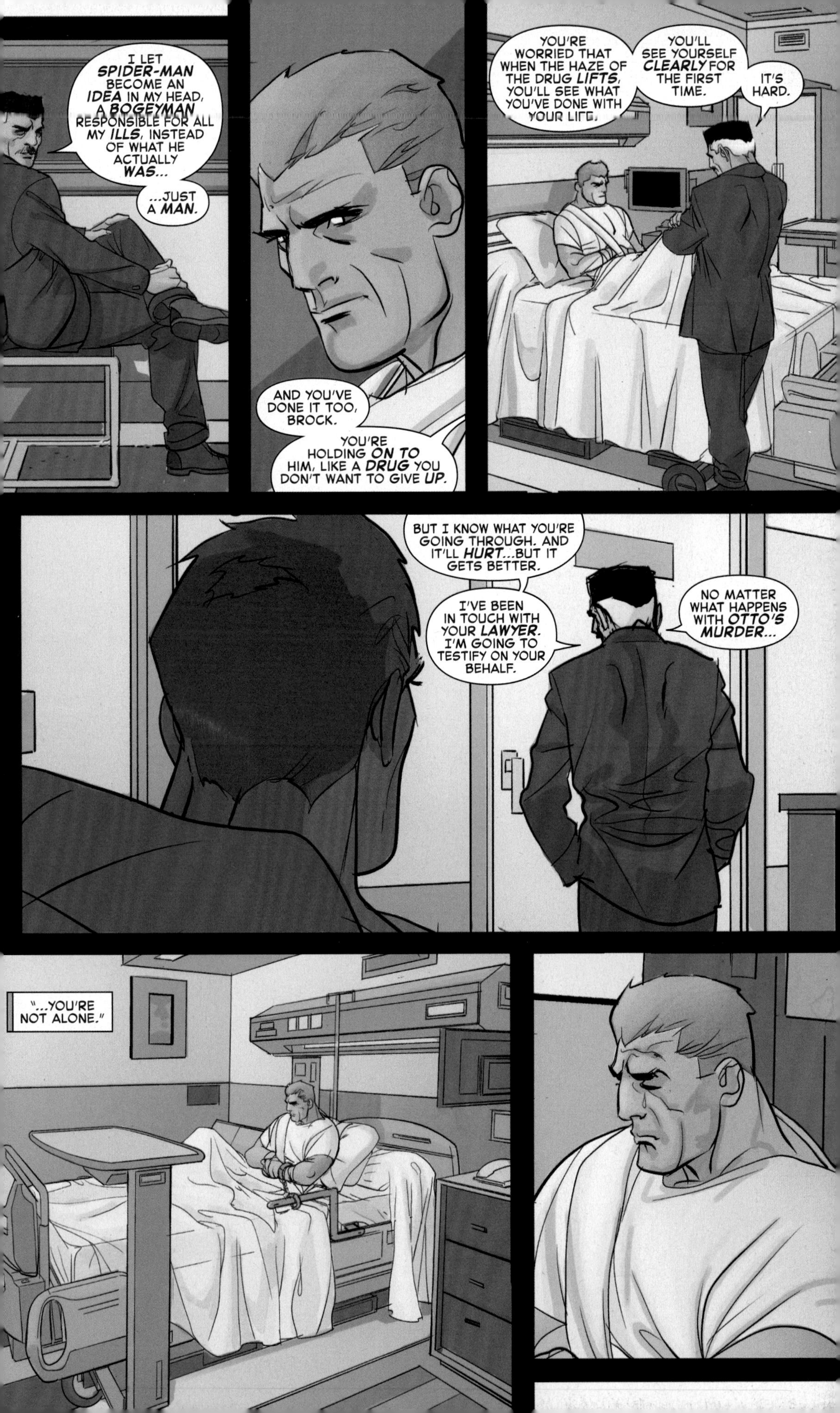
I LET SPIDER-MAN BECOME AN IDEA IN MY HEAD, A BOGEYMAN RESPONSIBLE FOR ALL MY ILLS, INSTEAD OF WHAT HE ACTUALLY WAS...
...JUST A MAN.
AND YOU'VE DONE IT TOO, BROCK.
YOU'RE HOLDING ON TO HIM, LIKE A DRUG YOU DON'T WANT TO GIVE UP.
YOU'RE WORRIED THAT WHEN THE HAZE OF THE DRUG LIFTS, YOU'LL SEE WHAT YOU'VE DONE WITH YOUR LIFE.
YOU'LL SEE YOURSELF CLEARLY FOR THE FIRST TIME.
IT'S HARD.
BUT I KNOW WHAT YOU'RE GOING THROUGH. AND IT'LL HURT...BUT IT GETS BETTER.
I'VE BEEN IN TOUCH WITH YOUR LAWYER. I'M GOING TO TESTIFY ON YOUR BEHALF.
NO MATTER WHAT HAPPENS WITH OTTO'S MURDER...
"...YOU'RE NOT ALONE."

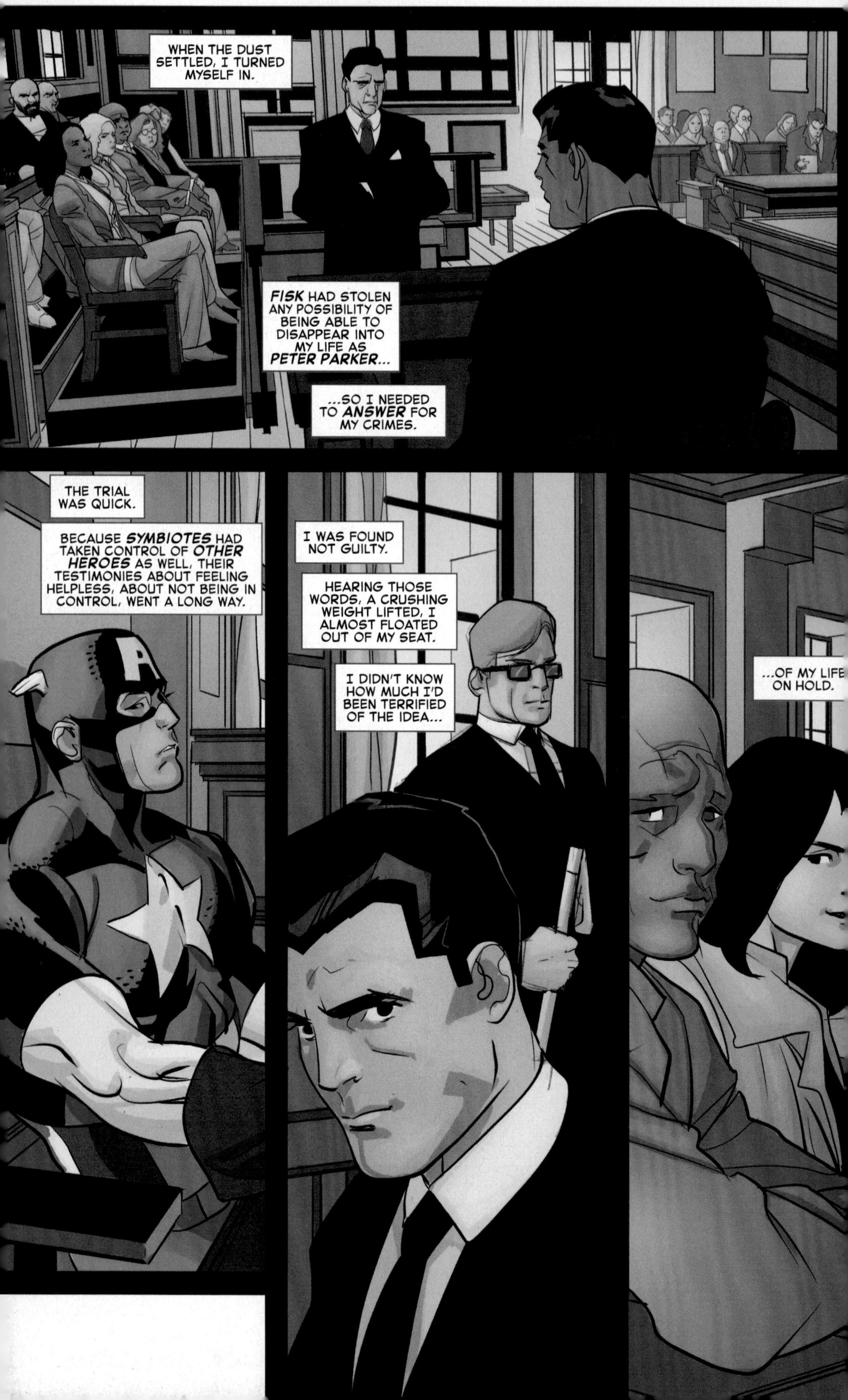
WHEN THE DUST SETTLED, I TURNED MYSELF IN.
FISK HAD STOLEN ANY POSSIBILITY OF BEING ABLE TO DISAPPEAR INTO MY LIFE AS PETER PARKER...
...SO I NEEDED TO ANSWER FOR MY CRIMES.
THE TRIAL WAS QUICK.
BECAUSE SYMBIOTES HAD TAKEN CONTROL OF OTHER HEROES AS WELL, THEIR TESTIMONIES ABOUT FEELING HELPLESS, ABOUT NOT BEING IN CONTROL, WENT A LONG WAY.
I WAS FOUND NOT GUILTY.
HEARING THOSE WORDS, A CRUSHING WEIGHT LIFTED, I ALMOST FLOATED OUT OF MY SEAT.
I DIDN'T KNOW HOW MUCH I'D BEEN TERRIFIED OF THE IDEA...
...OF MY LIFE ON HOLD.

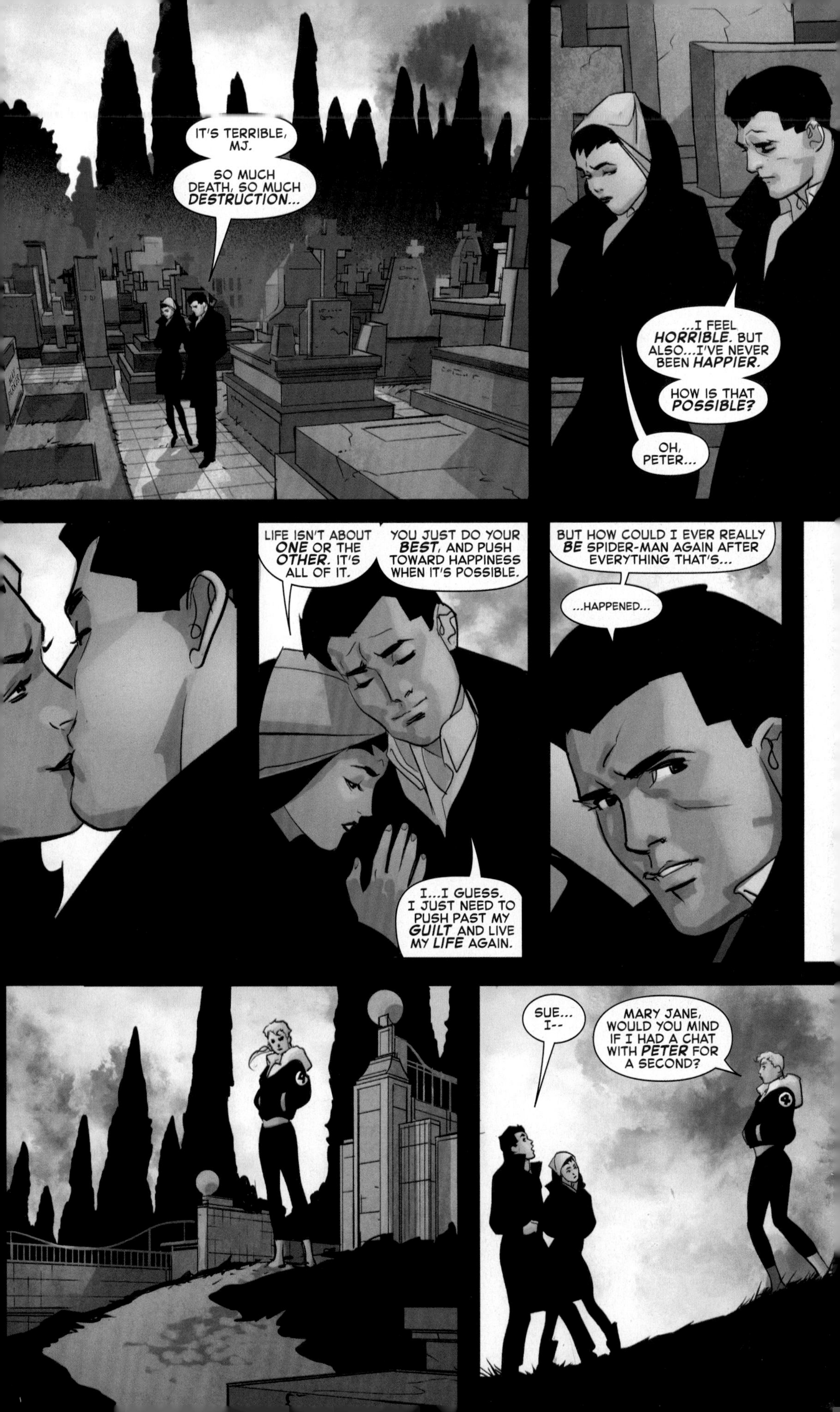
IT'S TERRIBLE, MJ.
SO MUCH DEATH, SO MUCH DESTRUCTION...
...I FEEL HORRIBLE. BUT ALSO...I'VE NEVER BEEN HAPPIER.
HOW IS THAT POSSIBLE?
OH, PETER...
LIFE ISN'T ABOUT ONE OR THE OTHER. IT'S ALL OF IT.
YOU JUST DO YOUR BEST, AND PUSH TOWARD HAPPINESS WHEN IT'S POSSIBLE.
I...I GUESS. I JUST NEED TO PUSH PAST MY GUILT AND LIVE MY LIFE AGAIN.
BUT HOW COULD I EVER REALLY BE SPIDER-MAN AGAIN AFTER EVERYTHING THAT'S...
...HAPPENED...
SUE... I--
MARY JANE, WOULD YOU MIND IF I HAD A CHAT WITH PETER FOR A SECOND?

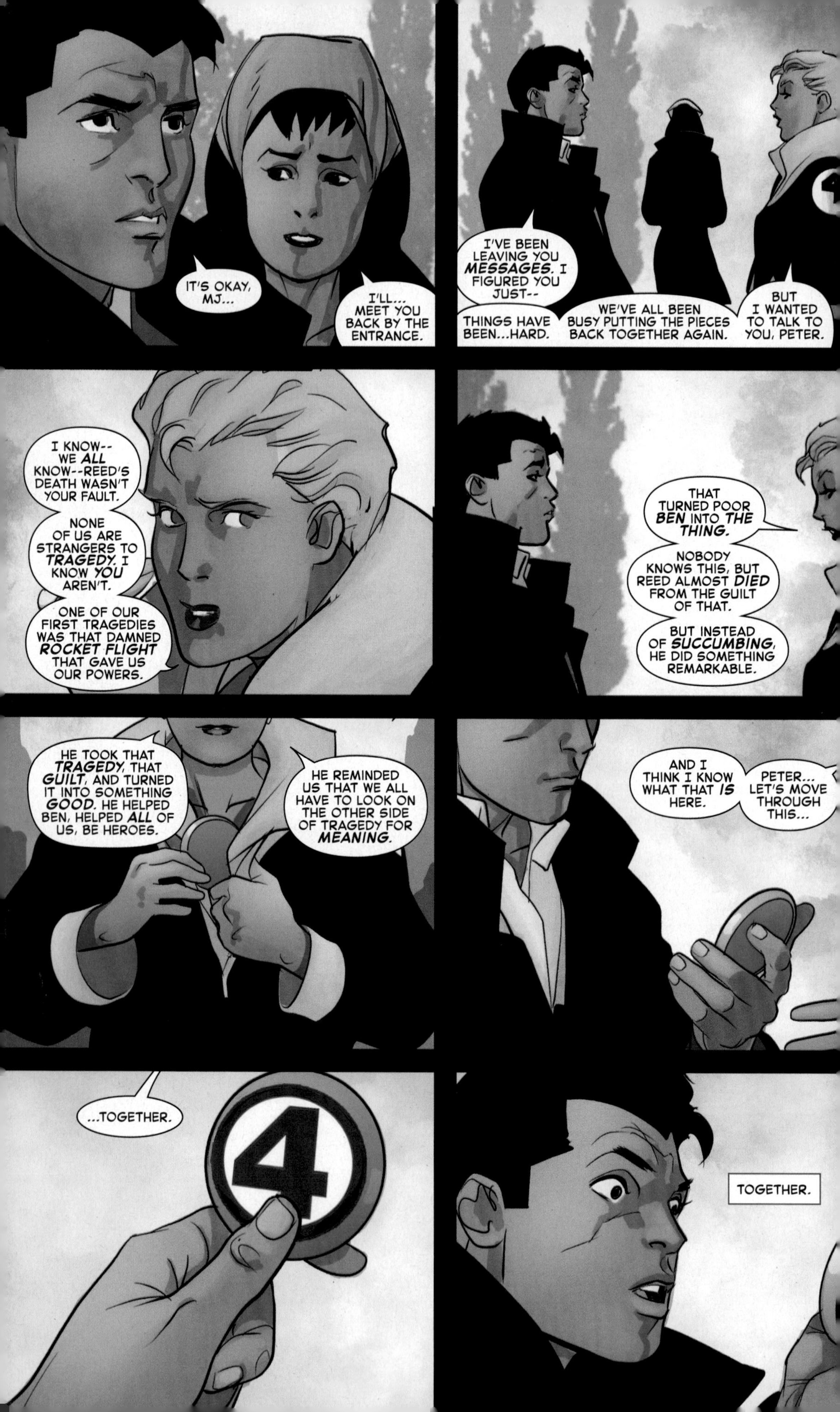
IT'S OKAY, MJ...
I'LL... MEET YOU BACK BY THE ENTRANCE.
I'VE BEEN LEAVING YOU MESSAGES. I FIGURED YOU JUST--
THINGS HAVE BEEN...HARD.
WE'VE ALL BEEN BUSY PUTTING THE PIECES BACK TOGETHER AGAIN.
BUT I WANTED TO TALK TO YOU, PETER.
I KNOW-- WE ALL KNOW--REED'S DEATH WASN'T YOUR FAULT.
NONE OF US ARE STRANGERS TO TRAGEDY. I KNOW YOU AREN'T.
ONE OF OUR FIRST TRAGEDIES WAS THAT DAMNED ROCKET FLIGHT THAT GAVE US OUR POWERS.
THAT TURNED POOR BEN INTO THE THING.
NOBODY KNOWS THIS, BUT REED ALMOST DIED FROM THE GUILT OF THAT.
BUT INSTEAD OF SUCCUMBING, HE DID SOMETHING REMARKABLE.
HE TOOK THAT TRAGEDY, THAT GUILT, AND TURNED IT INTO SOMETHING GOOD. HE HELPED BEN, HELPED ALL OF US, BE HEROES.
HE REMINDED US THAT WE ALL HAVE TO LOOK ON THE OTHER SIDE OF TRAGEDY FOR MEANING.
AND I THINK I KNOW WHAT THAT IS HERE.
PETER... LET'S MOVE THROUGH THIS...
...TOGETHER.
4
TOGETHER.

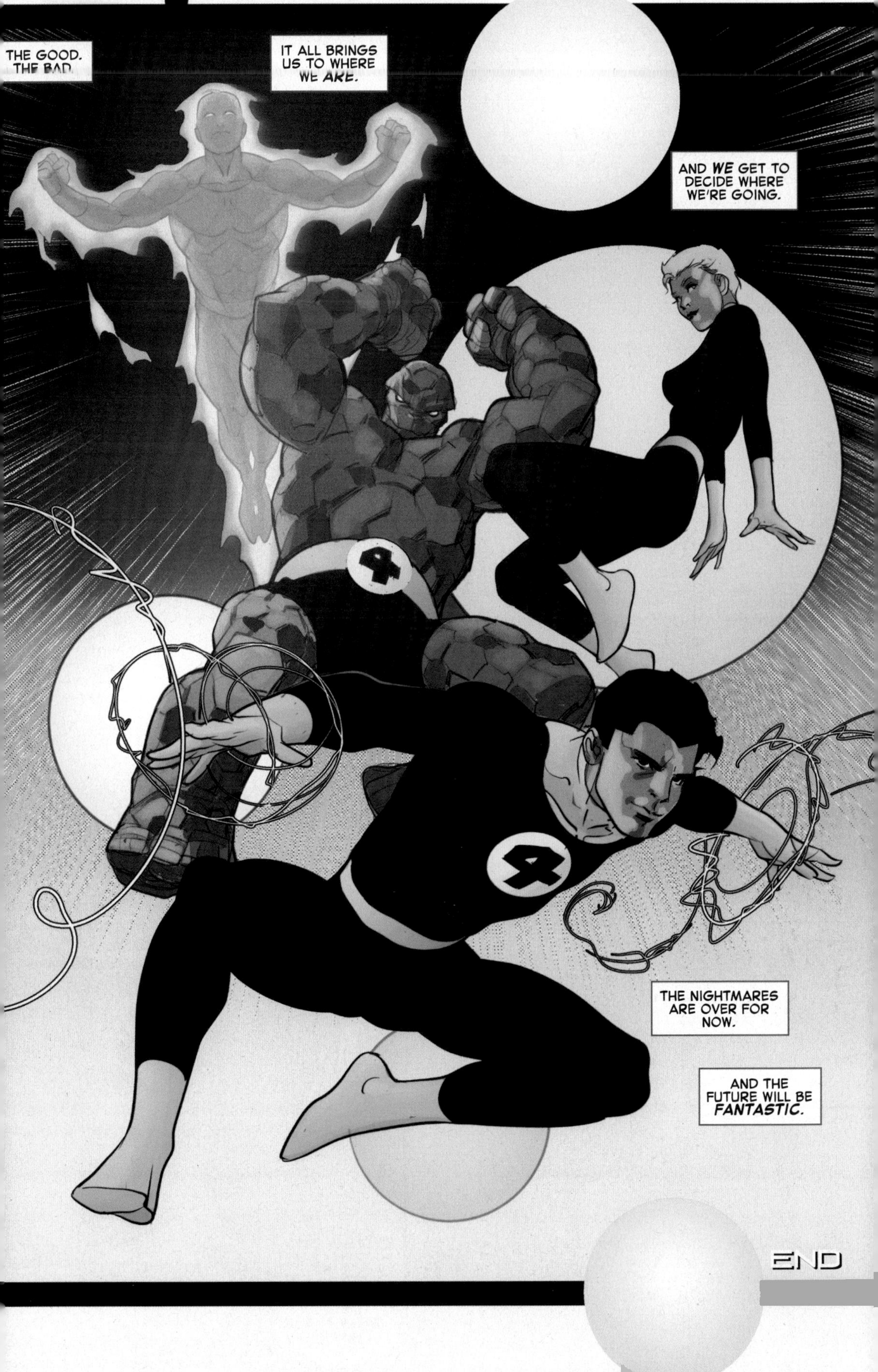
THE GOOD. THE BAD.
IT ALL BRINGS US TO WHERE WE ARE.
AND WE GET TO DECIDE WHERE WE'RE GOING.
THE NIGHTMARES ARE OVER FOR NOW.
AND THE FUTURE WILL BE FANTASTIC.
END

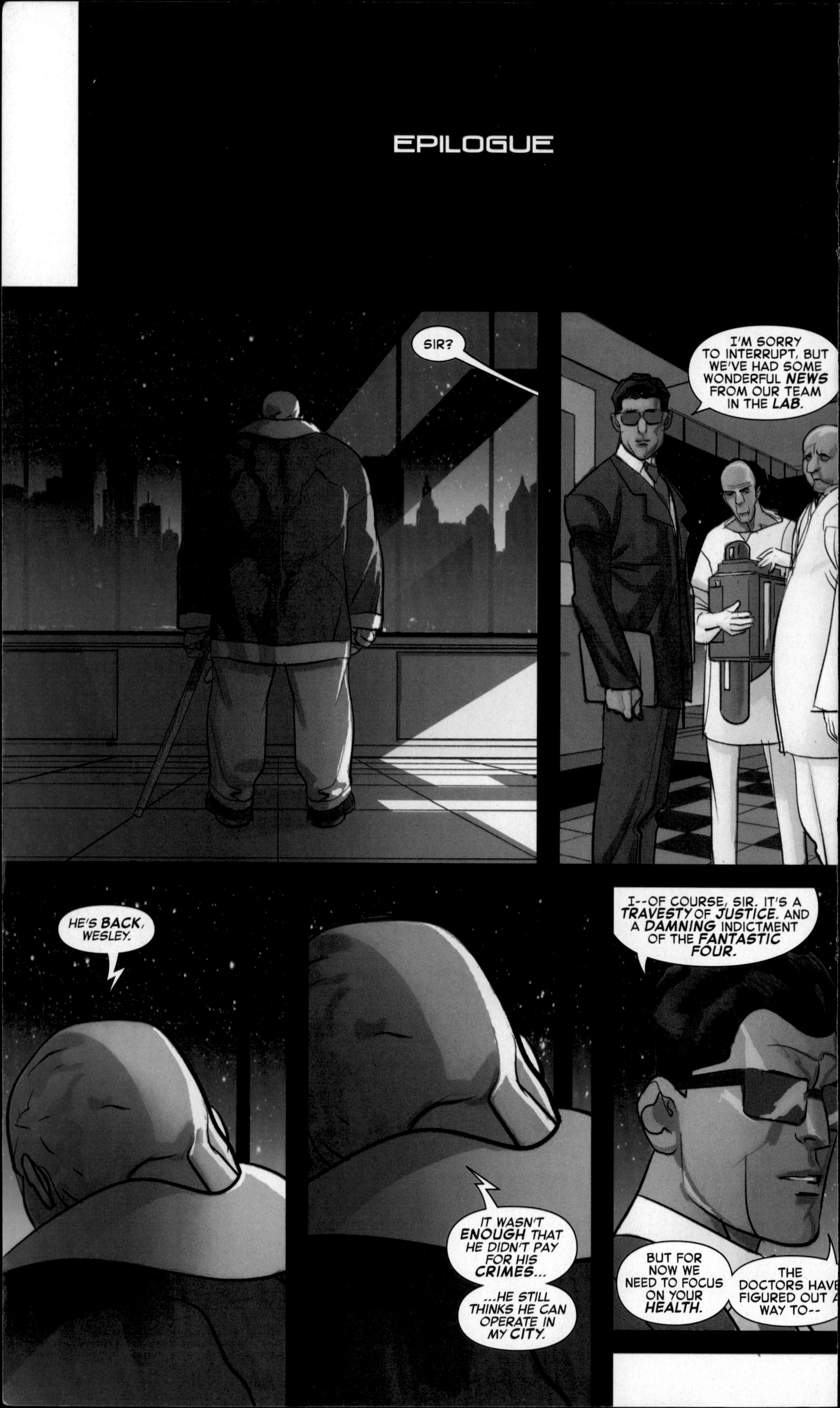
EPILOGUE
SIR?
I'M SORRY TO INTERRUPT, BUT WE'VE HAD SOME WONDERFUL NEWS FROM OUR TEAM IN THE LAB.
HE'S BACK, WESLEY.
IT WASN'T ENOUGH THAT HE DIDN'T PAY FOR HIS CRIMES...
...HE STILL THINKS HE CAN OPERATE IN MY CITY.
I--OF COURSE, SIR. IT'S A TRAVESTY OF JUSTICE. AND A DAMNING INDICTMENT OF THE FANTASTIC FOUR.
BUT FOR NOW WE NEED TO FOCUS ON YOUR HEALTH.
THE DOCTORS HAVE FIGURED OUT A WAY TO--

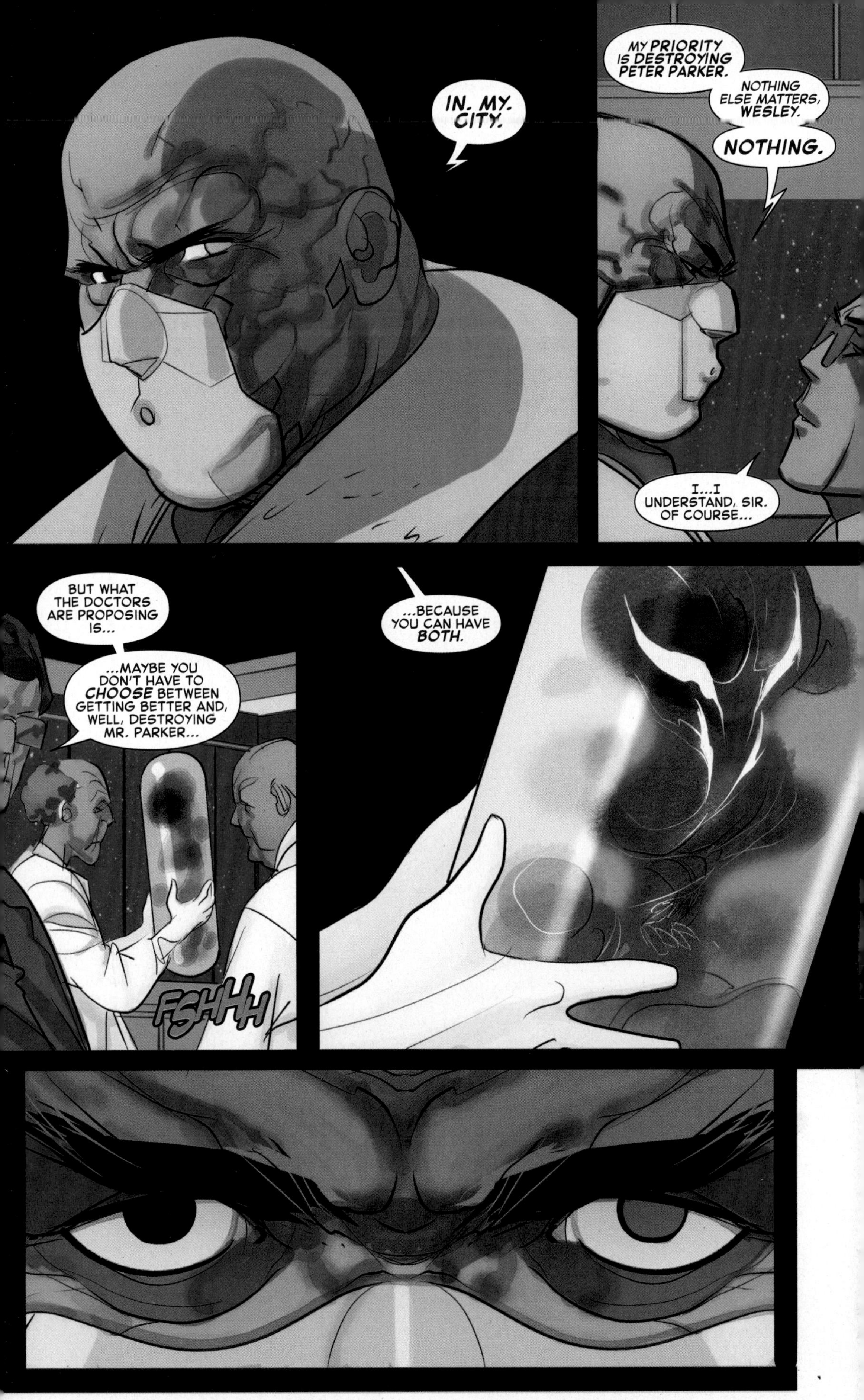
IN. MY. CITY.
MY PRIORITY IS DESTROYING PETER PARKER.
NOTHING ELSE MATTERS, WESLEY.
NOTHING.
I...I UNDERSTAND, SIR. OF COURSE...
BUT WHAT THE DOCTORS ARE PROPOSING IS...
...MAYBE YOU DON'T HAVE TO CHOOSE BETWEEN GETTING BETTER AND, WELL, DESTROYING MR. PARKER...
FSHHH
...BECAUSE YOU CAN HAVE BOTH.

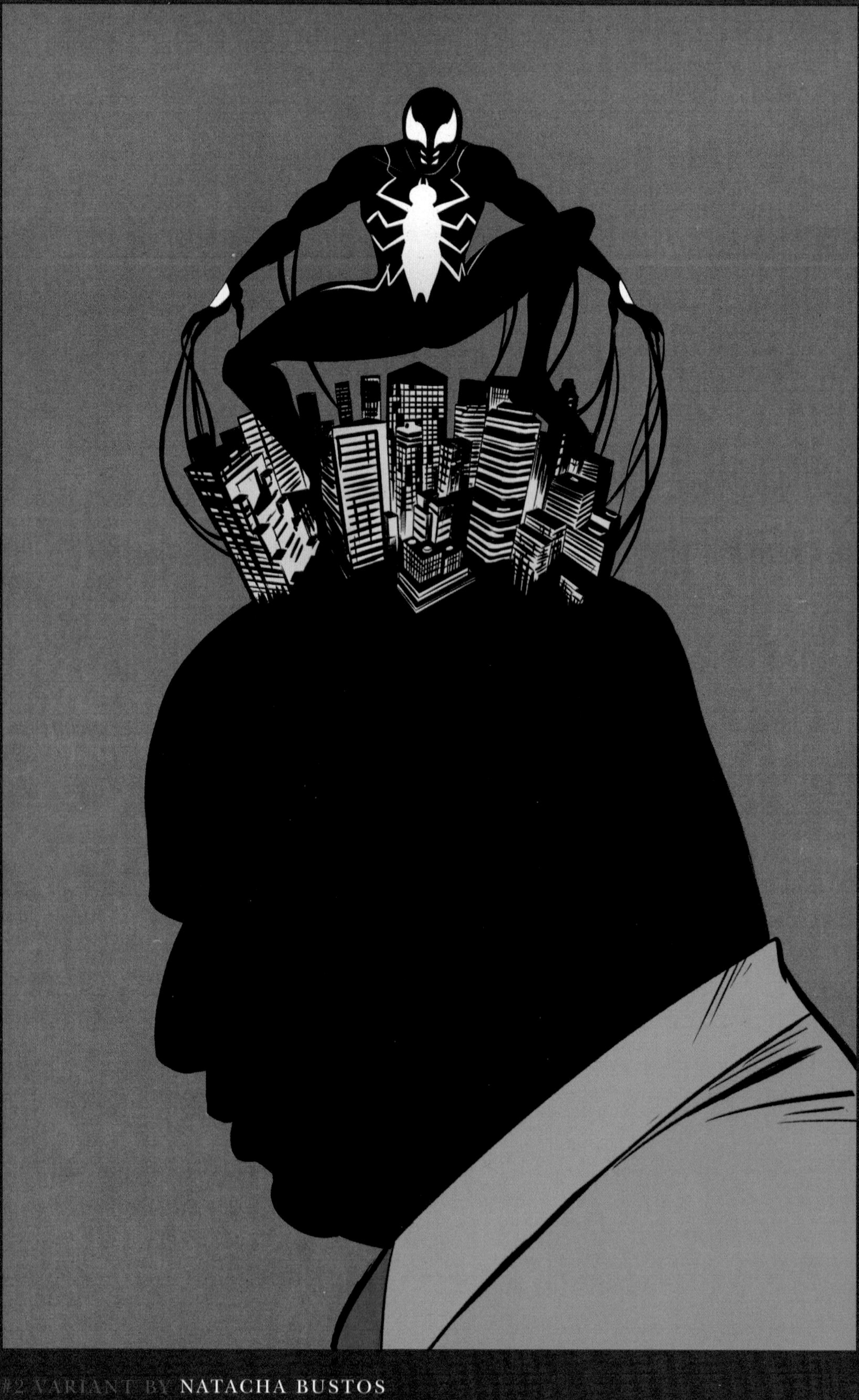

#2 VARIANT BY NATACHA BUSTOS

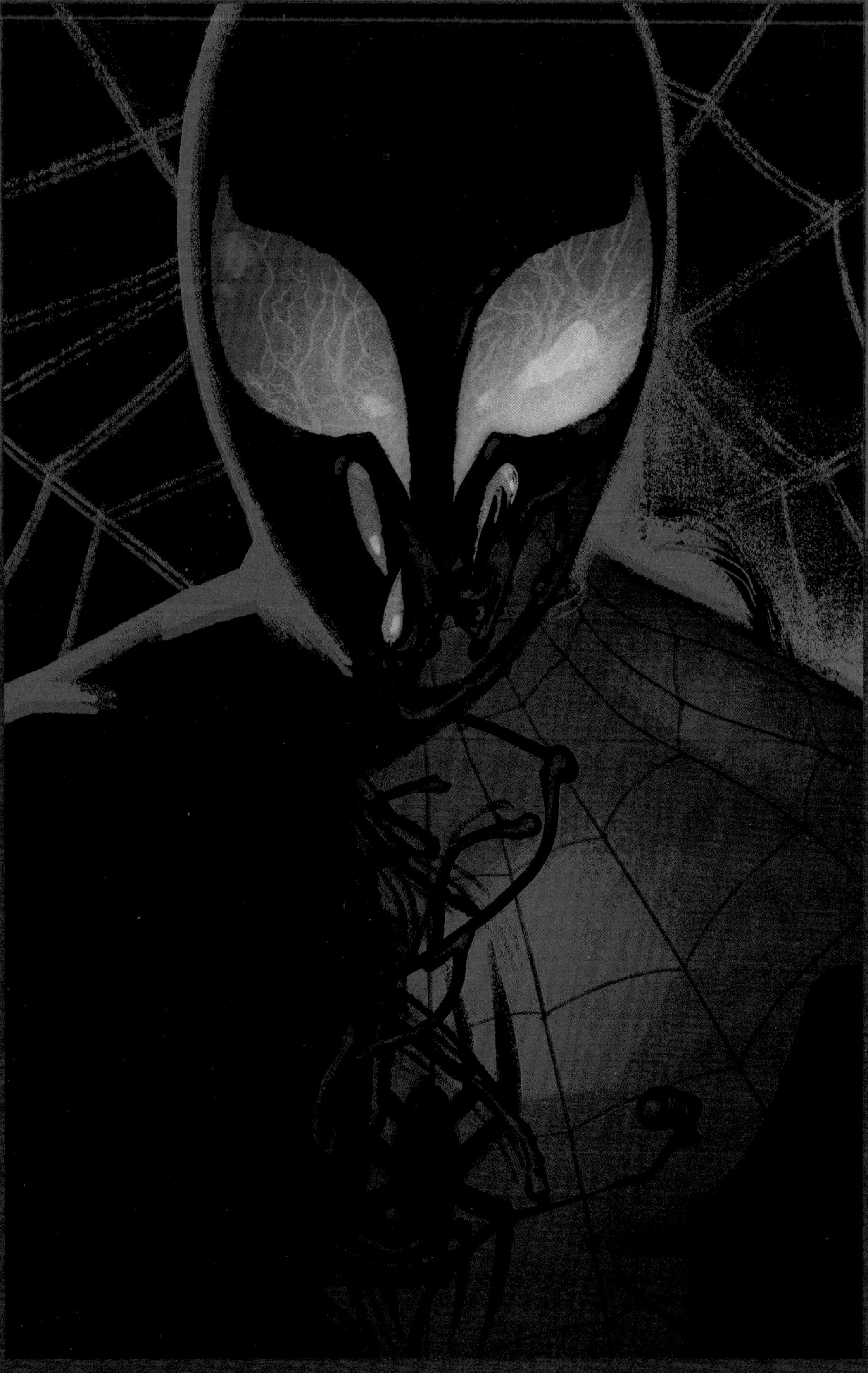

#3 VARIANT BY GREG SMALLWOOD

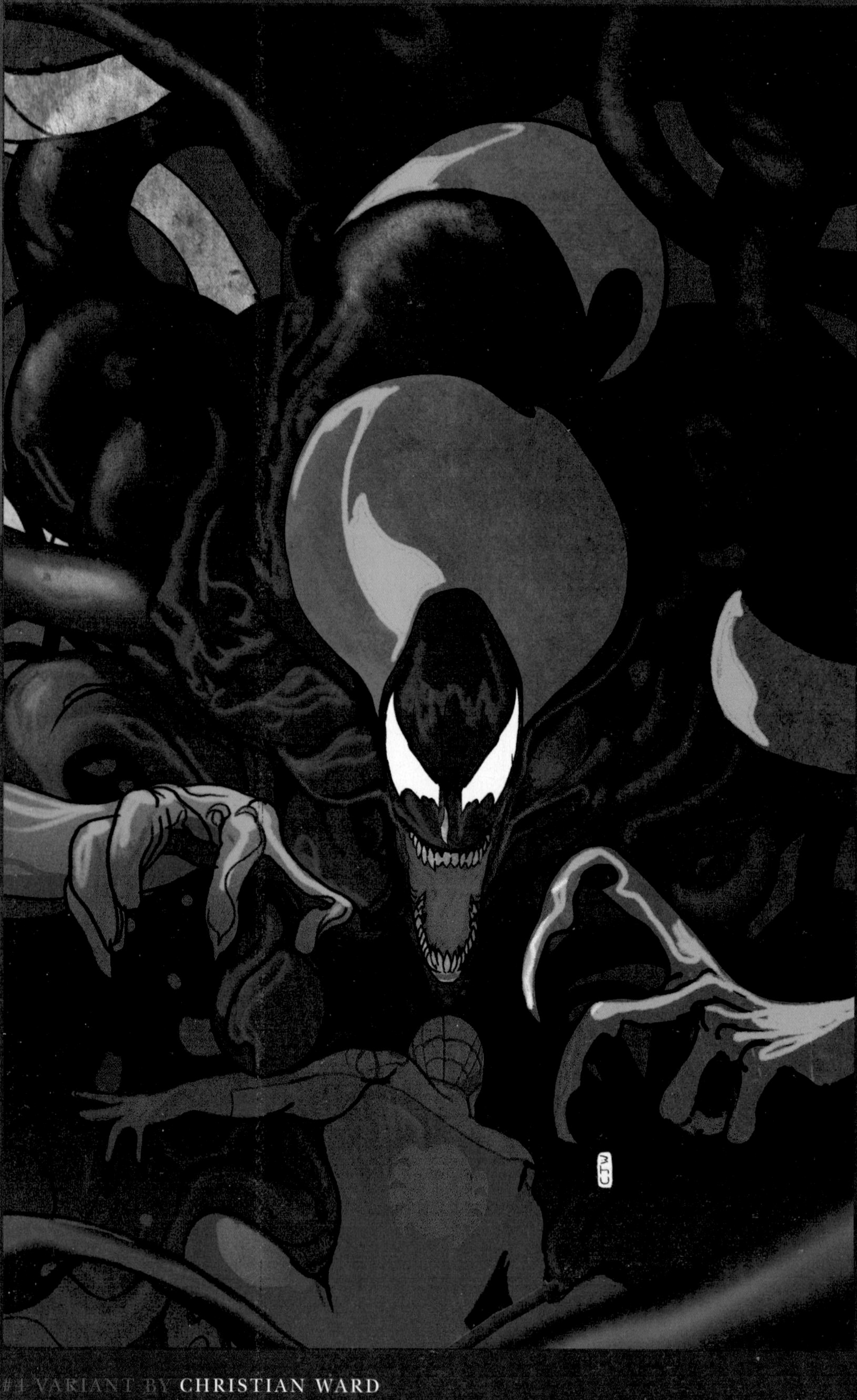

#1 VARIANT BY CHRISTIAN WARD